# THE SILENT REVOLUTION

## QUENTIN SEDDON

**BBC BOOKS**

# ACKNOWLEDGEMENTS

Farming has traditionally been the most generous of industries in sharing its resources and know-how. Any farmer who found out how to grow a better crop or raise a healthier animal has been only too willing to share his understanding and good fortune with a neighbour.

That kindly tradition, now sadly beginning to break down on the farm under the competitive pressures of modern life, makes it impossible for me to thank those who have helped towards the writing of this book. All those mentioned in its pages, as well as dozens who have not been, have given freely and generously of their time and experience. Without them, the book could never have been written.

The subject of modern farming is so vast and complicated that no one can begin to master the whole of it. So I must hope that those who have helped me will be at least as generous towards the inevitable errors and inadequacies of the story I have told as they were when trying to guide me in the telling of it.

Published by BBC Books,
a division of BBC Enterprises Limited,
Woodlands, 80 Wood Lane, London W12 0TT

First Published 1989

© Quentin Seddon 1989
ISBN 0 563 20632 2

Set in 10/13 Sabon Roman by Opus, Oxford
Printed and bound in Great Britain by Mackays of Chatham
Jacket printed by Belmont Press, Northampton

# CONTENTS

The author wishes to thank the following for permission to reproduce copyright material:

Basil Blackwell: *Rushall, The Story of an Organic Farm* by C.B. Wookey, Cambridge University Press: *The Bird of Time* by Norman Moore, East Anglian Magazine Publishing Ltd: *The Long Furrow* by Ashley Cooper, Sir John Eastwood: *The Eastwood Story*, Faber and Faber Ltd: 'Letter to Lord Byron' from *The English Auden: Poems, Essays and Dramatic Writings 1927–1939* by W.H. Auden, Farmers Weekly: an extract from A.G. Street's weekly column, 1947, Dr David G. Hessayon: an extract from a paper given in conference in Brighton, 1983, Clive Holloway Books: *The Story of a Norfolk Farm* by Henry Williamson, International Creative Management, Inc, New York: *Prophet of the New Age* by Robert Waller, Plas Enterprises: *Roots in the Soil* by Ralph Whitlock, Schering Agrochemicals Ltd: extracts from the company history of Pest Control Ltd.

The publishers have made every attempt to contact copyright holders for permission to use their material in this book. However, if any material has been used inadvertently without permission we would be delighted to hear from those concerned.

## PICTURE CREDITS

p123t ICI, b Farmers Weekly; p124–126t Institute of Agriculture & Museum of English Rural Life, University of Reading; p126b Farmers Weekly; p127 ICI; p128t Barnaby's Picture Library/Rudy Lewis; p128b–129t Farmers Weekly; p129b–130t MERL; p130b Farmers Weekly; p131 Massey-Ferguson; p132t Barnaby's Picture Library/Bill Meadows, b MERL; p133t Hulton Picture Company, b Farmers Weekly; p134t Farmer & Stockbreeder, b Barnaby's Picture Library/J J Buckland; p135t Hulton Picture Company, b Farmers Weekly; p136 Geoff Mahon; p137t Animal Biotechnology, Cambridge, Ltd, bl MERL, br Welsh Plant Breeding Station; p138t Massey-Ferguson, bl MERL, br R W Waltham Partnership.

ABBREVIATION  MERL = Institute of Agriculture & Museum of English Rural Life, University of Reading.

# Introduction

Over the last fifty years modern farming has been progressively more successful in meeting its task of feeding people. For the first time, the shortages and famines which used to be a constant of history now look to be nightmares of the past – though sadly as yet only in those countries whose political systems have allowed the development of modern farming. But, paradoxically, it sometimes seems that the more successful farming has become, the more it has been criticised.

Over the next fifty years farming's potential is even greater despite the fact that on a global scale its task will become much harder. Does that mean that farmers can expect the criticism to increase?

This dismal possibility will be avoided if two things happen: farmers must become more open to the demands and sensitivities of consumers; and critics must understand more about the technical developments and economic pressures which dominate the lives of farmers.

The Year of Food and Farming, 1989, is an attempt to encourage both of those things. This book is part of that process. It tells the story of modern farming's achievements and reminds us how much we have to be proud of, as well as explaining how and why we have arrived where we are today. It confronts the difficulties which have arisen, and describes some of the new thinking and new farming which have already started happening in response.

It also looks further ahead to sketch the possibilities which our deeper understanding of biology, especially of genetic engineering and biotechnology, will offer those who grow and those who consume. The term 'free radicals' sounds more like the progressive party of former times than an enemy which deeper biological understanding will help to keep at bay over the coming decades. The debate in this immensely rewarding but immensely difficult area is already joined – and here producers and consumers together must share the burden of technical and its economic consequences.

Farmers, environmentalists and consumers have often shouted at each other in the past. With the increasing need for man safely to harness the prodigious cyclical potential of the sun, there are encouraging signs of dialogue developing alongside the shouts. This book is a valuable contribution to that process.

*Simon Gourlay*
*President, National Farmers' Union*

# CHAPTER ONE

# From TB to UHT

'It was brought to the table with the mites or maggots round it so thick that they bring a spoon with them for you to eat the mites with as you do the cheese.' This was Daniel Defoe, on the subject of Stilton. One hundred and fifty years later, Louis Pasteur struck a blow against maggots when he evolved the process which now carries his name. One hundred years after that, ultra-heat treatment so sterilised milk as to put a stop to putrefaction completely.

Today, even those who like their cheese runny would blench at anyone bringing a spoon for them to eat the mites with. Hygiene has many more supporters than have the tasty maggots of Defoe; pasteurisation has won the day. In doing so, it has altered the dairy industry. It had to. The old town dairies may have relied on the 'black cow', or water pump, to bulk up their none too hygienic milk, but at least it could reach the consumer quickly. When they disappeared and all the milk was brought in from the countryside, the time spent in transit meant it was pasteurise or perish. Too often, it was perish. As late as the early 1950s we suffered more from tuberculosis than any comparable country.

Tuberculosis (TB) is a killer. Unchecked, it killed between 2000 and 3000 children a year outright, shortened the lives of many adults, and made invalids of thousands more both young and old. It also destroyed the lungs and other tissues of cattle, leading to their debility and early death as well.

Cattle and people infect each other with the disease. At one stage it was believed that tubercular milk could act like a vaccine against TB. Cowpox had given protection against smallpox – and every dairymaid, protected against the terrible pockmarks of smallpox, sang 'My face is my fortune' to prove it – so the belief was not surprising. It may even have been true for some; but a large number of others contracted TB from infected milk.

It was not until the affliction was stamped out in the cattle population that people were finally safe. That stamping out did not begin until 1950. Voluntary eradication schemes already operated, but in 1947 no more than one cow in seven came from a herd which had been tested and declared free of TB. In some herds, especially those in or near industrial areas which spent their entire lives in unhygienic and unventilated sheds, nearly all the cows were tubercular.

Milk could be made safe to drink by pasteurising it but farming families were still at risk because they drank raw milk. In any case not all milk was pasteurised. In 1946 the famous vet H.W. Steele Bodger reminded the Farmers' Club that 'American Forces in this country refused to drink English milk owing to the risk of transmitted disease'. This excessive GI sensitivity – forerunner of a stream of dietary fads from across the Atlantic – was a joking matter amongst the locals; but conditions in the cowshed often justified American fears.

There were 150 000 dairy herds in 1947 and of all those cows about 70 per cent were milked by hand. A small farmer usually had 10 cows for that was all one pair of hands could manage – while a bigger herd also meant more risk from tuberculosis and other diseases. Twice-daily milking was hard, painful work. On the rawest winter mornings, burning muscles were thrust gratefully into the icy flow from the cold tap. For years experts had said that the resulting scarcity of labour – especially that of women – for this demanding job would see the end of dairy farming.

The experts were wrong, partly because men and women laboured on willy nilly underneath the udder, and partly because of machines. The first attempt to get round the problem was simply a feather tube or quill thrust up the teat into the milk duct of the udder. A metal version of this hideous device was still sold in the first 30 years of this century, despite the fact that it rapidly destroyed the udder.

Two other approaches tried by early inventors were to imitate the sucking of the calf by a continuous vacuum, or the movements of hand-milking by pressure from rubber pads or rollers. Neither was workable, and both damaged the udder, but for all the painful muddle of those early experiments humane milking gradually evolved. By the 1920s successful machines using teat cups and pulsed or intermittent suction were on the market – although one history comments that the role of the cow as an interested party was not fully appreciated until the early 1940s.

In particular the let-down reflex, which is the cow's way of agreeing to release all the milk in the udder, became better understood, as did the dangers of continuing to milk when the udder was empty. Dairy farmers slowly learned not to put the machine on before the cow was ready and to take it off as soon as the job was done. The penalty for getting any of this wrong, whether in the working of the machine or the care of the cowman, was damage – often serious – to the udder.

All of this was known by the late 1940s, as were the economic advantages for even at pre-war labour costs machine milking had been cheaper. After the war, bringing in the machines lowered yearly labour costs by £2 to £3 a cow – or about half the weekly wage of one man – especially when herds were enlarged. So why were so many cows still hand-milked even after wartime labour shortages had forced a lot of farmers into using machines?

The machines were unreliable. This led to a reputation which manufacturers struggled to live down for years after the fighting had finished. The principles were well-enough understood; the trouble came from the materials used in the machines. Then they were described as utility; now they would be called dodgy. Dairying had to wait for cheap stainless steel, synthetic rubber, plastic and toughened glass – many of them invented to meet the demands of the war – before machines became reliable and hygienic.

As these developments slowly removed the aches and pains of hand-milking, so they contributed to milk purity. Bringing in machines often meant putting up a new parlour. Cows in the old, small herds had been chained by the neck in stalls through the winter. They stood or lay down, often enough in cold and semi-darkness, for six months with a concrete manger in front of them for food and a concrete channel behind them for dung. Hard-working farmers cleaned the dung channels daily, but under the circumstances hygiene could be a secondary consideration.

TB was not the only plague. Brucellosis caused abortion in the cows and flu-like symptoms in people. Anthrax still occurred despite the offer of free vaccines by the Ministry of Agriculture. Foot-and-mouth, which at least did not infect people as well as animals, broke out frequently. These afflictions left diseased and dying animals, all too often followed by cross-infection among people.

Pasteurisation, parlour hygiene, and disease eradication combined to produce healthy cows, healthy people and pure milk. Eradication involved the painful process of slaughtering – and often incinerating as well – any animal carrying the disease. Even so, it was not until the mid-1950s that the Ministry of Health could say 'the long drawn-out battle for safe milk has been won. Tuberculosis has followed cholera and plague into the limbo of the past. Childhood "glands in the neck", once an accepted feature of English life, have disappeared'. It was not finally until 1961 that the national herd was declared free from TB. In that year, 20 cows had to be slaughtered. At the height of the eradication campaign, more than 20 000 cows were killed each year to rid the country of the disease.

This world of plagues, peasants and pitifully diseased children is so remote today that the struggles to end it less than 40 years ago have already been forgotten. In the process we got a real taste for our milk and by the early 1950s drank 5 pints each a week. Milk modernisation was confirmed by commercial television in 1958 when the slogan 'Drinka Pinta Milka Day' pidgined the liquid into the language. Dairy farmers, who in 1947 had produced just over 500 gallons a year from each cow had set out on an expansion which went on until 1984.

The 150 000 small dairy farmers who after the war served their local communities with milk of uncertain quality, and the hundreds of small commercial dairies spreading it to markets only marginally wider, have today become 35 000 farmers and four huge concerns – Unigate, Express, Northern Foods and Dairy Crest – which dominate the dairy companies selling a vast range of cheeses, spreads, yoghurts, milks, creams and ice-creams. The small dairy farmer is now an endangered species himself in need of conservation.

The same pattern repeats itself everywhere – in food, plenty and diversity; in farming, size and specialisation. There is now so much diversity that we should talk about farmings rather than just farming. The specialist pig farmer has little or nothing in common with the specialist producer of tomatoes, potatoes, chickens, hill sheep, milling wheat or malting barley.

How did it happen? Why did it happen? How much is it changing? Where will it go next? The answers can only come through looking at the evolution of some of these farmings. They have met, and are still meeting, new demands. They have responded by changing their methods, by pursuing new technologies, by growing new crops and by learning new management practices. This is the story of that response.

# CHAPTER TWO

# Dan Bullen's Seasons

Melville Pooley looked at the pie on the polished table in front of the Prime Minister. The great man cut through the pastry crust, glanced at the contents, turned to Pooley and asked, 'What's this rubbish?'

The Director of the Meat and Livestock Division of the Ministry of Food faced a difficult moment. He was in the best possible position to know that the inaugural Woolton pie – named after his Minister, made of a mixture of potatoes and root vegetables in a pastry case with a dribble of gravy for flavour, and intended to help the nation through the crisis of wartime food rationing – was a poor substitute for a plateful of meat. He looked round the splendour of the Guildhall, scene of countless long-past banquets and a thoroughly unsuitable place to introduce such a pie to a meat-hungry nation, then down at the collection of brown-smeared vegetables which steamed feebly a few inches from Churchill's waistcoat. His explanation of the sad need for such wartime measures was cut short. 'Take it away', said the Prime Minister, 'and bring me beef'.

Not long afterwards, the country ran out of beef. Even with the difficulties caused by German submarines, it was a sacking matter for the Minister of Food to see the English cupboard barren of beef. Woolton was in Parliament preparing to make the shameful announcement when he was saved by the victory of Badia in the North African campaign. With the country starved of good news as well as meat, Woolton hid the bad news about beef in the good news about Badia and when at the end of his speech he asked rhetorically 'Beef or Badia?' the slogan saved him: the boos for beef were swamped by the cheers for Badia.

No beef was bad enough; but it was to be a long time before things improved. In 1946, a government report warned that wartime shortages would soon become worse. Before long, bread was rationed to just 9 ounces a day. No bread at all was to be served in catering establishments when a main meal was being eaten, and when this proved impossible to enforce it was declared that bread could be served, but only as a separate course. Soon potatoes were to be rationed too. No such restrictions had been needed throughout the whole course of the war.

If ever there was a farmer who could look on these straits with a lifetime's experience to guide him that man was Dan Bullen. His birthday in 1947 was a working day, which was nothing unusual for him even if he had just reached three figures. As if to underline the point, he farmed just on 100 acres at Carbrooke in Norfolk. He was born one year after the Repeal of the Corn Laws, an Act which was to dominate his life. For the first time in its history the country of his birth felt rich enough to give up growing its own food and buy it from others instead – as though a yeoman farmer, striking mineral wealth beneath his hard worked ground, had thrown away his hoe in the certain knowledge that mining was an easier way of getting rich quick than earthy toil.

The Repeal of the Corn Laws committed Dan Bullen to a lifetime of farming struggle. It did him less harm than some. A photograph taken in 1947 shows a splendidly robust man with a grizzled white beard and the level gaze of a youth of 50. He wears a high-necked winter coat with a neat, military collar, his shrewd eyes steady beneath the jauntily curled brim of a cut-down stovepipe hat. He is the original for the cartoon 'John Bull gets his ton'. From the nails in the soles of his boots to the felt in the crown of his hat, Dan Bullen stands there as the model of a man who could summer it and winter it. He knew what he was talking about when he described February, March and April of 1947 as the worst winter months he could remember.

That winter was to kill 25 per cent of the national sheep flock, to set spring planting back by nearly two months, and to cause floods which would leave 6000 fenland acres still unworkable and under water until June. As is so often the way with farming, the snow, ice and flooding were followed by drought. Denis Compton and other stars played charity cricket matches to help raise cash for an agricultural disaster fund – which became an embarrassment as the season improved, allowing parts of the country to harvest record crops.

These were hard blows for an exhausted country whose farmers and farm workers had been worn down by the toil of their six-year dig for victory, but one glance at Dan Bullen's square-shouldered stance shows a man who knew how to take them without flinching. It wasn't the winter which worried him, any more than it worried men and women who had farmed for only half, a quarter, as long as he had. Hard winters were an accepted part of the business he was in; make it twice as tough and it would hardly have been the weather that worried him. His shrewd determined gaze said he had lived through worse storms than these, and ones which blew up from quite a different quarter – such storms as had seen agriculture boom three times and go bust twice in his life.

Those booms and busts had swept in not from the North Pole or across the Steppes of Russia but from Westminster. The old man's steady gaze had seen seedtime and harvest through 100 years of rain and snow and sun, and what had changed three times through that century was not his farming. It was the national need. As a youngster in the early Victorian years, and again in two world wars, the nation needed his work. Twice, in the 1870s and the 1930s, he had seen what happened to his work when the nation no longer needed it. So now he strained his eyes to see whether the third bust of a lifetime's work was brewing up beneath Big Ben.

He was not the only one looking that way. The 1947 New Year editorial of the *Farmers Weekly* asked the same question: would farming once more be sold down the river? Alongside the column of print which asks that question there is another. It is a message from Tom Williams, Minister of Agriculture in Attlee's Labour government, who writes 'The land is our biggest asset and we must make full use of it. We cannot afford to do otherwise.'

On the other side of the editorial, there is a photograph. It is of two men using dung forks to spread shoddy, the sweepings from the cloth mills which helped to fertilise the soil. There is a determined but puzzled look on their faces, for in the early days of 1947, before the winter put a stop to spreading shoddy, they no more than the editor, or Dan Bullen, or any other farmers knew whether to believe the Minister – even when he emphasised his view by saying of the forthcoming Agriculture Act: 'This little bill is the biggest thing that any government has yet done in legislating for British agriculture.'

A lot of folk were uncertain about the new bill. A lot more, including farmers, straightforwardly opposed it. Farming had experienced tight control during the war through the War Ags – the County Agricultural Executive Committees in each county which told farmers what to grow and made sure they grew it well. Now the Labour government might stretch such central control into the years of peace.

One man who objected strongly to such a possibility was the well-known author and journalist A.G. Street. He was a believer in free markets and described the Agriculture Act as 'unEnglish, undemocratic and practically fascist'. Perhaps if he had spent more time talking to Dan Bullen, he would have better understood what free markets had meant over 100 years of one working life. But he didn't, and so found it hard to criticise those who wanted less state control and asserted that 'the main business of a farmer seems to be to bank the cheques he has got from government subsidies.'

Street did not like to hear such things said, but he could understand why people said them. Given foresight, many more farmers might have listened carefully to those words. Their author was Alderman Roberts, little-known owner of a grocer's corner shop. He must often have addressed them in private to members of his family; and as Mayor he had just addressed them publicly to a council meeting in Grantham.

Whatever Alderman Roberts and A.G. Street might say, however, shortages were rapidly growing so grim that bread rationing and the new Agriculture Act were not the only unEnglish things around. In July 1947 the Secretary of the Shire Horse Society was forced to publicise his fears. If the slaughter of horses, and especially foals, for food continued, there would be hardly any working horses left in Britain in 10 years. Some 45 000 foals were needed each year as replacements for worn-out work horses, and no more than 16 000 were being born – of which at least 2500 were being eaten. The Secretary was understandably less concerned about how many worn out working horses were also disappearing down the national gullet.

Other foods of equal strangeness turned up in the kitchen, snoek, whale, macon, as well as the now notorious Woolton pie which the nation, less fierce than its wartime prime minister, reluctantly ate. It was nourishing – indeed, the nation as a whole was better nourished than it had been in the pre-war days of apparent plenty when the poor had subsisted on a diet of bread and scrape – but it was damned dull. So dull was it that one of the immediate post-war hopes had been to add variety to the diet by increasing the feed rations available to livestock farmers, particularly for pigs and chickens. Instead, these rations had to be cut, from 25 per cent of the pre-war level to 15 per cent, thus sharply reducing the availability of the great British breakfast – although, showing an interesting judgment of the national need, the government decided to hold barley supplies for whisky at nearly 50 per cent the pre-war level.

Why, when a nation could feed itself in the face of bombs, submarines, rockets, all the devastation of warfare, could it no longer do so with the return of peace? A government report on world food shortages gave the short answer that we were on our own again. 'During the war, the United Kingdom was a bastion occupied by great Allied armies into which the nations for whom those armies were fighting were eager to pour supplies in order to maintain the fight.

'With the end of the war the United Kingdom ceased to occupy that privileged, though perilous, position; its claims upon supplies were now shared by vast liberated areas, some of them parts of Empire. The wide extension in claimants coincided with a sharp fall in world supplies.

'Moreover, our food imports had once more to be measured carefully in relation to balance of payment and dollar holdings.'

As the difficult year of 1947 went on, as potato flour was added to the bread, as the horses were eaten and the black markets in food grew larger, so ministerial speeches grew shriller in tone. Herbert Morrison told the farmers it was a question of produce or perish. Tom Williams declared: 'This is a national emergency with which all – the government, the farming industry and the general public – are now confronted. Without the utmost efforts of the agricultural industry, either under-nourishment or widespread unemployment may have to be faced, or some combination of the two.'

Dan Bullen might have called it a case of clogs to clogs in three generations. The country, once rich enough to abandon farming, now had no choice. It could farm or it could starve. Able to ignore the resources of its farmland and its farmers through 100 years of wealth, it could no longer afford this as a bankrupt. Gold and currency reserves were exhausted, little was being exported to replenish the coffers and the latest dollar loan was running out. In any case, bankrupt or not, the food wasn't available. World supplies were short or non-existent – except from America, and American farmers wanted dollars which we did not have.

Dollars, dollars, dollars were to dominate world trade for quarter of a century, and this country never had enough of them. The Chancellor Hugh Dalton wrote in his diary 'I was under no illusions as to what would follow if we got no dollar credit. We would go deeper into the dark valley of austerity than at any time during the war. Less food, except for bread and potatoes – less than an Irish peasant's standard of living – in particular less meat and sugar.' We lived with sterling crisis after sterling crisis, and Dalton knew better than anyone what he was talking about when he said, 'British Agriculture is the best dollar saver.' Farming had to expand as fast as possible both to grow the food and to save the dollars.

In short, after six years of war and two of peace, farming itself was now the battleground, and the language used was that of war. The government promised aggressive support for a great offensive – a combined operation to overcome bottlenecks that might prevent farming fulfilling its great service to the country in her hour of need – and to underline the importance of the battle, it was announced that there would be no military call-up for the men of agriculture for at least two years. They were doing their national service down on the farm. As Tom Williams put it in yet another plea: 'Never has the need been greater, never has the aim been higher, and never, I believe, will the response be more complete.'

They set about it, as farmers always have, with whatever came to hand. At first, here and elsewhere, they used the materials of war: 'Ammonium nitrate may go into fertilisers instead of shells; jeeps may serve as light tractors; bulldozers be used for making contour terraces; poison sprays, bombs and smokes for killing insects; flame-throwers for burning up weeds'. A stripped-down Sherman tank, weighing in at only 10 of its fighting 30 tons, was set to pulling an eight-furrow plough.

When at last, in the early autumn of 1947, the policy plans were published, they called for farming to achieve an expansion of 50 per cent above pre-war production. The date for meeting this target was 1951/52. It amounted to a five-year plan. As the *Farmers Weekly* of 29 August put it: 'For the first time during peace for more than 100 years the government of this industrial country frankly admitted that home agriculture was of primary importance to the well-being of the nation.'

A.G. Street and Alderman Roberts may not have liked the controls and the cash which together supported this expansion. The National Farmers Union (NFU) saw it differently. If compulsory extension of the potato, beet and wheat acreages were demanded, the NFU was ready. They saw clearly the urgency of the situation, and farmers young and old throughout the country followed them. The oldest of them all, old Dan Bullen himself, could have been forgiven if, for the first time in his 100 years, he'd blinked. He might now fairly believe he'd seen it all, his life's work come full circle.

And so he had. That year of 1947 was to begin a new era in British agriculture. The keynote was expressed in a speech, not by Agriculture Minister Tom Williams, nor by the President of the NFU James Turner, but by a young politician who was then President of the Board of Trade. Seventeen years later, the same man was to become Prime Minister after a general election campaign which extolled the white heat of technology as the answer to British economic woes. Now, faced with the food crisis, Harold Wilson said that 'the headway made by world agriculture would be governed by how modern aids of scientific techniques in crop growing, fertilisers and insecticide use and animal breeding were taken up.'

Sir John Boyd Orr, first Director-General of the Food and Agriculture Organisation, reinforced the point: 'If science is applied with the same intensity as it was applied for destructive ends during war, production can be increased faster than population can possibly grow.

'The full application of science would result in the higher standard of living and increased prosperity which are the only basis of world peace.'

It may not have looked very likely at the time but it did seem the only possible route. And in fact the truth of such statements did not become fully apparent for 30 years. That period saw farming science, farming policy and farming productivity bounding ahead together. Where famine and starvation had once threatened, now plenty flourished as farming for the first time in history found out how to follow seven fat years with seven times seven fatter ones. In essence, the story is the very familiar twentieth-century one of speed. Farming learned, as it had to if it was to feed the world, how to speed up both the natural cycles and the processes going on inside them. In an industrial age, it was imperative to forge an industrial agriculture.

These themes, of scarcity, subsidy and science, dominate the next three decades. 'Take it away and bring me beef,' was the confident Churchillian command which farming served. It included, first, the determination never to go short again and, second, the belief that what the nation needed was more animal protein — beef, pork and lamb, milk, butter, cheese and eggs. These farming increasingly supplied.

Towards the end of that period, success was so great that the themes changed to surplus, subsidy and science. Now subsidy is shrinking, and for the moment even surplus looks uncertain. Only one theme, science, has stayed unchanged, and always the farming science hare has outrun the farming policy tortoise. Farming and science are still learning and still going faster as they do. If the hare remains ahead, however, it is now clearer than ever that the race has many miles yet to go.

CHAPTER THREE

# George Stapledon Champions Grass

Anyone standing on the ramparts of Rockingham Castle in the autumn of 1942 and looking away to the West would have seen, day after day through the cold and grey, a figure always bent, often crawling, over the soggy winter pastures. These days the betting would be that the hunched figure was a bug hunter. Then it was George Stapledon.

He was trying to work out the secrets of the fattening pastures of the Welland Valley, traditionally some of the finest grassland in the country for taking in thin 30-month Irish store cattle in the spring and turning out prime fat three-year English beef in the autumn. What was it in those pastures which did the bullocks so well?

Sir George Stapledon – Stapes as he was known to his friends, admirers and pupils – was part scientist, part wizard, part practical man, part poet. When he died in 1960 a former Minister of Agriculture wrote: 'The fact that before the "hot" war started out farmers had already ploughed up and put to better use more than half a million acres of land must go to the credit of George Stapledon. He in his own field of endeavour won a mighty but unspectacular victory over our enemies.

'For my part I am convinced that without his victories we most certainly would have been starved of food and there would have been no military victories about which our generals now may argue.'

Among all the men who made the farming revolution – and it is almost entirely a story of men – Stapes is one of the most unusual. Robert Waller, author of Stapledon's biography, says, 'the names Aberystwyth-Stapledon should be joined in the public mind in the same way as El Alamein-Montgomery.'

If that is going too far, at least it gives the Dig for Victory campaign a leader and a hero. What Stapledon in fact did was to build the bridge between the old craft farming of the Norfolk four-course rotation and the new industrial farming of fertilisers, chemicals and machinery. He did it by championing the grass ley, which for centuries had been to the West Country what the four course rotation had been to East Anglia.

Stapes learnt his ley farming from the Cornish farmer Abraham Tribble, for whom he worked as a student in his twenties. Tribble, like his forebears, grew leys for fertility. Unlike his forebears he also used basic slag to fertilise the ground before he sowed his rye grass and clover. Helped by the slag, the clover in these pastures allowed him to carry more livestock, while the manure left behind could then be cashed through arable crops when the ley was eventually ploughed out. Tribble knew that ploughing an old clover ley released the very large quantities of nitrogen essential to secure high yields of wheat and barley. His system was an effective way of manipulating the nitrogen cycle to gain a heavy harvest of corn.

The lesson happily learnt in Cornwall was repeated harshly in the Cotswolds when Stapledon worked briefly at the Royal Agricultural College. There he first saw the tumbledown grass of a countryside slumped into the agricultural depression of the 1930s. Once fertile land was now derelict, as were the beautiful Cotswold towns and villages where an energetic farming community had raised their families, their livestock and their crops. These experiences lay behind a career which took him first to direct the newly established National Institute of Agricultural Botany, then to the Welsh Plant Breeding Station in Aberystwyth, of which he was both founder and first director.

One of his staff there described Stapledon's work: 'He was sorting out the grasses of the world, and said that as far as we were concerned there were only half a dozen grasses that mattered and he called them the followers of man. Where man congregated with his animals there was ryegrass, cocksfoot, timothy, the fescues and the wild white clover becoming more and more evident. He was very thrilled one day when I drew his attention to a story, one of the most ancient tales of Europe, in the collection known as the

Mabinogion. It said that "wherever Olwen trod four white trefoils sprang up." The point is the treading, the treading brought up the clover, which Stapledon observed to be true. The Red Indians of North America call white clover "White man's footsteps". It is not indigenous but has spread with the colonisation of the white man.'

Stapledon devoted himself to restoring fertility through the ley. He knew that grass, livestock and crops flourished together, and his lifelong interest was in the whole rotation – the relationship through the seasons between soil, plant, crop, animals and farmer. His approach was described by one of his early collaborators, Captain Bennett-Evans:

'Stapledon's great idea was to scratch, scratch, scratch: lime and phosphate; and oversow. This scratching business was rather slow and tedious and I'm a bit of an impatient chap. I said to him one day "If you think all this going up and down the hill is economic, I don't. We've got no tilth at the end of it."

'We were using a New Zealand harrow, a pretty drastic one, it certainly did a bit of ripping, but it was bouncing about too much. I got tired of watching it, so I said: "Look here, I'm going to buy a plough." Stapledon said: "Oh, are you? Well, ploughing is completely out of date. But it's your land, you carry on if you want to and I'll lend you all the help I can, but I'm against it."

'I said: "Very well, I'll plough alongside your scratchings and I'll do it in plots, controlled, and all the rest of it, and then we can compare which is the better." He went off shaking his head: but I did buy a plough, a three-furrow disc plough, and ploughed very carefully by the side of his scratchings.

'We let a winter pass to break down the furrow and then we disced it and harrowed it, and in a very short time the ploughed area was a beautiful emerald green. Stapledon was delighted. He brought the world and his wife to see it.

'Mind you, the scratchings did well too, they came on later. The fact is that improvement is not so complete under the plough, but it's quicker, and you can't wait for ever for your returns. It takes as long as 10 years to get a good sward by that method.

'Stapledon was right. I've given up ploughing now and have gone back to scratching. But that ploughing was a damn good advert for him: the scratching doesn't produce such a nice emerald green. The scratching method brings in white clover, the foundations of fertility, the mother of milk.

'You can tell that this scratching/discing method works because of the increase of worms and moles; they do a lot of the cultivating for you.'

Stapes was to return the compliment. Many years later he wrote: 'I remember motoring into Aberystwyth from Stratford-upon-Avon on a dull and cold winter morning and suddenly being aroused from my apathy by the sight of Bennett-Evans' green patches vibrant against the lowering background of dark and forbidding hills, the first vivid green to meet my eyes since I had bundled myself into my car early that morning.

'I wondered rather morosely as I drove on, who cared? Who of the thousands who passed over that road on a normal summer gave those patches a moment's thought, or even noticed them? Were there any who had been suddenly thrilled? Who wished to know what like of man lived in that bleak, isolated spot in that strange home built of stone and railway carriages?'

Previously, the accepted rule had been that climate imposed fertility. Therefore the Welsh hills could not be made fertile. The experiments with Bennett-Evans proved that fertility could be created at will by manuring with artificial fertiliser, especially phosphate and lime, sowing the wild white clover and supporting the new ley by more intense, controlled grazing. The seeds, manures and implements could be carried almost anywhere by tractor, especially by caterpillar tractor.

Stapledon's ideas went far beyond rehabilitating the grass: 'I wanted to acquire a block of anything up to 50 000 acres of hill land and then to set about its rehabilitation. I wanted to cater for agriculture, forestry and the holidaymaker. I wanted to set up a scheme of parent and filial farms. The parent farm would be fully equipped for contracting and would be a hive of industry in work ancillary to forestry and agriculture. There would have been holiday camps and hostels around the filial farms. Nothing, of course, happened.'

Stapes may have been convinced that the plough was out of date for restoring grassland. But ever since his involvement with farming in the First World War, he had argued for 'ploughing up the Midlands, sending the stock away to the west, and creating a great wheat and bean belt. I have been advocating ploughing up England ever since. My optimism (or my madness) has never deserted me, and it never will – ENGLAND MUST BE PLOUGHED UP.'

He knew that the British climate and countryside grew grass excellently, and insisted that grass was the best feed for cows. If this sounds obvious, the debate even today is not finally concluded. Then, grass was a widely under-valued feed and cows were fed mainly on oilseed cake and other imported feeds. He said with sadness at the time, 'Abundant and cheap supplies of imported foodstuffs were the foundation of the system of farming practised' and he no more liked to see it than did the wartime merchant navy whose sailors died in their thousands because of this prodigal system.

Stapes knew that grassland could not be put into cold storage and that it depreciates like machinery when it is not properly managed. Not only did he teach others how to manage it, he searched the world for varieties and strains of grass which would flourish. As a result, the first of the Aberystwyth-bred grasses was put on the market in 1932, and from then on the Station produced a stream of new ryegrasses, clovers, cocksfoots and timothys suitable for British farming.

Their influence in turn was worldwide. One of Stapledon's colleagues, visiting America, arrived at Yale University. Asked where he came from he replied Wales. The Americans shook their heads, so he tried Aberystwyth. Immediately they grinned and said 'the Welsh Plant Breeding Station'.

Stapledon's contribution was immense. But towards the end of his life he had doubts. He had always concerned himself with the whole rather than the parts; now he worried about increasing specialisation. 'The chemicalisation of agriculture may unknowingly build up disaster if it is too rapid and ill-considered. We must develop the state of mind of looking for other consequences as well as those we aim at. Why this unseemly hurry?'

In 1956, in a message to the summer meeting of the British Grassland Society he had helped to found, he said, 'Today, technology has begun to run riot and amazingly enough perhaps nowhere more so than on the most progressive farms. The red lights, if as yet only on the sub-threshold, are there for those who can discern them.' What he looked for was production without destruction, optimum production rather than maximum production. These feelings, much more widespread today, were rare when he began to express them in the 1950s.

There is a marvellous description of Stapes at the time, written by Cressida Ridley: 'Most people, as they grow old, become heavier, staider and duller of response. George Stapledon merely became more fragile. He seemed to blow across a room like a leaf blown on a faint breeze. He did not drop into a chair but settled on it weightlessly like a butterfly. His remarkable good looks, with the profile of a small and kindly hawk, the thistle-head of hair, brilliant blue eyes and shell pink complexion resisted both age and illness. Though his body failed him and his brain was no longer capable of the sustained effort he demanded, his mind kept all its acuteness and, perhaps to his discomfort, its restless energy.'

Stapledon had begun as a revolutionary, driven by the miseries of the 1920s and 1930s, then of the war, to his life's work on grass. It was he who made a later generation realise that grass is to both livestock and arable farming what the air cushion is to a hovercraft. Take away the grass and the industry will capsize, sinking slowly lower in the water until it disappears. By contrast, the more strongly the grass grows, the higher the craft of farming rides – so that some of today's grasses, building on Stapledon's early work, rise more like a helicopter than a hovercraft. If at the end he came to mistrust the helicopter, to urge farming to make haste slowly, it was not because he came to reject the new but because he wanted to see secure bridges built between tradition and progress.

The next stage in this work was to be carried out by the Grassland Research Institute (GRI) at Hurley outside Reading, which he helped establish in 1949 and whose first director was Stapledon's friend and colleague William Davies, described by Heathcoat Amory when Minister for Agriculture as 'the best export we have'. He meant that Davies's knowledge had led him to advise on grassland everywhere from the Falkland Islands to New Zealand.

Davies pursued two quarries. The first was to boost ley farming, the second to grasp the interactions between soil, plant, crop, animal and environment. He was attacked from one side by those who believed in the productivity of permanent pasture, from the other by those who believed in the productivity of permanent cereals. The arguments still go on today; neither 40 years more farming experience nor much scientific detective work have been able to decide the matter definitively.

Some soils are suited to one, some to another of these systems. Stapledon was right. No rules can be laid down in isolation from soil, climate, management, and the environment they create between them. But Davies was then in a strong position for the day of the ley was at hand. Much grass had been ploughed up during the war to grow cereals, potatoes and sugar beet. When the fighting finished, farmers worried that these newly ploughed soils would lose fertility. Combined with the arguments of Stapledon and Davies, these fears gave force to the ley/arable corner of the debate.

Leys offered the advantage over oilseed cake that you could have your grass and eat it. The more productive the grass, the more animals it fed. The more animals it fed, the more fertile it became. The more fertile it became, the better the next crop of corn grew. The points Stapes had been making for years became part of everyday farming.

No sooner had it started than it stopped. Within a short time it was clear that new seeds mattered much less than improved fertility. And fertility could now be bought and sold by the bagful. Artificial nitrogen fertiliser gave instant fertility, and that gave a starving nation more food fast.

In 1947 the use of bagged nitrogen fertiliser on grassland was non-existent. Across the country, it averaged 7 pounds an acre. By the early 1950s, Davies and the GRI knew that 1 pound of fertiliser would give at least 20 and often 30 times as many pounds of grass. They knew this worked when 100, 200 or 300 pounds of fertiliser were put on. In some experiments, 400 pounds an acre went on and still the yield went up 20 times. ICI who made the nitrogen knew it; so did the National Agricultural Advisory Service (NAAS), which had replaced the wartime County Agricultural Executive Commitees. Together, they swamped the country in meetings, open days, discussion groups, all repeating the same message. The unity was such that some thought the NAAS a division of ICI, others that ICI was part of the government.

What was true for grass was true for crops. With nitrogen the crops of wheat and barley, potatoes and sugar beet grew green and gold and copious. In a world crying out for food, not to use fertiliser was to be thought a lunatic or a criminal. Where was the sense in growing clover, keeping animals to graze it and three or four years later ploughing in the ley to release the nitrogen, when the best crop of clover ever grown on the most heavily dunged field in the land could not grow the crops bagged fertiliser could? Stapledon might have his worries about this. They could keep. Given the knowledge of what nitrogen did, grassland farmers were astonishingly moderate. What Davies knew in 1950 most farmers still ignored in 1970, when average use was still well under 100 pounds an acre. But when farmers started to say that the best grass seed came out of a blue bag, the message began to get through. The reference was to the colour of the plastic in which ICI fertiliser was delivered, and the meaning was quite clear: more nitrogen grows more grass whatever seeds you start with.

To reach that position took all the energy of enthusiasts who loud-hailed at farmers through every one of those 20 years. Specialist grassland advisers had never been heard of before. All of a sudden in the 1950s there were eight of them. One scattered his seeds so widely he was known as Timothy Meadow Fescue Jones. He considered the two grasses together with white clover so tolerant of bad management, so idiot-proof, he called them Muggins' Mixture, and patches of the scattered olive green pastures spread rapidly from Gloucester to Cornwall.

The aim of all the advisers was the same – to give a grazing animal the largest amount of the best and most suitable food most quickly. But since suitable food must include at least nine major groups, from proteins and fats to minerals and vitamins, there were plenty of things which could go wrong. For all the work of folk like Timothy Meadow Fescue Jones, pasture grasses were far less uniform and reliable as a feed than any other agricultural product. They were certainly less reliable than the cake which Stapledon despised.

Only a very small amount of all this often unreliable grass is of direct benefit to the farmer. For example, 33 per cent of what a beef animal eats when grazing is passed out in dung; 20 per cent of what is left is passed out in urine, or in methane when the grazing animal belches ruminatively; and almost all the remainder is used either to grow bone and fat or to maintain body functions like keeping warm, or simply to digest the food itself. Only one mouthful in 20 of the grass which is grazed goes to putting on the weight which the farmer has to sell.

Grass is difficult. One grass farmer in an upland district described his calling as 'the most refined form of slavery in the world'. No doubt the remark was made at the end of a long, hard winter, in one of those wet, cold, late springs when it seems that nothing will ever start growing again. Day after day the spiky grass remains steely blue in colour and to the endless chores of winter feeding are added the worries of fodder supplies running low. No doubt a few days later the sun was shining, the cows were out in fields of translucent emerald, and the farmer – filled with the adolescent optimism of springtime which can still catch the most enslaved old stockman by surprise – leant across the gate gazing happily into the hazy distance.

There are fierce human and social problems in living with long winters, short days and incessant rain. And, while not all grassland farming is carried on in the cold, wet uplands, it could only have been a couple who had spent their life in that way who could come back from their first holiday in 20 years to tell the neighbours, 'funny places those hotels. You know there's nobody about and nothing at all to do at five in the morning. Why, you can't even get breakfast'.

Most grassland farmers are much more interested in their animals than their grass. Those animals always want the same amount to eat while the grass grows different amounts in different months as well as from year to year. The obvious way to keep grass-fed animals content is to keep far fewer beasts than the grass can carry. The problem is real. The GRI grew more than twice as much grass in its best year as in its worst. In wetter parts of the country the difference is not so large – but in wetter parts of the country a lot of the grass can be trampled uselessly into the mud after incessant rain.

The decisions the farmer takes are often less to do with grass, more to do with risk. Many small producers do not want the risks of making the largest profits by relying heavily on their grass; they want to avoid a bad year. They don't care for the fast track; they just want to keep on nice and steady. Decades of advice from experts have not made a great deal of difference, because the experts have been talking to the plant and the animal, not to the farmer.

Difficulties multiply when the grass must first be conserved as hay or silage – and it must be so conserved because for at least six months of the year it grows scarcely or not at all. Badly done, such conservation produces something less like a feed than a poison. Faced by this, farmers remained stubbornly cautious. They would grow more grass, but they would not rely on it. Despite Stapledon, Davies, the GRI, ICI, the NAAS and people like Timothy Meadow Fescue Jones who worked in it, despite the enthusiasts and the publicity, even despite the clear truth of the claims that all these people made, grass refused to catch on. It was not reliable and it was only briefly fashionable – except among a slowly growing band of enthusiasts who kept the flagleaf flying.

In some places the blast for grass got up the nose. Alderman Jacobs, Chairman of a County Agricultural Executive Committee in the Fens, remarked that so far as he was concerned grass was no more than waste space out of doors. Since the War Ags had the power to make farmers change their ways, such views were very influential.

# CHAPTER FOUR

# Richard Waltham and the Dorset Wedge

Mention in the local pub you're cutting for silage the next day and the talk passes to more interesting topics. Mention, in a spell of settled weather, that you're cutting for hay and there comes the sound of sharply indrawn breath, then silence. The oldest person present may give a short, harsh laugh. Looking up from his pint, the haymaker sees other heads slowly shaking. The words are unspoken but say clearly enough, 'I wouldn't cut tomorrow. Not if it was my crop I wouldn't.'

A day or two later the drizzle comes down, and in the taproom someone will make a statement which traditionally takes the form of the question 'Got some hay down, have you?' A week or so later the blackening stuff in the field will receive a kick with the comment, 'Tis better than snowballs.' A pause and then, doubtfully, '. . . I suppose'.

The only way to avoid all this is to wait for a dismally wet evening. As the rain thumps down, the casual mention that you're cutting hay tomorrow provokes cautious nodding, and a knowing look which says that there are still some who know more than they let on.

Haymaking is midsummer madness. We have been doing it for thousands of years, which dignifies the habit, but why, given silage, people should still make hay in our climate is now a question for psychologists. Yet year after year it is made, and year after year farmers up and down the country will say the same thing: 'But I do like a bit of good hay.'

The Romans made hay because they had no choice, though even they tried different ways of lessening the pain. Thereafter for centuries the grass was cut, turned, carted and ricked by hand. It needed a lot of people. One picture of haymaking before machines shows 122 people in a single field. While the workers struggled with the crop they were diverted by Morris dancers, musicians and a large catering corps.

Through all those seasons it was not the farmer who made the hay, it was the sun. It still is, or – much more often – is not. To make hay, the sun must evaporate between 6 and 8 tons of water an acre from the mown grass. Meanwhile, bacteria and fungi begin to decompose the moist dead tissue. The haymaker is in a race to get the crop dry before losing too much food value.

In our climate, obstacles are placed in the way, making this race a hard one to win. Often enough, when all but won, rain arrives to push the finishing tape back – as well as directly washing further nutrients out of the drying grass. When the job goes badly, the haymaker may lose more than 50 per cent of the feeding value of fresh grass. When it goes well, losses of 30 per cent are common. Not surprisingly, this process is known ironically in some parts of the world as 'saving the hay', and a heavy and obvious blow delivered to an ill-prepared opponent is still known as a 'haymaker'.

The task was eased by machinery, but even that led to much thoughtful straw-chewing. Here is what A.G. Street had to say at a time when the baler was a recent and uncertain arrival on the farm:

'I shall never go back to stacking loose hay if I can avoid it. But baling is a tricky business and, although this is my third season with it, I haven't made up my mind about one thing.

'This is whether to bale the stuff very gay and leave the bales out in the field to make, or to bale a day or so later, and stack the bales immediately. I don't know which method is the better, and should welcome the opinions of others on this matter.

'I thought I was being very clever the other week. We baled some gayish stuff on two successive evenings, and decided to leave them in the field for a week. But on the Friday morning I smelt rain, for once agreeing with the official forecast. So after dinner I told my stalwarts to get those bales under cover. At 5.30 pm it came on to rain, and rained most of that night and the next day.

'Next morning I felt very pleased with myself. But by Monday those loads were hot as love on a Sunday, and hotter. Will their contents come out as good fodder as those from subsequent bales that have weathered a full week in isolation on end in the open air?

'I have memories of visiting one farm where they were baling hay fast and furious, and stacking the output immediately in a huge Dutch barn. I climbed on to the stack in the making, and it was much too hot for my liking.

'When I forced my hand into a bale that had been stacked the day before I drew out stuff like dung that was almost too hot to touch. Yet the farmer assured me that the stack would not overheat, and that the hay would come out as first-class stuff the following winter.'

Street owned one of the first balers to be used. He bought it because it took much less time, trouble and labour than using hay sweeps to gather in the crop – so modern methods do help. In today's field high-output mowers cut; conditioners bruise or scrape; whizzlers, haybobs, acrobats and tedders spread and turn; balers square and round, large and small wrap; sledges collect and a great variety of mechanical donkeys cart the crop. Some of this has speeded up haymaking, all of it has reduced the labour and lessened backache, but only the possibility of barn-drying using powerful fans gives modern haymakers a significantly better chance of beating the weather than Street experienced 40 years ago.

The arrival of silage which did in two days what could take the haymaker two weeks should have swept hay aside in a season. Farmers took one look and, in a triumph of hope over English summers, resolutely went back to their haymaking. It was as though housewives had stuck to Monday mornings and the laundry copper decades after washing machines became widely available.

Official histories tell us that 'since the introduction of ensiling in the middle of the nineteenth century there had been repeated campaigns to encourage the adoption of silage making'. Nobody cared. By 1950 these campaigns had persuaded farmers to make 1 ton of silage for each 20 tons of hay. The official version goes on: 'Results obtained with silages on farms were highly variable. In many instances losses of dry matter during ensiling were high and the levels of production by animals fed silage were disappointingly low.'

It was not surprising. The early accounts of silage and its problems now seem so bizarre it is surprising anyone bothered with it at all. Gordon Newman was one of the pioneers and, after 40 years at the clamp face, admits that mysteries still exist between silage maker, silage and cow. He enters our story standing on top of the silage at Reading University, where he was then Farms' Manager. He is watering the heap with a hose while muttering, 'It's too dry. It's too dry.' It was a small crisis of faith in new technology.

Near this muttering watering figure stood the old technology – a concrete tower silo some 25 feet across. From field to filling, that had required a workforce of at least 15 people, and once filled had to be emptied the same way – by hand. The tower produced a well-made feed which the cows ate happily, but the labour for such games no longer existed, which was one reason why many farmers refused to consider silage making.

In fact ensiling could now be carried out with the Ferguson tractor and the Paterson buckrake, which allowed a much smaller workforce to dump cut grass readily on to a heap. On such a pile, described by him as 'a monstrous molehill' stood Newman with his hose. Not for the first time, he was in conflict with official views, which said let the grass heat up.

This was rotten advice. Silage and compost both start with a heap of grass. Leave them be and air is drawn into the hot decaying heap until it becomes compost. The silage maker must stop the rot, and Newman's hose was meant to cool down and compact his molehill and keep out the air. This strangles the plant cells, and releases their sugars. Bacteria ferment the sugars to acids, killing the other microbes which lead to rottenness. Decay stops and, instead of compost, the heap becomes a stable somewhat acidic clamp of silage, smelling slightly cheesy. When this goes wrong the smell – and taste – is of rancid butter. As with all decay, much ammonia is given off, adding to the unwelcome farmyard pong.

Other early aids to excluding air were soil, limestone and chalk, or farmyard manure, which last made its own distinctive contribution to the perfume of the heap. To feed this material, a thick layer of decay was removed. The underlying silage was then hacked out daily by a strong man wielding a type of immense hand-operated guillotine.

Many weird ideas were tried to stop the rot and with it these rancid butter mountains. Vast concrete tubs, monstrous manure-covered molehills, pits suitable for elephant traps, grass-filled sausages sized for giants and vacuumed into submission – all were tried at one time or another. It took straight thinking, black plastic and a Dorset farmer called Richard Waltham to restore sanity. Between them they evolved the Dorset wedge, which is the basis of many modern systems of silage making.

Richard Waltham fed his cows on hay, silage, kale and mangels. 'One old boy was kept busy cutting the kale with a hook. Then the carter went up, forked it all up with a pick and dropped it in a grass field, and the cows came out by day and ate it.

'The carter was a little chap, just about 5 foot nothing, off with his two horses every morning happy as could be. There was nothing he loved so much as his two old horses. He got older and older and slower and slower and so did his horses, but I couldn't tell him the time had come for him to finish. It would have broken his heart.

'But one miserable day he was out in the field picking up the kale and he just turned to me and said he couldn't go on. What a relief it was. We worked out his two horses together came to 45 years between them. One was 22 and the other 23. I never did find out how much the three of them together came to.'

While the cows ate their kale the cowman put the hay into racks in the shippons where the animals were tied up the rest of the time. A lot of cows stayed where they were all through the eight-month winter, but Richard Waltham's went out into a dry field for their kale unless the weather was too fierce. They also got a ration of mangels, pulled by hand, thrown up on to the tractor and trailer and brought back to a clamp in the yard.

The animals were machine-milked in a parlour. They were let out in sixes, popped over to the parlour and let back to the shippons. By the time you'd fed them and milked them and dealt with the dung it came to a lot of dodging about.

By 1958 there were 50 dairy cows kept in this manner. No one could have decribed it as a system, so the boss planned to improve things. He went up to see a pioneer of self-feed silage, Sam Morton in Leamington Spa. Waltham planned to adapt what he saw there, which was loose housing for the cows and self-feed silage from a covered clamp. They put the buildings up in 1959.

There were no building standards issued by the Ministry so he got hold of a civil engineer from Sherborne. Waltham knew nothing about building and the engineer nothing about farming but between them they worked out how to build a covered clamp with reinforced walls 9 feet high. Then they had their first go at filling it with silage.

'There was a fair bit of advice around but the criteria seemed to change every year. The view was that you had to have heat to make silage, there were dangers involved if you didn't get heat for good fermentation. The NAAS believed it, and also that by the time silage went down a cow's throat it had lost a third of the feeding value of fresh grass. Heat and fermentation went together. The view was you started on a Friday, by Monday it would have heated up enough to go on.'

The silage team had a new green forage harvester which cut the crop with spade-shaped flails. They filled the whole floor of the clamp 8 inches deep, 75 feet by 40 feet, with a covering of grass and went on up 8 inches a day like a layer cake. The other bit of new technology was a polythene sheet, which covered the cake once they'd cooked it.

When they opened the clamp to feed, the cows were deeply unimpressed. The grass had overheated, was too dry, too tightly compressed, very poorly fermented because of the earth and mud which the spade flails had picked up with it, and had got very hard. Richard Waltham grins ruefully and vigorously scratches the back of his head as he cheerfully admits all this. 'We'd made as many mistakes in one year as you could get into one year. We were left with a good bit the cows never did eat.'

For most people that was the signal to go back to hay. But Richard Waltham has a fund of good-humoured common sense and no backlog of prejudices – and he had his new buildings which he wanted for their designed purpose. He also has the virtue of thinking things through simply. Indeed, as he tells the story now, the whole thing was quite simple. But ICI had spent 13 years trying to work out just how to make silage down the road at Henley Manor, and the NAAS still advised that heat was needed. So Waltham's cheerful view that he could never quite understand what all the fuss was about must be taken with a good dose of additive.

If the grass got too hot, make it cooler; put it on in thick layers of 3 feet not thin ones of 8 inches. If the harvester picked up soil, get another harvester. George Richards down the road was using a double chop New Holland with sickle flails which he liked the look of, so he outed the green monster and bought one of those. But, he says, 'It's not the money you spend it's the methods you use.' And, grinning again, 'The changes were so obvious you couldn't come to any other conclusion.' Maybe not, but no one else had got there by 1960.

A 3-foot layer of grass had to go in on a slope to go in at all, so they made a wedge. At the end of the day they covered it with polythene to keep the air out, and next day put another wedge on top of it. They went on until they finished, when they covered the whole wedge carefully and left it for the winter. 'When we opened it, the stuff looked quite different, much like silage looks today. It was a nice sort of yellow colour, it hadn't got too hot, had a nice consistency and a nice smell, and the cows gobbled their way through it and finished it off by the second week in February.

'The third year we matched the quantity to the cows, and went steadily on doing it in the same way for the next few years.'

The NAAS and Richard Waltham measured the loss of feed value in his clamp. It came to just over 10 per cent. This was a staggering result compared to the accepted loss of more than 30 per cent, but although the NAAS wrote up the results nothing more happened. Waltham put the bit of a report away in the farm office and got on making his silage.

In 1966 he went up to a gathering at the Grassland Research Institute outside Reading. There he asked Frank Raymond, the Deputy Director, whether he would come and talk to the local Dorset discussion group. The Agricultural Research Council had recently changed its established policy that scientists should not talk to farmers. Now they were to get out and about more with their message, so Raymond willingly agreed. He arrived early at Manor Farm, and the two men put on their boots to go and look at the cows. When Raymond saw them feeding at the clamp he asked immediately, 'Why isn't there any waste?'

'There ought not to be any waste.'

'But there always is.'

Frank Raymond was at once convinced that he was looking at something remarkable, and from that moment, Richard Waltham became unofficial silage adviser to the nation. The engineers from Silsoe came down with a work study team; ICI came several times from Henley Manor; Fisons came from North Wyke; and above all, grassland farmers came from everywhere, every Monday, to an informal discussion group and get-together which might have up to 50 people present. The Dorset Wedge, as Frank Raymond christened it, had arrived. It appeared in the GRI Bulletin Number One and in the ICI advisory leaflets on silage-making.

Through it all, Richard Waltham remained delightfully unimpressed; the only thing which surprised him was that anyone was surprised. It all seemed so obvious. 'All it amounts to is this. Previously, a whole lot of criteria had been chucked around. All the Dorset Wedge technique said was that about six things were important. If you missed any of them you made a mess. It made silage making predictable. People knew all this already but no one had put it together as a programme to ensure you hit all those targets. All the Dorset Wedge amounted to was a procedure which put the various related factors which are important into some sort of order.'

Frank Raymond only made one mistake. He should have christened it the Waltham Wedge.

Today, silage making follows Richard Waltham's practice. As he says, the rules have not changed, though the machinery has got much bigger. 'Then a big tractor was 40 horse-power. It would cut 9 or 10 acres a day, so unless you filled on a slope and did the covering with polythene you'd get overheating. Now, 100 horse-power is common, and 200 horse-power self-propelled machines not uncommon. You can cut up to 50 acres a day, so it's become a different game altogether. But it's played by the same rules and the machinery makes it easier to hit the targets.'

Silage psychosis had finally been broken. As farmers grew confident, they made more and more of the stuff. Once, the aim was to make 6 tons a cow; today, 10 tonnes a cow are common. The animals come off grass in October and stay indoors until April. Grassland management has become much more effective as a result.

While these developments were taking place in Dorset, Newman, never a man to do things by halves, had called in the Royal Engineers to blow up his old concrete cast tower silo at

Reading. The University cows and the University cowman now had the latest in self-feed silos, the cows would enjoy a far better diet and the cowman would no longer need to labour as he daily forked out the silage. Get rid of the tower and Newman could turn his restless energies to other things. The Engineers did their spectacular job and kindly bulldozed away the rubble, leaving cows, cowman and Newman looking at one final heap of extremely old silage in the pit hollowed out at the foot of the tower.

For the last time, the cowman sweated to throw out the feed. It was oat and vetch silage, which had been made by passing sheaves of the two crops through a chopper-blower into the tower. When the stuff had all been dug out, it was thrown down as rubbish to soak up the slurry behind the cows feeding at the face of the new silo. The University cows turned herd about from the self-feed silage in their smart new silo, shoved hard ahead to get at the material being chucked away behind them. It was another unexpected pointer to the future.

The cows liked the old oat and vetch silage because it was dry, they disliked the grass silage in its up-to-the-minute self-feed setting because it was wet. It is hard to make good silage from wet material and to do it at all the end product must be made more acid. A cow does not have to be at university for long to know that wet, acid, badly made silage fails the exam. This lesson led to the practice of wilting grass in the field before making the silage. When the weather made that impossible, the farmer added sugar or acid to the crop. Both helped the silage-making bacteria do their work.

Over the years, Gordon Newman has simplified the results of all these struggles into the dairy farmer's four-part wife test. First, take some handfuls of silage and squeeze as much liquid as you can out of them. Second, wipe your hands vigorously across the front of your shirt. Third, go in and hug the wife. Fourth, stand back.

If she hugs you warmly then your cows will hug you too. If she looks thoughtful and sends you straight outside again, ammonia levels are rising and the decay is getting worrying. If she backs off instantly, turns away and insists you sleep in a separate room, you have a disaster on your hands. Proper use of modern methods ensures she hugs you back.

For years, however, farmers and their wives remained suspicious. It was not until 1984 that more silage was made than hay. The early difficulties were one important reason for this very slow uptake. The other was Bobby Boutflour.

# CHAPTER FIVE

# Bobby Boutflour and the Cake Bag

Sir George Stapledon was the scientist and prophet of British grassland. Professor Bobby Boutflour was the hard-headed commercial operator. Where Stapledon thought biologically and believed in grass, Boutflour thought economically and backed cake – the cheap by-product which was left after imported oilseeds had been crushed to extract the oil for making margarine and soap. It was a high-energy food and cows happily ate it in quantity.

Boutflour began his career in pre-war Wiltshire. Arthur Court, the well-known West Country farmer and journalist, describes in his autobiography how he met 'a small but dynamic man who toured the villages telling farmers to change their ideas about feeding cows. We should regard the milking cow as a machine! You put in a certain amount of food and don't forget plenty of water to drink, and you should get a gallon of milk for each 4 pounds of balanced cake or meal you feed. Well! Who could resist this young man who preached the gospel so very well?'

In those days the Court family farmed 70 Shorthorns which in total ate 4 tons of cake a year, while producing 500 gallons of milk each. Boutflour's advice would have meant feeding a ton of cake a head, but as Court said, 'Bobby was one of those people who, by subtle exaggeration, made his audience believe there was something in his ideas. The only thing which stopped an explosion of milk was the potential of the breed'. Few Dairy Shorthorns were able to produce more than 500 gallons.

Boutflour didn't persuade everyone. Rex Paterson set up a cheap grass-based system which was so successful he ended up farming a large part of the Hampshire plains – 7000 acres given over to 70 herds on 100-acre units in which each cow gave 700 gallons a year. So unorthodox was this approach when he first pursued it that the War Ag put out an order to have his land taken over as improperly farmed. Paterson successfully fought the order and expanded his enterprise, but there were few to follow his example at the time. Most followed Boutflour's advice. When he became Principal of the Royal Agricultural College at Cirencester he had a standing bet, on offer to anyone who would take it: given two cows bought at random in the market, he could get more milk from one than his opponent could get from the other. He always won.

Sometimes he could be persuaded to admit the secret. It was an armful of hay. Late at night he would go into the cowstalls with the hay – and feed it to the opposition cow. His argument was simply that there was a limit to how much a cow can eat. As they were given more cake to increase milk production, so roughage – grass, hay or silage – must be cut back. The Steadings herd at Cirencester was to average 2000 gallons a cow at a time when the national average was less than one-third of that and this, combined with Boutflour's position and personality, added up to heavy firepower – even if his cows did have to eat 30 pounds of cake a day each to back him up. The difficulty was that after the cowman had stuffed that quantity down their throats there wasn't much room for anything else. The high-energy food goes rapidly into the true (or second) stomach and the neglected rumen (or first stomach) shrinks.

That seems a perverse way to treat an organ so well-suited to fermenting grass as the rumen, and of course it collapsed in wartime when there wasn't any cake about. But in the unrationed post-war environment both cows and people went on a binge. Just as bagged nitrogen fertiliser was a cheap and very effective way to grow the larger crops which the nation demanded, so bagged concentrated cattle cake was an excellent answer to the cry for more milk. When cattle feeds came off ration in the early 1950s, Boutflourism was bound to flourish.

As late as 1972, the husband and wife team of the Donaldsons, authors of the excellent *Farming in Britain Today* could write: 'Probably the most important and certainly the most colourful pioneer in the field of nutrition was the late Professor Boutflour.

For better or worse, the Boutflour system has left a lasting mark on the UK dairy industry'. In the long run, however, Stapledon's arguments for grass were the stronger. The realities faced by Boutflour were economic and would change rapidly with circumstances: the realities faced by Stapledon were biological, and would change little if at all as economic conditions altered.

Bob Ørskov of the Rowett Research Institute outside Aberdeen knows as much about this biology as anyone. He wrote recently 'the feeding of ruminants has been surrounded by a great deal of mystery and indeed still is. The stomach is a large fermentation vat where a multitude of micro-organisms flourish. Like any other fermentation it is important that conditions are stable. It may well be compared to winemaking, with each animal having its own fermentation vat. The stockman is able to influence the fermentation in the stomach in much the same way as the winemaker producing wine.' And, like the gallon jar of fermenting dandelion or elderberry, ruminants are very much influenced by their relationship with their environment, including the winemaker or stockman. This striking picture of the country's farmyards filled with arguing amateur winemakers, each carefully tending as many as 200 separate four-legged fermentation vats, stands in sharp contrast to the beliefs of Boutflourism. In particular, it tells us that too much cake upsets the wine vat.

As good wine starts with grapes, good milk starts with grass, and particularly the fibre called cellulose. So fibrous is cellulose that it is used in the textile industry to make cotton or linen, neither of which is obviously a nourishing food. Nevertheless, fermentation in the rumen turns cellulose into rich, creamy milk. The trick is worked by bacteria which stick to the fibrous grasses swallowed by the cow and slowly break them down into more digestible foods. While the cow clearly gains by keeping these bacteria busy in her rumen, there are also some losses, partly through the heat of fermentation and partly through the gases which, as every winemaker knows, come bubbling off the top. When the bacteria have digested the fibre they are carried on to the true stomach where they are digested themselves as the major source of protein. As Ørskov puts it, 'the animal's reward to the microbes for their service in making feed available to it is to digest them afterwards!'

The problem for Boutflourism is that high-energy cake upsets the balance of these bacteria, with results familiar to a winemaker when the brew turns to vinegar. Just as our stomachs are likely to be acid after too much Christmas cake, so is the cow's after too much cake. The secret of feeding dairy cows is thus to maintain ideal conditions for the bacteria which ferment cellulose, and the secret of that is saliva. Saliva counteracts acid. A cow can produce about a 45-gallon barrel of the stuff a day, which is enough to counteract a lot of acid, but she can only do this if she spends much of her time cudding and ruminating, which she does when she has large quantities of rather indigestible food – like cellulose.

Boutflour's easily digested cake not only produced much more acid, it also produced much less saliva. This hardly mattered when the hay or grass which accompanied the cake was itself low in feed value and helped counteract the acidity caused by the cake. But this balance was to change with the slowly increasing popularity of silage, which is itself an acid feed. For cows, every day became Christmas Day, which was a great deal too much of a good thing. Dairy herds throughout the country began to display daily symptoms of the morning after the night before.

The situation was not helped by advances in oil extraction. BOCM and other crushers were making margarine more cheaply by squeezing more oil from their cake, and the energy held by the oil was replaced in dairy rations by starch or fat. Both made the rumen more acid, which meant less creamy milk.

Butter and margarine have fought a war for the fats market over the years, and butter has generally had the worst of it. Since the extra oil squeezed out of the seeds meant more margarine and less cream, butter was hit from both directions in this skirmish, which left a particularly bitter taste in the cud.

Alka Seltzer deals with the symptoms of Boxing Day disease, and cowmen can and do feed bicarb. Much better is to remove the cause, an aim which Gordon Newman has been promoting through a National Society for the Promotion of Cudding in Cows. Membership means feeding more forage. But while a cow will eat up to 100 kg a day (around 220 pounds) of fresh grass, she won't force down much more than 60 kg of silage. She will eat good hay in larger amounts, if the summer has allowed any good hay to be saved, but otherwise she will be looking round for something more.

More might mean various things. It can be cake. It can be treated straw. It can be maize silage. Or it can be something like maize gluten, brewers' grains, molassed sugar beet pulp, fishmeal or even pressed citrus pulp. None of these alter the aim of keeping the rumen a happy place for the cellulose-fermenting bacteria.

# CHAPTER SIX

# Joe Edwards and AI

Boutflour's influence spread beyond food to sex. His success in pushing up milk production led farmers to think feeding was more important than breeding. 'All the pedigree goes in through the mouth' they said, which echoed the grassland farmer's belief that the best grass seed came out of a blue bag.

This attitude was unhelpful to a cattle industry within which British breeds were already slipping from their proud position of bloodstock suppliers to the world. By 1947 this belief, though often expressed, was no longer firmly based. One geneticist remarked that 'there are many people who consider that our dairy breeding is still little better than a hesitant groping in the half light of a meagre knowledge, but this is, for the ordinary breeder, as a noon-day blaze compared with the conditions under which the user of a beef bull works.' Another, speaking at the first Royal Show held since the end of the war, said sharply: 'Make the shows over from something akin to greyhound racing or football, from very fine spectacles for the betting farmer, into an important factor in his progress as a businessman.'

For centuries breeding had been a numbers' game more like bingo than greyhound racing and, for the winners, it was still a rich one. With bingo, the more cards you have the more likely you are to win. With breeding, the more cows you've got the more likely it is that one of them will hit the jackpot. You pays your money and you takes your choice, and the more money you pay the wider your choice can be.

The great breeders of the eighteenth century, above all Bakewell, had bred for fat. 'It was his maxim that, the fat being the most valuable part of the carcase, it could not be too abundant.' In

Bakewell's day there were none of the cooking oils we know now, and in the absence of other lighting materials tallow was very valuable for producing candles. The energy in fat was thus highly valued in itself, and the value attached itself to the meat in the belief that fat gave the joint its flavour. The situation is rather similar with the extraordinarily fat pigs produced in China today.

Bakewell's decisions show how important it is first to choose the right qualities, and second to choose the animals which can pass them on to their offspring. Some animals, like some human beings, look splendid and hand on to their children some very undesirable qualities indeed. All too often, this was the fate of pedigree cattle.

It could work the other way, as it did for Amos Cruickshank who established the Scottish Shorthorn. The breed began with the English bull Lancaster Comet – but when Cruickshank first set eyes on this particular beast he was so appalled that he left it, far from any further chance of disturbing the view, in a distant corner of his remotest farm. By the end of his first fierce Scottish winter, the exiled Lancaster Comet was dead. But before he died he bred. One of his sons, Champion of England, was to become the sire on which the Scottish Shorthorn was established.

So there was luck as well as judgment. Sometimes the judgment got confused, and style – a patch of colour here or a shape of head there – became more important than performance. So far as milk yield went, all sorts of things were tried as indicators, from appearance to size of milk vein to udder shape to teat size. This 'Crufts' factor' became so important, above all in the beef show ring, that it was remarkable when a breeder and a butcher chose the same animal as champion.

By 1947 breeding attitudes were changing, and artificial insemination (AI) and the Milk Marketing Board (MMB) were showing the way. The battle for AI saw three men of firm confidence on one side. They were John Hammond, Arthur Walton and Joseph Edwards at the School of Agriculture in Cambridge, where Hammond had worked for more than 20 years on how farm animals grow, and especially on when and why they lay down bone, muscle and fat. In the course of this work he had put livestock breeding on a scientific basis for the first time. These three early champions of AI were soon to be joined by a scattering of enlightened farmers and the MMB.

On the other side stood the rest. Farmers, breeders and, so far as they cared, the public all rejected AI because it would lead to infertility, imbalance of the sexes, abnormalities, inbreeding and injury. It was immoral – which led the farm manager at progressive Dartington Hall to say there was enough scandal around the place without going in for AI. It was expensive. It would threaten existing Breed Societies, and British status as bloodstock breeders to the world. Above all, it was new. In those days, the semen used in AI was first mixed with a protective fluid which included egg yolk. Some feared their calves would emerge covered in hen's feathers. Although the technique had been in use in other countries for several years, once again it was wartime pressure which eventually overcame the opposition, When in 1941 AI finally got the ministerial nod, Joe Edwards went to work.

Dr Joseph Edwards is today an 80-year-old so vigorous his life's work seems to have given him back more energy than he has put into it. He is not the only grand old man of the dairy industry who seems to have found the secret of eternal youth, and his butter-fired enthusiasm was much needed in the battle to establish and spread AI, first for dairy cows and then for beef.

Edwards's revolution was built on fighting the fashion for appearance – the colour or texture of coat, the size of udder, even the shape of horn – which the traditional breeders still supported. What concerned him was performance. Appearance was irrelevant. As he puts it, 'if production and type are connected, breed for production and type will come with it. If you reverse that argument, you're lost.'

Pedigrees alone won't do. At one testing station for many years the best and worst results in progeny tests were held by full brothers. The only way to avoid the Lancaster Comet problem is to ignore appearance and record what each bull's daughters do, then use only those bulls with the best daughters. This battle for performance against appearance was to take much longer to win than introducing AI. Other things apart, there was huge money still to be made from bingo. The finest house full of them all was not finally called until the Perth bull sales of 1963.

Torquil Munro and Lindertis Evulse were the two who held the winning card. At this distance it might be fair to wonder which was the breeder, which the bull. In fact they entered the game in the order mentioned, breeder first, bull second, and when all the numbers were called and the card full it was Lindertis Evulse who had a new owner. Jack Dick paid £63 000 for the animal and took it back to Blackwatch Farms in New York State. In today's money, that would be £750 000.

Lindertis Evulse was an Oxo cube on legs. The chosen goals on this bingo card had been a very compact, short-legged, deeply fleshed, early maturing animal. The breeders had aimed at it for decades, and the prize for getting there was rich. Small beasts of this sort were wanted by New World ranchers, where conditions led to bulls becoming gaunt and rangy. The breeders in America and Argentina came back year after year to Perth for bulls to correct this tendency, and the breeders in this country made fortunes supplying them.

The idea of such early-maturing bulls, born in the age of Bakewell, thus reached its peak at a time when fat was still beautiful, lean was mean, and we drooled at the thought of succulent slices of roast beef circled by thick frills of savoury fat whose juices flavoured a rich gravy. The bulls to meet such needs then found themselves in a dead end when suddenly fat was seen as a killer.

There were in fact other arguments in favour of such animals. Hammond himself had supported them, on the grounds that families were getting smaller and no longer bought the traditional 14-pound Sunday roast from the huge traditional ox; and, as he pointed out, small muscles were tender muscles. But this quality was expensive, and for all Hammond's work on how animals put on flesh it brought with it that legacy of fat which lay like an immense bolster across the Herd Books. Lindertis Evulse reached the end of this road – a terminus symbolically and expensively marked by the fact that he never managed to father a calf.

Edwards attacked all this by measuring production through recording the performance of daughters. He knew which daughters came from which bulls, so could then use these fathers to improve herd performance. There was no other way of finding good bulls.

This method takes time. A bull will be seven years old before his daughters' records can be added up, and by then he may be past his prime or even dead. This made AI essential. Left to his own seductive devices, a bull will father around 60 calves a year. If such a seducer cannot be used until he's seven and can then only get 60 calves a year, a lot of bovine Don Juans must stand around twiddling their tails. AI means a bull can father 500, 5000, or even, as the technique developed, 50 000 calves a year – which hugely lowers the rate of tail twiddling.

Edwards's testing and recording therefore had to go together with AI, and the whole package meant a growing interest in identifying the genetics of a bull which might father 50 000 calves. With the Cambridge and District Cattle Breeders' Society he set up a farmer co-operative, registered under the Friendly Societies Act, which began work on 1 November 1942. The average size of the Cambridgeshire herds which he first inseminated was seven cows, and 75 per cent of these herds had no bull.

Until Edwards came on the scene, the cows in such herds were served to get them in milk without thought for the quality of the calf. Sometimes they used a neighbour's bull, at best unimproved and at worst a disease-ridden mongrel. Sometimes the Ministry supplied premium bulls which stood in the village. But these were over-fat beef Shorthorns so they were a very odd sort of premium, and were justified by the then widely held belief that only the mother carried the genes important for dairying so the contribution of the father could be ignored.

The Ministry wanted the new service to be free. Edwards was determined to charge for it. If farmers were going to say AI was against nature, then only payment would convince them of its value. The fee was set at twice the charge for the Ministry's fat-filled premium bulls.

Support from small farmers came rapidly and was widespread. Traditional dairy breeders may have achieved no more than the half light of a meagre knowledge, but as we have seen none of it shone on the milking herd of 10 cows. Their keepers wanted the new Friesian blood because of the volume of milk it produced. AI meant they could afford it. Don't use the bull, use the telephone, became their breeding philosophy. Breed societies also enthused. Their top males were in greater demand, and they enjoyed increased demand for females.

In 1943 the Chairman of the MMB visited Cambridge, and later that year agreed to establish a national AI service on behalf of milk producers. In 1945, Joe Edwards moved to the MMB for three years to start its new Breeding and Production Organisation. He was to stay there until he retired 23 years later. By 1957, 700 bulls were used to serve 50 per cent of the cows in England and Wales by AI; the other 50 per cent were served by some 60 000 farmyard bulls. Yields had risen to nearly 3500 litres, or 700 gallons a cow. Nearly all of this improvement in fact came from better feeding, but genetic improvement of the national herd, courtesy of AI, was at last picking up speed. Gradually, Edwards proved that the pedigree did not go in through the mouth.

If dairy breeding was on the move, the only light which shone on beef breeding came, as we have seen, from fashionable photographers snapping the bidders in the front row at the Perth bull sale – snaps which were rushed to London to be reproduced in the next issue of the *Tatler*. Nevertheless, as early as 1947 this too began to change when Joe Edwards was called into the Ministry of Food and told to extend the developing AI service to beef. He refused, wishing to concentrate on dairy. His objections foundered on the unexpected rock of President Peron of Argentina.

The President knew well the British love of beef, knew better the shortages which still constricted beef supply and knew best of all how to exploit them. Three times, seeking more cash to satisfy national or personal needs, he jacked up the contract price of beef exports at the last moment. The Ministry decided the time had come for action. Beef bulls were to be stationed at AI centres with inseminations offered free.

Edwards was compelled to agree. Testing for beef offspring was added to the existing scheme for dairy, and slowly began to influence beef breeding in a similar way. As with dairy, however, the biggest influence was not to come from better home-bred beasts as much as from new breeds from outside. Even as Lindertis Evulse sailed westward across the Atlantic, an assault was being mounted across the Channel. It had started two years before the triumph of the Oxo cube with the first importation of French cattle. Within a few years, the invasion led by these 16 Charolais and their successors was to dethrone Evulse and all his kind.

These battles for change in both meat and milk may have been long and fierce, but victory was inevitable, because people's needs were different. They changed for two main reasons — the internal combustion engine and central heating. Engines — in cars, lorries, tractors, hoists, chainsaws, milling and rolling machines and a thousand other devices — replaced muscles, and so fuel replaced food. Hard physical labour went out of fashion. 'These days', one landowner remarked, 'my farm staff would use the mechanical digger to bury the farmyard cat'. Central heating saw two woolly vests, a flannel shirt, waistcoat, worsted jacket, gabardine topcoat and felt hat replaced by rayon, and so fuel again replaced food. The vast fat-enriched meals and immense flagons and firkins of beer, wine or cider which our ancestors downed whenever they could get them — essential foods for hard muscular work and warmth — gave way over the years to fast foods, television dinners and vegetarianism.

People's sensitivities also increased. They had been blunted by the brutalities of war, but reappeared more strongly as the long period of peace developed. W.H. Auden put it like this:

The Higher Mind's outgrowing the Barbarian,
It's hardly thought hygienic now to kiss;
The world is surely turning vegetarian;
And as it grows too sensitive for this,
It won't be long before we find there is
A society of Everybody's Aunts
For the Prevention of Cruelty to Plants.

Widespread recognition of all this would take a long time. For at least 20 years after the war a necessary reaction to shortage, hardship and danger saw consumption and indugence rising greedily under such banners as 'I'm all right Jack', 'You've never had it so good', or the Swinging Sixties. The ownership of cars, fridges, television sets and tape recorders increased steadily, the Continental holiday became an annual event. The entire circus was all the while supported by fuel which had never been so cheap, a steadily rising flood of oil from the Middle East at a few shillings a barrel.

Agriculture was having a binge as much as the rest of the economy. Cheap fuel encouraged production and use of fertilisers, tractors, chemicals, and imported and home-grown feedstuffs, whose consumption stuffed the fields, the crops and livestock of our farms. The result was a growing cornucopia to parallel the long post-war boom in our towns and cities. Amongst a few there was also a recognition that cheap fuel and a novel way of burying the farmyard cat were steadily putting the fat into fatal.

It was this which led to the import of the Charolais. They were needed to produce cheap lean meat and counteract the Perth bull sale effect. Big animals could produce cheaply, and big animals tended to be thin. So much energy went into growing size there was little left for growing fat. Big thin dairy cows produced more milk with less cream and big thin beef animals produced more lean and less fat.

The battle for the new beef breeds took longer than the battle to introduce Friesians. Once again Edwards was backed by the MMB and the Ministry, and opposed by the breeders who argued that the foundations of British bloodstock supremacy – not to mention the chance of selling £63 000 Aberdeen Angus bulls – would be destroyed for ever.

Such men, spurning French, Swiss, German and American cows – cows of every nationality, shape and colour but their own – kept the tourniquet tight for six years. In 1955, Edwards asked for permission to import Charolais semen. So strongly did the Breed Societies maintain their resistance that in the end the matter had to be placed before a Commission under the guidance of Lord Terrington. There, in an action bizarrely suited to a cattle rearing drama, traditional breeders slit their own throats. Terrington announced that, just because the opposition to the imports was so great, he knew at once there must be value in them. He advised the Minister of Agriculture, Christopher Soames, to allow the importation. The first beasts arrived in 1961.

In the nineteenth century the French breed had been known as Durham Charolais, for then the needs had been reversed and France had imported Durham Shorthorns to improve their own native stock. Today, the MMB inseminates more cows with Continental than with native beef bulls. Some would now argue that the change has gone too far, that lean Continental beef is tough, flavourless beef, that what we need in milk is more Channel Island quality. But for the time being the rangy new beef breeds appear more and more often on British farms, while the triumph of the black and white cow from Friesland has long since been confirmed.

Before these triumphs were complete, one further development was needed. To be fully effective, a way had to be found to store semen for longer than the two or three days possible when AI was first introduced commercially.

# CHAPTER SEVEN

# Chris Polge and Embryo Transplants

Artificial insemination broke new ground by breaking the natural link. What had gone was the most familiar farmyard story in the world, the story of boy meets girl. It was a slow old story which for centuries had governed the generations of our cattle, sheep, pigs – all our livestock. That ageless drama had finally been rewritten. Now that boy no longer needed to meet girl, traditional reproduction, always frustratingly slow for the impatient breeder, could at last be speeded up.

There were other developments to come which would take sex right out of the straw yard and put it in the laboratory test tube. The men in white coats were about to move in, their influence spreading rapidly from animal to human lives. Of all the parts of the farming story where human and animal mix it is the most dramatic – and it is the animals which have led the way. Fertility drugs, test tube babies, embryo transplants, surrogate mothers and the heartbreak and courtroom dramas that can go with them, all started life down on the farm. Human sexual morality is still struggling to adjust to the extraordinary changes which science has added to nature.

Christopher Polge was the man who did it. He is a comfortable, friendly man whose deliberate and helpful manner does not seem to have altered as a result of his achievement in boosting the breeding cycle of farm animals into low orbit. Not long after you meet him, he will show you a photograph of Isabelle, a Limousin, standing outside British Livestock Embryos Ltd near Royston with her 19 magnificent calves around her. Isabelle is another part of the revolution which replaced Lindertis Evulse.

Her story starts in 1948, fully 15 years before the jackpot was hit that day in Perth. It was then that Polge, later to join the same group at Cambridge which had developed AI, was given the task of trying to preserve fowl semen by freezing. For a long time there had been reports that semen survived freezing to very low temperatures, and could then successfully fertilise a hen. If they were true, AI would become a much more flexible and powerful breeding tool.

Polge tried the recommended technique. He took a solution of fructose, the sugar which gives fruit its sweetness. He diluted the semen in the fructose and froze it rapidly to the temperature of solid carbon dioxide. The semen died. He tried again, with the same result. He kept trying. The semen kept dying. Finally, he decided the reports had been wrong. After months of effort, he gave up the work. AI looked as though it would be limited to live semen, with all the restrictions of timing and transport which that implied. The answer came through one of those odd accidents which frequently come to the rescue of puzzled scientists. The chance came to renew the work and when it did, Polge, undeterred by earlier failure, sent for the remains of his fructose solution.

Immediately there was a change. Far from emerging dead the semen came out of solution leaping with life. An equally lively biologist did not stop to ask awkward questions. He set to work to inseminate his chickens. At last from several hundred carefully manhandled eggs there finally pecked its way into the unexpected light of the laboratory a single chick.

This tiny survivor emerged from its sealed life in the egg to mark the next stage of the breeding revolution. Diminishing stocks of fructose were rapidly replenished so the work could go on. But once again no semen would survive freezing. That was when the questions began. Chris Polge accumulated the minute remaining quantity of successful fructose solution and sent it for analysis.

The solution contained no sugar at all. But it did contain glycerol, the stuff you put in your car radiator to stop it freezing in the winter. It also contained a lot of protein. It was a case of mistaken identity. Somehow the fructose label had ended up on a similar bottle containing Meyer's solution. This mixture of glycerol and egg white was often used in the laboratory, and it was that bottle which had been sent across from the cold store when the work began again.

This lucky chance meant that at last Polge knew how to keep frozen semen alive. There were still a lot of snags, as there were with similar work going on at the same time to preserve blood by freezing – work which laid the foundations for today's blood transfusion services. One by one, they overcame the difficulties. In due course, numerous chicks were raised from frozen semen – the first living animals ever to have been produced in this way by a definable, reliable method.

This was the breakthrough which allowed the AI revolution in cattle to take off. Once you could preserve semen by freezing and successfully fertilise cows with it, you had limitless access to the best bulls. A top bull could fertilise females thousands of miles away, or years after he was dead. Boy no longer needed to meet girl and excellence, unlimited by time and place, could be carried round in a flask of liquid nitrogen.

This was fine for bulls. But what about cows? They carried half the excellence in their eggs, but as things stood after Chris Polge's early work it was only the male seed which could be rapidly spread. That was all about to change as well in a revolution which went back to the 1890s. Then, an embryo had been taken from a rabbit and transplanted into a Belgian hare. There it survived, and in due time gave rise to another rabbit. Since no one had known whether the offspring would be a rare or a habbit, this was an advance in knowledge. Further experiments took place during the 1930s when John Hammond had worked with the oddly matched pair of a Shire horse and a Shetland pony. But progress was slow, and it was not until the 1950s that inability to exploit the excellence of females was again seen as a major problem.

Four things were needed to change this. They were a quantity of eggs, their fertilisation, their removal from the womb, and their safe transfer to a borrowed womb in which a borrowed mother could bring them to successful birth.

Eggs were easy. Egg production could be stimulated by hormones. The human use of this method is now familiar from fertility drugs and the multiple births which result. But, while in humans as many as six or seven babies may be born, a cow can produce 30 or more eggs with heavy doses of the right drugs. Once the eggs have been flushed from the ovaries by hormones, the cow is fertilised by AI. Then the fertilised eggs must be removed. At first, that meant surgery. This was not just messy and difficult; it was also costly, time-consuming and of limited use since a build-up of scar tissue stopped it working more than two or three times for any one cow. The same muddles were then repeated when the fertilised embryo was placed in the foster mother. These difficulties put a stop to the use of embryo transplants for commercial breeding. The technique seemed stuck in the laboratory.

Simple non-surgical methods were needed for embryo transplants to be a practical farmyard proposition. One answer turned out to be a pump. By carefully pumping fluid into the uterus, the fertilised eggs could be flushed out and sucessfully collected in a small dish. With the help of a microscope they could be picked out for temporary storage. It then became possible to pass them down a fine tube into the wombs of other mothers waiting to receive them. There were many difficulties to be overcome among the winding tubes and complicated chemicals of a cow's insides. Like AI in males, the end result was to allow the genes of superior females to be spread rapidly.

The trick of breeding is not to look for the Arnold Schwarzeneggers or Marilyn Monroes of the animal world, but to look for their fathers and mothers. There is only one reliable way to find such parents. Alas, it is statistics. When you have decided exactly what it is you want – rapid liveweight gain, more milk, better conformation, disease resistance, less fat – you have to be able to measure how successfully that quality is passed on to the next generation. To do this needs careful counting, which has removed much of the hit and miss from the business of breeding.

These methods hugely speeded up genetic improvement. Now, a totally new accelerator has appeared. It is, of course, genetic engineering. It started in a laboratory close to Hammond's when James Watson and Francis Crick unravelled the genetic code of DNA and announced they had discovered 'the secret of life'. There is no evidence that the old scientist, still to be seen cycling round Cambridge on his bike, knew what the two young scientists were doing; but his understanding of how mammals work would link with theirs on how this information is handed down the generations. Together, the two would revolutionise animal breeding.

Before that happened, there were other consequences. In 1978 another breeding first took place in Cambridge. Less than 30 years after Chris Polge first watched a chick peck its way out of an egg into the laboratory, Dr Robert Edwards, of the well-named Bourn Hall Clinic, brought together the egg of a woman and the seed of a man in a test tube. The successfully fertilised egg was then returned to the mother's womb. Nine months later Louise Brown was born to parents who, without Chris Polge and Isabelle, without all the intervening work in farmyard and laboratory, would never have been able to hold their own baby in their arms.

Now, hundreds of parents who would otherwise have remained barren have also held their own babies, born in the same way, in their arms. The commercial pressures on farming which drove on the experiments have led to joy for many families. If the reliability is less than with animals, it is partly because we leave the test tube until last, partly because we can't experiment with humans as we can with animals, partly because of moral sensitivities about working with human embryos. As a result, we are still uncomfortably ignorant about test tube babies. There is a good deal of trial and error with women who want to have babies this way and the failure rate is high. So far, the best answer has been to keep on trying.

# CHAPTER EIGHT

# Broadbalk and Fertility

Two hundred years ago the English dug up the battlefields of Europe for bones. They were much reviled for it. The practice was stimulated by phosphatic fertiliser, not necrophilia. The bones were treated with acid to make the phosphate available to plants. J.B. Lawes, father of agricultural chemistry in this country, patented a process to use rock phosphate instead and started the bagged or artificial fertiliser industry.

Over 40 years ago, the *Farmers Weekly* of 5 September 1947 carried the headline 'Rothamsted Director Trounces "Witchdoctor" Critics'. Rothamsted, founded by the same J.B. Lawes whom Europeans cracked into for digging up bones, is the oldest agricultural research station anywhere in the world. It has unrivalled experience of using both natural and artificial fertilisers in continuous experiments going back to 1843. The names of fields at Rothamsted are as well known to farming as battlefields to the military.

The director in 1947 was William Gammie Ogg, and he was answering 'virulent and unprovoked attacks on the practice of using fertilisers, and [those] who claimed it poisoned the soil and injured the health of plants, animals and human beings'. The Scottish indignation still slices through Ogg's words: 'Those holding the most extreme view not only reject fertilisers but engage in rituals recalling the magical practices of the alchemists or the antics of the witch doctors'. But, instead of telling us what those fascinating practices were, he rather lets us down: 'Some base their beliefs on curious anthroposophic philosophies; others simply dislike chemicals.'

Ogg went on to cover ground much cultivated since. Fertilisers do not remove natural fertility; they do not reduce worm populations or those of other soil-dwelling creatures; they do not open crops to attack by insects or diseases; they are not recommended by modern science to the exclusion of manure, but as complementary to it. Opinion today would agree with most if not all of this; but Ogg included most of the issues which are still debated, often in almost the same words.

Nitrogen is a plant food and there must be enough of it to make plant growth take off. Plants no more grow without nitrogen in the soil than birds or aeroplanes fly without wings. The wings of a plant are its leaves, and to work – that is, to raise the plant from a poor, spindly wisp to vigorous leafy lift-off – they must have enough nitrogen. Yields sufficient to feed ourselves in this country depend on adequate supplies of nitrogen.

Broadbalk, perhaps the best-known field at Rothamsted, has grown a crop of wheat every year for 146 years. Some of the field has never been fertilised but still today has nearly 3 tonnes of nitrogen in the top 10 inches. This nitrogen is held in the soil organic matter or humus and seems likely to remain there for at least another 150 and perhaps even another 1500 years.

Sow a wheat crop in this ground, however, and it produces meagre, wispy plants. The nitrogen in humus is so tightly locked up in the soil the plant can make little use of it. An acre of wheat grown there would keep an adult on a European diet alive for a little under three months. But add a good dressing of fertiliser, whether organic manure or bagged nitrogen, to the same soil and at once it will grow a wheat crop to support an adult on a European diet for rather more than 13 months.

The nitrogen in Broadbalk came from raw nitrogen gas, which must be cooked before plants can use it. The cooks are bacteria in the soil – and if that sounds an unlikely spot for a kitchen, it is worth remembering we have long used bacterial cooks to make foods like cheese and yoghurt. These cooks have been changing nitrogen gas into plant food for millions of years, and the nitrogen now locked away in large quantities in the soil of Broadbalk comes from their work. Among them is a group of master chefs called the Rhizobia. They convert atmospheric nitrogen into plant food, a process known as 'fixing' it; and they have gone into partnership with plants known as legumes. Legumes supply Rhizobia with food (mostly sugars) and housing (called nodules) in exchange for nitrogen fixed direct from the atmosphere. When the deal is working well, legumes and bacteria together fix large quantities of nitrogen.

Farmers first put in a takeover bid for this partnership thousands of years ago – though they did not begin to understand how it worked until 100 years ago. Now, legumes specially bred for agriculture are very widely used. George Stapledon described the partnership like this: 'The legume's unique feature which makes it so important is its ability to form root nodules with Rhizobium bacteria. As the root nodule grows the bacteria inside it can take nitrogen gas from the air and transform it into substantial quantities of nitrogenous compounds which are then immediately available for plant growth.' This makes legumes the cornerstone of land improvement in all parts of the world.

Today, bacteria worldwide fix around 90 million tonnes of nitrogen a year, but only what is fixed in farmers' fields is available for a farming takeover. The most widely used legume in this country is clover, though vetches, lucerne, sainfoin, peas and beans are also grown. An acre of well-farmed wheat after three years of clover will produce enough food to keep an adult on a modern European diet alive for nearly 10 months.

This is an excellent return, but there are practical difficulties. Three years of clover to grow one year of wheat means three fields of clover for each field of wheat. That means a lot of animals to graze the clover. Growing peas and beans as well as clover makes a dent in all this cudding, but not big enough to alter the conclusion – that we should produce as much legume nitrogen as we can, but by itself that won't be enough to feed either plants or ourselves fully.

Nitrogen for plants is also available from other microbial cooks. When turning dead plant material into humus, microbes can pass a single atom of nitrogen between them several times in the course of a morning. Some of it becomes available to plant roots as nitrate in a process called mineralisation. Just as farmers have for centuries used legumes, so they have used mineralisation. They have added dung or compost, both of which contribute to the soil kitchen where the microbial cooks are working. The product is excellent but, like legume nitrogen, it is hard to get enough of it.

When, a few hundred years ago, we learnt how to keep farm animals alive through the winter instead of killing them every Michaelmas, there was more farmyard manure. Beef animals, brought into yards for the winter to tread dung and straw into farmyard manure, became the foot soldiers of fertility, while the golden hooves of sheep trod in additional fertility as well. From then on, most arable fields would have received a blowout of this excellent material once every four or five years. Traditional farming was just this partnership between farmers, dung and microbes to supply nitrogen which plants could use, and very laborious it was too. It's too wet to work you'd better go muckspreading, was the endless theme. Short of hoeing, manure-spreading was the most arduous job on the pre-mechanised farm.

As late as 1953 – the year Mount Everest was climbed for the first time – about half the farms in this country were still loading and spreading muck manually. Gnarled hands wrapped around the four-pronged fork, horny tendons prised the straw and dung from the floor of cramped calf house or cow byre and aching muscles threw the forkful on to a cart. Often enough the load was dumped on a large heap in the field, sometimes it was placed in small heaps spaced evenly across the field – either way it was spread across the soil with the same four-pronged fork. The labour took at least four times as long as mechanical spreading. Farmyard manure is terrific stuff. Given an adequate dressing, an acre of wheat can feed an adult on a European diet for 15 months. But, as we have seen, it is very hard to get enough of it.

There are two other ways of turning atmospheric nitrogen into plant food. One is with lightning, but that, at best, is a hit and miss affair. The other is to use a large pressure cooker. At the beginning of this century, a German chemist called Haber discovered how to do industrially what Rhizobia do naturally in nodules. His cooking was as unlike a nodule, as unlike an old farmhouse kitchen, as anything could be. Even today, modern versions are to a nodule as volcanoes to a glow worm. They are pressure cookers at the top end of the heavy chemical industry which, with great ingenuity and force, manage to control massive and continuous explosions and turn them into ammonia, then into nitrates, both of which are chemically identical to the bacterial products. Like farmyard manure, this too is terrific stuff, so good it has been described by switched-on farmers as 'electric shit'.

A typical ammonia plant has vast furnaces and pressure vessels, miles of gleaming piping, endless dials and huge quantities of lubricating fluids, all combining to churn out cooked nitrogen. Around 25 per cent of all the energy used in agriculture goes into producing nitrogen fertilisers. Cereals are particularly heavy users, but in exchange wheat or barley will yield 3 units of energy for every 1 put into them. And they have been getting better at using nitrogen. Wheat grown on Broadbalk 100 years ago recovered 30 per cent of the nitrogen fertiliser applied to it. Ten years ago recovery had improved to nearly 70 per cent of the applied nitrogen. Five years ago, the figure reached 80 per cent. Industrial chemists now make 50 million tonnes of nitrogen fertiliser each year by the Haber process, which is more than 50 per cent of the 90 million tonnes of nitrogen fixed by the bacterial cooks. An acre of fertile soil which has had a full dressing of bagged nitrogen can grow enough wheat to keep an adult on a European diet alive for two years.

For all that Haber achieved, however, the traditional bacterial cooks still hold their place in the kitchen and always will do. But they work slowly, while the human population grows faster and faster; and this has forced farmers to learn how to speed things up. Bagged nitrogen is almost the ultimate in fast foods and has spread among farmers at least as rapidly as hamburgers, pizzas and southern fried chicken have spread among the rest of us.

Hamburger joints have their critics. It wasn't long before fast-food nitrogen came in for criticism too. Since all increases in speed bring with them increases in stress, the question was soon asked whether the speed and stress which came from Haber's pressure cooker were damaging our soils. It was to this question that Ogg gave answer in 1947.

Ogg's predecessor at Rothamsted, Sir John Russell, put it this way: 'Farmers had to obtain high yields in order to remain solvent, and they knew they could never make the hundreds of tons of compost annually required to give even moderate crop increases. So they continued to use artificials.' Russell referred to the wartime years. But through the 1950s the demand for food continued to increase, and this practical necessity overwhelmed the doubters. Farmers gained additional confidence from rising yields as the new methods were better understood, and the great majority felt that the fears were groundless.

After nitrogen, phosphorus is most widely added to crops as a fertiliser. Animal manure, composts, and plant remains are valuable sources of phosphate as well as the bones and the rock phosphate which were treated by Lawes. The organic forms are very stable, so they release phosphorus slowly and over long periods of time. Phosphate fertilisers are particularly important for seedlings and young plants. Lack of phosphorus leads to stunted roots and stems and discoloured leaves. The fertiliser is applied in a variety of forms, and whether it is organic or bagged it does not leach through the soil. It attaches itself to the soil in a trial marriage, and then locks itself to its partner. The other major fertiliser, potash, is important for the growth of seeds and fruits. It also attaches itself intimately to the soil and is especially fond of clay. The attachment means that it does not leach like nitrogen, yet plants can get at it more readily than at phosphates.

# CHAPTER NINE

# Harry Ferguson Cuts the Backache

Farming is a spread and gather operation. Every year we spread 1 million tonnes of cereal seed and gather 25 million; half a million tonnes of potatoes and gather six million; 50 million tonnes of hay, silage and other feeds – in front of animals – and gather well over 50 million tonnes of wastes behind them, spread in its turn on the land and gathered in again as another harvest.

For most of history all these materials have been handled by muscle, human and animal. The observation 'any tool with a wooden handle is made for hard work' was embodied in the horny hands of a million workers. As working horses and wooden handles disappeared, so we have relied on machinery to complete this gigantic labour. For some, the change came too slowly. George Ewart Evans, the celebrated historian of traditional East Anglian farming, records the old farm worker James Seely saying this about the First World War:

'We had a proper training at the beginning of the war, but I remember later drafts coming out to us. They joined the army, had leave, were sent to France and were killed – all in eight weeks. Young kids! Passchendaele was the worst because of the mud and water. You couldn't make trenches because if you dug down more than a foot or so it would fill up straight away with water. We had to make a hollow in the mud, and we lay there like swallows: we used to long for the dark so we could stand up and straighten our legs.

'But do you know, I think the happiest time I ever had was in the army.'

Of this unbelievable preference for the trench over the furrow Evans observes quietly that the countryside 'may have been idyllic to some but evidently not to people who lived as close to the land as James Seely did'.

The man who made the largest single contribution to changing all this was Harry Ferguson, a sharp-eyed visionary and a driving genius. The photographs show aquiline features, rimless spectacles, a wide, determined yet quirkily humorous mouth and an unusually high forehead. It is not the face of the farm worker he was born to be – work which, like James Seely, he hated.

Ferguson was an outstanding engineer – Henry Ford, with whom he worked closely, ranked him with Bell, Edison and the Wright brothers – a determined entrepreneur, a brilliant salesman, an inexhaustible organiser, an obsessive, an enthusiast and a dreamer. His immense skills were devoted to producing a cheap and efficient mechanical system as a means to the end of his personal rainbow. The pot of gold which lay there was neither wealth nor status but cheap and plentiful food, which he believed would cure most of the world's ills.

What Ferguson achieved was to turn the tractor – until then as its name implies a mere hauler – from a mechanical horse into an efficient, lightweight engineering system. Before this, implements could only be trailed behind the tractor, or lifted by the driver who left his seat to swear and heave. There was also a drawback with the drawbar: the pull of the implement tended to swing the tractor up on to its rear wheels and topple it over backwards on to the driver. Ferguson devised a three-point rear linkage on which equipment could be mounted, controlled by a hydraulic lifting mechanism in such a way that the downward force of the implement was transferred to the rear of tractor. This greatly improved traction as well as sharply reducing toppling and swearing – though there was and still is a good deal of swearing in the environment of heavy agricultural machinery.

The prototype, first seen in 1933, was so small and light it was dismissed as absurd. Ferguson outfaced the ridicule by matching his tractor against others in competitive working demonstrations which fully justified his claims. His revolution began to roll off the production line in 1936. It established the basic principles of the modern tractor, and the fundamentals have not altered since. Until very recently the only other major development this century was the introduction of the pneumatic tyre, which changed the machine from a traction vehicle in a field to one which could also be used for transport – and dealt the final blow to the horse.

Ferguson's achievement places him in the same league as Watt, Stevenson and Brunel; as a feat of engineering it ranks with the artificial manufacture of nitrogen for fertiliser as one of the two great pillars on which modern agriculture stands. An excellent description of the introduction of the Fergie is given by Henry Williamson in his *Story of a Norfolk Farm*.

'I turned away from the failure of my scheme and regarded the new tractor. It was as beautiful as the cottages were sordid. It was half the weight of an ordinary tractor, built of aluminium and of immensely strong steel, and it carried its twin-furrow plow under its tail, on three arms that looked like a grashopper's hind legs. On pulling a lever like the short gear-change lever of a racing car, the twin plows lifted up out of the ground.

'Instead of lugging a heavy sledge of plows around the field, bibbling, as Bob said, in the corners, this new design of tractor lifted its tail, and, put into reverse, moved back to exactly where one wanted to drop the implements.

'Both Bob and Jimmy were sceptical of its performance. "You won't beat horses on that ould sud of a Hilly Piece. No tractor can git up that."

'So, as soon as it was run off the planks of the lorry, I took it up Hilly Piece. The field in August was silver-grey with thistles hiding the thin stalks bearing "mouse-ear" barley.

'It was twilight when I got to the field. I took the tractor to the bottom of the steepest part. The engine purred almost silently. I pushed down the lever controlling the hydraulic gear, which dropped the twin plows. I put it in plowing gear, let in the clutch and opened the throttle.

'The little machine went up without the least falter. Its thin spiky wheels pressed the ground lighter than horse-hoofs would have done. Its twin shares bit into the sullen soil and turned it over, exposing a tangle of white roots. I heard Bob mutter: "Blast, I like that patent." This was the highest praise from one who regarded many of my schemes with hard-eyed caution. I was beginning to realise with the early Victorian author of *The Chronicles of Clay Farm* that the hardest part of farming lay in the stubborness of the human ideas.'

It did the job better and it did it more cheaply. One man who has followed the consequences, from the Fergie to the future, is Claude Culpin. His book *Farm Machinery* has been in print for 50 years and has gone through 11 editions, each of which amounts to the latest chapter in the story of the takeover by pistons from muscles on the farm. 'In 1947,' he writes, 'British agriculture had become in some ways more highly mechanised than that of any other country in the world.' The war had given mechanisation a tremendous boost, both because of the shortage of labour and because of the resulting rise in labour costs. Once the war was over and Culpin was established in what had once been Lady de Grey's cupid-bedecked boudoir at Wrest Park, Silsoe, there he stayed, organising the ministerial forces of farm machinery advisers and pouring out information on the latest developments in the industry.

The third edition of his book was published in 1947. It gives a state of the art account of the machinery available at the time. Strikingly, everything we are familiar with today, from grain dryers to self-propelled root harvesters to automatic trenching and drain-laying machines, is included. All the machines were ready and waiting; the manufacturers had already determined where to go next. The debate was about how fast they could persuade the farmers to follow them.

Culpin and the Ministry helped them out, and the arithmetic was simple. One man can develop one-eighth of the power of a horse. With wages at 90 shillings a week, he costs 15 shillings per horse-power hour. Give him two horses to work with and the cost comes down to two shillings and sixpence per horse-power hour. Give him a small tractor and it falls to sixpence per horse-power hour. Conclusion? 'It may safely be claimed that the future of agricultural progress depends largely on the extent to which mechanical power and machinery can be employed to render labour more productive.'

Bob, Jimmy and Williamson himself would have agreed, but none was to farm long enough to find out that once you have a small tractor you are more than halfway towards getting a big one. Bigger tractors are faster and economically more efficient; since one driver can do much more work, the sixpence becomes threepence and then three-halfpence. All these costings drove farmers relentlessly towards size and speed.

To work fast, a big tractor needs big implements behind it and plenty of space. That is why farmers take out the hedges. According to Sturrock and Cathie, two Cambridge economists, 'Fields surrounded by hedges may provide a charming landscape for the town dweller but to the farmer they are his factory floor.

'Field size depended on farm size and very small farms had tiny fields. While horses were used to cultivate the land, small fields were not too much of a disadvantage. Even a 5-acre field could keep a ploughman occupied for a week, but with a tractor he could finish it in a morning and then waste time moving to another field.

'It is not surprising therefore that as tractors and implements increase in size, small fields are regarded as a nuisance by the arable farmer who is tempted to pull out hedges to amalgamate fields.'

Sturrock and Cathie have measured the effects of field size on work rates, and their figures show that a tractor working with an implement 10 feet wide in that 5-acre field spends just about a third of its time cultivating the body of the field. The other two-thirds are spent turning, cultivating the headlands (which are the ends of the field where the tractor turns round) and changing fields or implements.

In a 25-acre field, effective working time rises towards two-thirds, and in a 100-acre field it gets to nearly three-quarters. Similar advantages come from using bigger implements, and more advantages again from using even bigger and faster tractors. Put all these factors together and the differences become enormous. When tractor, implement, speed and field size are small to middling, the work rate is around 10 acres a day. When everything is huge, 115 acres a day can be covered.

This speed is very important quite apart from the economies of scale. It adds up to good farming. Ask what the difference is between a good farmer and a bad one and, 20 years ago, the answer would have been a fortnight. Today, inevitably, the answer is less, and in some cases it may be down to a few hours. One farmer said recently about a particular task that those who sat down to watch the Cup Final missed their only opportunity that spring to get the job done at the right time. Perhaps he exaggerated. But it shows the pressures which drove farmers to take out hedges.

Farmers do not, though, see a hedge just as time and money. Traditionally, a hedge is a good guard, as boundary to field and farm, and as shelter for stock, as well as birds and insects which benefit farming purposes. It is a bad thief, stealing light and fertility from nearby crops – a hedgerow tree may steal both for up to 40 feet into a field – while some of the birds, insects and weeds in hedges will steal directly from the crops and stock which farmers struggle to husband. As for the beauty of a hedge, opinions will vary; but a sensible owner will consult more than one opinion on this difficult question.

Before the nineteenth-century invention of barbed wire, farmers had no choice in the matter. When they needed guards, they needed hedges, except in some uncompromising parts of the country where they used stone. Historically, we know that hedges have come and gone, and many of the ones now going were installed during the enclosures which stretch across 300 years of our history. How much hedge has gone? No one is sure, but Dr Norman Moore of the Nature Conservancy estimated that in 1947 there were around 620 000 miles and that now somewhere close to 500 000 miles remain.

From the point of view of wildlife, especially birds, what is more important than the quantity is the quality of the hedges we still have. One survey by the great hedgeman Dr Max Hooper, the proposer of Hooper's Hedge Rule, counted the birds' nests on three farms. He showed that one farm with half as many hedges as the other two had the same number of nests, because it had twice as many nests per mile of hedge. Another study by Moore showed that, when hedges are allowed to grow bulky by trimming only every few years, the number of birds is greatly increased. When the bottom of the hedge is allowed to thicken out into an A-shape, the number of species can increase to twice that of a tightly clipped or layered hedge.

Sturrock and Cathie summarise the debate over hedges and birds like this: 'If fields are quadrupled in size from 25 acres to 100 acres, hedges will be reduced by about half. If the remaining hedges are well distributed about the farm and allowed to grow for five or ten years (between trimmings) they could accommodate many more birds per 100 yards.'

Management is thus very important. Without it, hedges deteriorate and in time disappear. With it, their value both for us to look at and for wildlife to live in can be increased. This management costs money. It is money which farmers would pay more happily if they knew more about the consequences. They don't and, as Norman Moore has pointed out, no more does anyone else. 'Far too little research has been done to determine the exact value of hedges. We simply do not know the extent to which natural predators in hedges can reduce the need to use pesticides; we know very little about the significance of different densities of hedge in reducing soil erosion.

'Only governments can fund the long-term research which is necessary; so far, regrettably little has been done. Until more facts are available it will be extremely difficult to use the agricultural value of hedges as a convincing reason for their retention.' Oddly, this plea was made 100 years earlier from the other side of the fence, when C.W. Hoskyns, author of *Talpa or the Chronicles of a Clay Farm* wrote of hedges that 'it would be a difficult but interesting task to make out a calculation of the economy per acre of the riddance of these hideous and useless strongholds of roots, weeds, birds and vermin that afflicts the farms of merry England. Unproductive in themselves of anything that is good – for even the timber they contain is rarely so – they are equally an obstruction to the plough that toils for bread and the eye that wanders for beauty.'

It was not just the plough and then the tractor which needed more space, it was also the combine harvester, the second great mechanical accelerator of modern farming. 'Fifty years ago the normal method of cutting corn was with the scythe, and one man could then mow about an acre a day. With a binder and two teams of three horses each, 10 acres a day can now be cut and tied by one man; while if two men are equipped with a tractor and a combine harvester, they can cut and thrash up to 20 acres a day. This illustrates the imperative need for present-day farmers to appreciate the economic possibilities of mechanisation.' Thus Culpin summarised the position in the preface to his first edition, published in 1938. The same is true wherever you look. A horse mower with two men took more than 2 man hours to cut an acre of grass, a tractor mower with one man took an hour. A gang of potato planters working without machinery took 18 man hours to sow an acre, while automatic planting took under 6 man hours. More than one farmer would complain that he employed men, not man hours; but such results could drive the industry in only one direction.

The first combine, an American invention of course, arrived in Britain in 1927. By 1945 they had established their superiority in speed and economy but even so there were no more than 3000 in the country. Much of the crop was still cut and bound in sheaves – indeed, there were still men with scythes who cut round the outside of the field to open up the crop for the binder. There were no grain dryers, so the sheaves were stooked in the fields to dry. These stooks or shocks were then ricked and later threshed.

The really laborious business was threshing. It was described by Jack Cornell to Ashley Cooper in his excellent book *The Long Furrow*. The machinery needed came as traction engine, to provide the power, and drum, to do the threshing. It took a lot of labour.

'I used to reckon about 10 to keep the drum going and then you'd need a couple or three more to load and convey the sacks to the barn. You see, it was like this, two men came with the machine, the driver and the feeder. In addition, you'd have one man to take off the threshed corn from the drum; one man would be bagging off the chaff and another would take the chaff to the barn and collect the water for the engine. Then there would be two or three men pitching from the stack on to the threshing machine where the feeder received their sheaves. Finally you'd need another couple of men to build a stack of the loose straw that came off the elevator.'

All crops benefited from the mechanical harvesting which replaced these labour-intensive methods. Colonel Uvedale Corbet, who was to make his mark by setting up Sun Valley poultry in Hereford, employed 50 women from the town every year to harvest a similar acreage of blackcurrants. Today he grows more than 100 acres of the fruit. He has to, because a modern harvester demands that acreage for economic working – yet requires fewer than 10 people to keep it running. Wherever crops were grown the story was the same: smaller workforce, larger machines, bigger fields and faster work rates.

Claude Culpin is absolutely confident of the benefits: 'The prime objective was always to find ways of getting one man to do a job where more than one had done it before. The aim was to increase profitability and to get rid of manual labour which was unpleasant and unpopular.'

Culpin's crusade was to get rid of wooden handles. But as an extreme example of unpleasantness he cites carrying the 4-bushel wheat sacks from the back of the threshing machine to the barn. A 4-bushel sack weighed over 2 hundredweight – that is 9 of them weighed more than a ton. The work was not especially unpopular. In fact in the manner of a tougher and more physical time, the ability to hump these monsters was a matter of pride among farm workers. Strong men carried two, one under each arm, but one on its own was enough to do fearful damage to spine and hips. Other organs also suffered. Clouds of dust and moulds were vigorously inhaled by hard-working lungs, which meant widespread infection with the disease known inevitably as farmers' lung. Jack Cornell described the threshing machine as the dirtiest thing ever invented. There were rats everywhere.

Machinery transformed spreading and gathering, as well as ploughing and cultivating. All are still hard work, but most of the aches and pains have gone. Today there is no aspect of that once fearsome physical labour which cannot be done mechanically.

Although economic factors were pre-eminent, in muck-spreading, in harvesting, in hoeing and in planting, there were other factors at work as well. In the third edition of his book Culpin wrote: 'Compared with sugar beet singling, and potato or beet harvesting, potato planting requires little labour. A gang of 12 Fen women will plant 10 to 12 acres a day of unchitted seed, or 7 to 9 of chitted; and so long as good labour is available farmers in such districts are unlikely to be greatly interested in mechanical planters. It seems possible, however, that the days of large labour gangs are numbered, and it would not be surprising if many farmers who have no use for potato planters today may be unable to do without them in a few years' time.'

The Fen gangs, the Hereford blackcurrant harvesters, the working horses – all were to go. Forty years ago there were still more than half a million horses. Now those patient, docile, faithful animals have all gone, to be replaced by the even more patient and docile tractor. By the middle of the 1950s tractors outnumbered horses; by the middle of the 1970s they outnumbered farm workers. Now there are getting on for half a million tractors. In terms of horse-power the increase has been stupendous: modern farming can call on the equivalent of 25 million horses, 50 times as many as there were just after the war, to get the work done on time.

This delights Claude Culpin. His quiet, unassuming and helpful manner hides a clear example of the man who knows his own mind. He has consistently resisted attempts to divert him from his central concern and interest. Sir Miles Thomas of Nuffield tried to get him into business when he advised the company on the design and manufacture of its first tractor. The Ministry of Agriculture offered him many ladders into wider and more powerful areas of operation. He has resisted them all and stuck faithfully to the machines which have taken the backache out of spreading and gathering.

Although the end of the wooden handle was the beginning of easier working, the story is incomplete without a footnote. George Scales, a leader of organised farm labour in the then NUAAW, has said that the greatest invention in farming was the wellie. Machines may have seen hands less horny: wellies put a stop to centuries of soaking feet.

# CHAPTER TEN

# Joe Nickerson and Plant Breeding

Wheat is the Daley Thompson of British crops. What are the 10 things it does best? It makes bread, biscuits, breakfast cereals, flour and whisky, as well as being a nutritious animal feed. It is used to make syrups for food-processing and glues to make cardboard and paper, and can be used to make plastics. It is supple, versatile and strong – but it did not start out that way.

It began its life as a 7-stone weakling, and everyone kicked sand in its face. The pre-war wheat crop, spindly, sickly, and weedy, produced a small amount of our bread, a few of our biscuits and a bit of chicken feed from the left-over tailcorn. The contrast between today's muscular athlete and yesterday's wimp could scarcely be greater. Then we bought 7 in every 10 tons of wheat from North Americans or Australians; now we sell wheat to the world. The change came because we have the climate for wheat-growing, and the scientific, technical and management skills to take advantage of it. Wheat is a huge home-grown success story, and will continue to be so.

The few pre-war fields of sparse, straggly cereals full of weeds and unknown, unrecognised diseases, yielding around a ton an acre – about the world average today – did not displease the eye of the farmer because it had seen no better. The demands of war and the immediate post-war years saw rapid improvements, even though the technical demands for growing the crop were still small. There were a few chemical weedkillers and insecticides, but no disease killers at all. Once the seeds had been sown the chief task was to keep the gate shut and most of the animals out until harvest.

Harvesting was increasingly mechanised, but the level of technical demand is illuminated by the General Proficiency test of the Women's Land Army, then still in its wartime glory and contributing much to the muscle-power required. Two of the six skills tested were pitching straw and loading straw. The other four were harnessing and driving a horse, beet singling, swapping – and spreading manure. As well as dung, men and women also fertilised the land by heaving soot, marl, chalk and lime, shoddy, blood and bone meal, basic slag and even the occasional trainload of sprats.

A modern combine would have left as much as 75 per cent of this sorry crop in the field, as a mixture of straw and weeds. As a direct result of these methods of growing wheat, the Atlantic and Channel ports swarmed with dockers, the skyline was crowded with silos, elevators, flour and feed mills; the streets of Liverpool, Bristol and Southampton thronged with the workers in these enterprises. Vast quantities of our food and animal feed came to us through the businesses which established themselves around these deep water ports.

Today, much of this activity has moved to wheat fields, silos, elevators and mills spread throughout the country. The docks of Liverpool stand silent. Where there is still activity in the ports it has swung to the opposite side of the country, to the North Sea, and now the wheat is pouring out, not in. Cheap fuel and the internal combustion engine hastened these changes while rapidly easing the crushing burdens on millions of muscles. But they were far from the only technical improvements on the way, and the one which was perhaps chief among them slides into our story over the snow-covered Lincolnshire landscape on a sledge. Ralph Whitlock has described the scene: 'When the arranged date for the journey arrived, Lincolnshire was buried in snow many feet deep. In that winter, the roads around Rothwell were blocked by snowdrifts for about 10 weeks.

'Ted Drury and Len Templeman, based in the town, had been instructed to meet J.N. at a certain time on the main London road, which had been kept fairly clear for traffic. They arrived wondering how he would be able to negotiate the snow-blocked lanes of the steep-sided valley leading up from Rothwell. They were not kept waiting. Within a few minutes they saw J.N. speeding over the windswept fields in a horse-drawn sleigh.'

J.N. was, and is, Sir Joseph Nickerson, and the description is taken from Whitlock's biography of him, *Roots in the Soil*. He is a man with the bearing and can do of a Guards' officer. Perhaps this explains his passion for cereals, which at his command have been drilled in massed ranks across the fields of England. He has driven himself, his company and his crops with the precision of the parade ground, but above his spruce military moustache has always gleamed an eye as sharp for tactics and strategy as for square-bashing. That eye, screwed up against the cold and glare, saw clearly not the glitter of the undulating Linclonshire snow fields but the golden sea of harvest, and the new varieties of wheat and barley which would grow there to feed the post-war world.

Nickerson realised that European breeders were far ahead of the British. In fact, there was no barley breeding in Britain at all except 'for HM Government, who had one variety, bred in those days in an old shed by the late Professor Bell.'

Bell had bred barley for many years. His greatest success came in the early 1950s with Proctor, which at its peak was to occupy 4 out of every 5 acres sown to barley in this country. This immensely successful variety helped barley production rise from 2 million tons a year to 6 million tons by the early 1960s.

If there was little breeding with barley, there was less with wheat. We sowed foreign seeds with names like Atle, Champlein, and above all the famous Cappelle Desprez. But wheat was stirring too in Bell's old shed, soon to be transformed into the post-war Plant Breeding Institute where in due course our home-grown wheats would be transformed into today's world-beaters. The reason the new varieties came from across the Channel, and not from Rothwell or Cambridge, was that European breeders could collect royalties to reward them for the risks they took. Those risks were very large.

To breed a new wheat, the breeder must become an insect. This is because wheat, a self-pollinating plant, breeds true from one generation to the next. To make a cross – that is to produce a different wheat – a breeder must first prevent self-pollination, then bring in pollen from another plant as insects do when they pollinate plants which cross-breed naturally. When the wheat plant flowers, the breeder delicately snips the male organ from every flower so that no pollen can be produced. Each castrated ear is then sealed into a plastic bag with a carefully chosen partner so that its remaining female organs are fertilised by the partner's pollen. This gives the first cross.

This finicky operation must be repeated hundreds of times. A large breeder will make more than 1000 crosses a year. This gives around 2 million plants a year later, all of which the breeder must examine for signs of improvement on their parents. The main goal is higher yield. Other aims are improved quality or better disease resistance. The huge majority of crosses fail this test, but some 50 000 of them are good enough to be sown again for the next year. Ten or 12 years later, one or two of these plants may have survived to produce a new variety for farmers.

Not surprisingly, such labour, patience and investment were uncommon when a new variety belonged to everyone as soon as it was released. That meant the breeder could profit from it only in the first year of its introduction. After that, anyone could grow it on. As late as 1956 a leading journalist could write: 'The few varieties which have been bred in this country are the product not of the private plant breeder but of government stations. For the seed firms who indulge in breeding, it is chiefly a matter of prestige. They get a certain amount of publicity from producing a new variety but precious little else. It just does not pay to produce a new variety in this country.'

Such difficulties did not discourage Nickerson. He collected breeding material across the Continent, and soon had contracts with 100 breeders. Within a few years, Rothwell would embark on its own programmes of breeding for cereal varieties particularly suited to this country.

He was not just an entrepreneur of unusual clarity and vigour. He was also a practical farmer. Whitlock tells how he instructed his representatives always to carry a piece of string, a pocket-knife, cigarettes even if they did not smoke, and chocolate bars for the farmers' children. 'You won't be in the company of a farmer for long,' said J.N., 'before he will need either string or a knife. This is where you will gain points by producing either.'

Thus armed, the Nickerson organisation started down a very successful road. Meanwhile, the founder worked away behind the scenes to underpin plant breeding with something more substantial than scissors, pocket-knives and string. The results of this lobbying were to end in Nickerson holding open house for 10 days in a suite in the Dorchester Hotel, where he briefed Members of Parliament and others who might help in securing the introduction of Plant Breeders' Rights. The Plant Varieties and Seeds Act, which was passed in 1964, largely as a result of these activities, has rewarded breeders with royalty payments ever since.

The results were to be dramatic both for Nickerson and farmers, because new cereal varieties are the most important single factor in pushing up yields. About half the increase is brought about by better seeds – and in the 15 years after Nickerson's 1947 sledge ride, yields of wheat doubled to around two tons an acre.

For farmers, this meant that growing cereals became very profitable. 'For 20 years up to 1964, one of the easiest, pleasantest and most certain ways of making an income was to grow corn.' Through those years, governments encouraged farmers to grow all the corn they could. Farmers who did so got to know the pleasures of the weekend, probably for the first time in the history of farming. They made so much from corn, potatoes and sugar beet they could get rid of all their livestock. This was attractive because of the poor returns from sheep and beef, quite apart from putting an end to Sunday working.

Wheat had made nearly £30 a ton in the early 1950s. It came back to £25 in the 1960s, but higher yields allowed farmers to absorb both that and a chunk of their higher costs. These yields were needed. At the beginning of the decade, growing 26 hundredweight gave a good profit; by the middle, it broke even; by the end, it made a loss. Still, without excessive effort or outstanding skill, most made profits of from £10 to £20 an acre through the period. Every farmer who could, and some who couldn't, wanted to get in on it, and the wheat and barley acreage expanded, very much at the expense of the oats which were no longer needed to feed the horses.

The bonanza stuttered in 1963 when Christopher Soames summoned the Russian Ambassador to the Ministry of Agriculture. (In those days, the state of home-grown production was such that we bought corn from Russia.) When Soames heard that year's asking price for barley from the Steppes, he looked sombre. The Ambassador promptly named a lower figure. Such bargaining had become part of his job, and it came as no surprise to see the Minister shake his head again. Then, when the Russian refused to go lower, Soames burst out with the plea not for a price cut but for a rise.

Now it was the Ambassador's turn to shake his head. He had learned the skills of grain trading, he had struggled with his hosts' sense of humour and nowhere more than with the ministerial brand of it, but here was a new sort of trade, a different joke. When he realised Soames was serious, he shook his head some more: if he ever understood English humour, he would never understand capitalism.

However, the reasoning was simple. Farmers received deficiency payments which made up the difference between the market price and the price guaranteed by the Ministry. Cheap supplies from overseas drove down the market price and increased the gap to be covered by deficiency payments. Soames's little chat, so confusing to the Ambassador, was a signal that the government had reached its limit. Minimum imports prices were one sign of this. Standard quantities were another; they restricted the amount of a commodity on which deficiency payments could be made, and so put a ceiling on Treasury support.

From then until we joined the Common Market, further attempts were made to cut back – apart from periodic economic crises when agriculture was again pushed forward in its import-saving role. But, although the profitability of corn growing was a little less certain, it was still easy and pleasant. The technical revolution, of which plant breeding was a part, rolled on in other spheres. If half the increased yields which gave governments their problems had come from Proctor and Cappelle Desprez, the other half came from the wider use of machines and nitrogen fertiliser, and from the early use of chemical pesticides.

# CHAPTER ELEVEN

# The Magical Chemical Hoe

We have seen how British muscles have long forgotten the worst strains of labouring on the land. Our only memories of it are in words. Ashley Cooper, in his book *The Long Furrow*, considered pulling sugar beet by hand one of the worst jobs. Bob Daniels, who had done it in his youth, told him 'I used to bind up my arms and wrists to give them support. When it was rough and cold I just carried on with the job and after a while forgot about the discomfort'.

Years earlier, Rider Haggard had taken up farming in Norfolk, where he wrote: 'to contemplate the spectacle of two men commencing to drain a great expanse of 6 or 8 acres of stiff clay land on some dull and cheerless day in January is to understand the splendid patience of developed man. The task looks so vast in the miserable grey light; it seems almost impossible that two men should find the strength to dig out all those long lines of trenches, or at least that they should have the spirit to attempt it. Yet if you speak to them you will find that they are not in the least depressed at the prospect, in fact the only thing which troubles them is the fear lest frost or snow should force them to pause in their monotonous labour.'

When Cooper asked one farm worker what he thought about in the fields all day, the old man replied 'What the hell does any young man think about in a damn great field when he's all by himself for days on end?' Perhaps Rider Haggard underestimated the frustration – though he did not underestimate another muscle-cracking task when he remarked 'truly of weeds there is no end'. If that seems doubtful today, the beginning of weeds will remain forever far from view since, contrary to popular belief, hoeing is the oldest profession.

The hoe gives more than a healthy appetite. Throughout history it has done damage not just to plants but to people, very often women: 'In traditional cropping systems, the labour available for weed control is the limiting factor for the area which can be planted (never plant a garden larger than your wife can weed).'

The hoe was to a farm what the mop was to a house. Both kept the place clean. As today's house has supplemented mops and muscles with vacuum cleaners, washing machines, food processors, fridges, detergents, disinfectants, cleaners for windows and bathrooms, powders for flies and spiders, poisons for mice and rats, treatments for rots dry and wet; so today's farm has replaced armies of labourers with a similar range of machines and chemicals. More muscles and time are saved on farms by modern weed control methods than by any other innovation.

The horse hoe, still in use in the 1950s and 1960s, had been the first great improvement on hand hoeing, but even the horse hoe had its critics. One old farm worker remarked to Rider Haggard that farming with the hoe instead of with the plough was what made the weeds. In his boyhood, weeds were ploughed down, as many as four times if that was necessary to clean a piece of ground. With or without the horse, however, the hoe often worked but poorly.

'The weeding that is performed is generally done by women and children, and so soon as the thistle, cockle, and other rubbish are sufficiently grown to be cut by the weed hook, or drawn by hand: the most common and injurious weeds, and those stated to be most difficult to subdue, are charlock and coltsfoot; these seem to have taken their permanent, and often undisturbed residence in many places in the district.'

The long summer holiday that school children enjoy today is in part a hangover of the time when children were needed to keep the fields clean during late spring and early summer, and then later to help with harvest. Even in those tough days good farmers kept on top of weeds. Crop rotations helped; so did knowledge of weed behaviour. As long ago as 1855 the Professor of Botany at Cirencester could write of weeds 'there is perhaps no object in nature which is so well understood'.

The professor, right in theory, was wrong in practice. As well as knowledge, something else was needed – masses of cheap labour.

Shortly after he spoke, the farming depression saw a steep decline in the workforce, and weeds rapidly repossessed the fields from which they had been so laboriously uprooted. Industrialisation ensured the labour would never be available again. Weeds stayed in possession until the arrival of chemical hoes nearly 100 years later.

Farmed crops are very poor competitors with other plants; they demand bare soil, high fertility and the minimum of competition to thrive. In this they are like weeds, and from the very start of farming, crops and weeds have mimicked each other. Some people even argue that farming started in a dustbin. Weedy crop plants flourished in the trash heaps of the earliest settlements because they were the sort of open, fertile habitats which such plants preferred. Supporters of this theory argue that these 'habitation weeds' sought out humans as much as we sought them; indeed that weeds need people, and above all farmers, to survive and flourish.

The crops and weeds which started out in this tangle of intimacy stayed that way for thousands of years. This was long accepted as a fact of life; neither the Greeks nor the Romans had a word for weeds. They ate the weeds as often as the crops, often without knowing or caring which was which. The two often swapped roles, for as crops like barley were taken to cooler regions, the weeds – like rye, oats or vetches – thrived until they became the crop and the crop the weed.

This mimicry gave weeds weapons for survival. Above all, they produce a lot of seeds which stay alive for years. Sir Edward Salisbury, whose patience might have astonished even Rider Haggard, counted 480 000 seeds from one poppy plant. Other workers, almost equally patient, found the average number of weed seeds buried in today's arable fields to be around 5000 a square metre. Weedy fields may contain five times this quantity, and as many as 100 000 have been recorded in infested fields.

John Fryer, who has devoted his life to the subject, believes that peasant farmers lose 25 per cent of their crops to weeds. Recent work at Long Ashton Research Station on poppies tells us that each pair of beautiful redheads, so seductive when seen from the roadside, replaces one wheat plant. Sir Edward Salisbury, still counting, found an average poppy produced 17 000 seeds so some 8000 wheat plants are threatened when a poppy goes unweeded.

Cleavers are the most aggressive of all arable weeds in this country; one will hack down seven wheat plants. Wild oats come second, each felling more than two plants, while poppies and mayweeds are equal third. At the seedling stage such weeds can throttle a crop completely, which is why most hoeing is done at crop emergence. All this explains why it seemed miraculous to farmers when tens of thousands of years of hoeing misery disappeared in a puff of spray. They had never seen anything more dramatic than this rapid, powerful, selective chemical control.

The first hint of this puff had come in 1926 when F.W. Went, working in Holland, identified a naturally-occurring chemical which could regulate the growth processes in plants. He summed up his reactions, with Dutch brevity and unhelpful circularity, by stating 'no growth without growth substance'. Ten years later, workers at ICI's Jealott's Hill laboratory observed that these plant hormones could make a plant exhaust itself by outgrowing its own strength.

Before the miracle happened there were a number of false starts. Sulphuric acid was one of these. You can still see the metal helmets worn by early users, riddled with holes eaten through the crown and brim. Other unpromising materials included arsenic and DNOC, both of which were highly poisonous and killed insects, mammals and – if used without protective clothing – humans before their use was banned. Sodium chlorate was less destructive but like DNOC had the unfortunate side effect of bursting unexpectedly into flames. Many was the pair of unwary trousers which caught fire in this way.

The use of these chemicals was accelerated by war. The only fields full of farm workers were battlefields, food was desperately needed, and anything which would increase food production was thrown into the fray. Even so it is difficult, today, to understand why people should risk flaming trousers and worse for weed control. The story becomes clearer if, instead of looking at what farmers did, we look at the commercial development of these techniques.

Pest Control Ltd was one of the earliest companies dealing in the new methods of control. Its company history describes the environment it faced.

'The late 1930s were nearing the end of a long period of agricultural depression and technological stagnation in the UK and Europe. The farming industry was labour-intensive, with a poorly paid and relatively unskilled labour force. Capital equipment was minimal with the horse still the main prime mover, fertiliser input was low and so were yields and commodity prices.

'Control of pests and diseases was confined to a few high-value crops and the chemicals used were for the most part discovered in the nineteenth century. Weed control was still largely based on the plough, hoe and hand.'

The new company emerged from this background through the unlikely collaboration of an elderly British insect imperialist with an energetic Austrian-American insect entrepreneur. Sir Guy Marshall had built up the Imperial Institute of Entomology to advise plantation agriculturalists, but realised his research would lead nowhere if farmers could not apply it. Dr Walter Ripper was collecting European parasites to help control pests introduced into America. Both men dreamed of an organisation which would do for the farmers' crops what the medical profession did for his health. They wanted to 'make it as socially respectable for the entomologist to turn his profession into a profitable business as it was for the GP to pocket his traditional guineas'.

Their timing could not have been better: 'The development of the Company during its formative years was profoundly affected by war conditions. The very foundation of the firm was encouraged by the national drive for home food production. The rising farm profits and falling labour force created an opportunity for contractors trying to exploit the market. Farmers who might have been doubtful whether their crops really needed spraying were persuaded by the Ministry's advisers it would be foolish to take a chance with the nation's food supply.'

Cometh the hour, cometh the chemical, pretty much summed up the early response. Pest Control Ltd was established in a disused roadside petrol station near Hauxton Mill in Cambridgeshire, near the Chequers public house. It was to become a significant location in the developing era of scientific pest control.

That science was still of the suck-it-and-see school. There is a photograph of Dr Ripper walking behind a three-wheeled tractor which puffs along at 1 mile an hour trailing a 'gasproof' dragsheet, the whole emitting enough smoke for a fair-sized dragon. It was the first time nicotine gassing had been taken out of the glasshouse and into the field. 'Oddly enough, the operations did not result in any serious incidents, and only non-smokers seemed affected by exposure to the vapour or dust,' says the official history.

If early tractor-drawn models were Heath Robinson, they were more than matched by the first helicopter spraying which took place in September 1945: 'The spray boom was removed from the back of a normal tractor-drawn spraying machine and hung on a Sikorsky R-4 helicopter. A 100-foot hose connected the sprayer on the ground to the aerial boom. The tractor driver, Mr W. Cornwell, then drove the spraying machine at the normal pace through the crop. Dr Ripper and Dr Greenslade walked behind supporting the hose, and Mr Marsh, the RAF pilot, flew behind, trying to keep the hose taut and the boom no more than 4 feet above the crop. The laden helicopter contraption was so unstable that when released from the hosepipe the pilot considered it safer to return to his base flying backwards.'

As bizarre, at least to European eyes, is a photograph showing the youthful King Hussein of Jordan observing with interest the world's first camel-mounted sprayer, a device whose extraordinary nature is emphasised by the amazed yet characteristically haughty expression not of the monarch but of the camel. Rather than trail spray tank and boom behind on a wheeled cart, like a horse-drawn sprayer, the tank was mounted for'ard and the boom immediately astern of the camel's hump.

These early devices worked. The nicotine vaporiser killed 99 out of 100 aphids and left their natural enemies unharmed. It was so successful it spread to crop dusting, with the copper sulphate dust used to control potato blight also trapped beneath the 25-foot dragsheet. But it was expensive so, to increase use of the machines, weed control was offered as a contracting service, at first with sulphuric acid, then with DNOC, which was more selective but, as we have seen, in its own way just as unpleasant. 'There were,' comments the company history, 'several hair-raising incidents when the concentrate just took fire as it was being loaded into sprayers in the field.'

At first there was no ill-health among operators. Then workers in the manufacturing plant went sick, so regulations for manufacture and use were carefully reviewed. But in field conditions some operators took short cuts, and although the dangers led to the development of air-conditioned spray cabs this was not before eight operators had died from inadequate protection. A mandatory scheme for protecting employees and a voluntary scheme for clearing new products were then introduced. The second, the Pesticides Safety Precaution Scheme remained in effect for nearly 30 years until it was replaced in 1985 by the Food and Environment Protection Act.

All this, however, was still well into the future in the late 1940s, when the industry was almost entirely unregulated. It was hardly surprising that farmers were happy to leave application of messy, yellow-staining and toxic substances like DNOC to the self-styled experts. Thus, despite the problems, the years from the end of the war to the mid 1950s saw the first great period of expansion. Pest Control Ltd became an established leader within the new industry. The company realised that the arrival of low-volume spraying machines and 'safe' hormone herbicides like MCPA would undermine its contracting activities, and moved towards becoming a research-based company. 'The mainstay of Pest Control business in the early 1950s was the manufacture, sale and application of selective weedkillers in farm crops.' These were the products emerging from the work in Holland and then by ICI, as well as by scientists at Rothamsted.

Farmers initially displayed a characteristic suspicion of such new-fangledness. One early commercial rival to Pest Control Ltd, driven from the farmyard by an unpersuaded farmer, turned into a field of wheat and traced with his sprayer the outline of the Union Jack. As the weeds grew in the rest of the crop, the patriotic advertisement displayed its message until harvest finally erased it.

In the midst of all this competition, development and sheer technological excitement, management had been suffering at Pest Control. The company found itself constantly expanding but, because there never seemed to be time for consolidation, it remained unprofitable – as though, sprayed with one of its own hormone herbicides, it was constantly outgrowing its own strength.

The conflict between rapid growth and insufficient control continued until in the mid-1950s a change of management became unavoidable. In 1954 Fisons, whose agricultural interests were in fertilisers, took over the pioneer crop protection company, whose name was changed to Fisons Pest Control Ltd. Later, Fisons itself was to be taken over – but the site at Hauxton has remained in use throughout.

Thus the new businesses boomed and went on booming. As the Pest Control history put it: 'new classes of pre-emergence herbicides began to appear, non-poisonous, non-explosive and of such low solubility they could be applied to the soil and left to lie in wait for the germination of the weeds, without fear rain would quickly wash them away.' The first generation of hormone herbicides was soon to be followed by a new group which worked differently, by attacking photosynthesis, the mechanism which plants use to convert the energy of sunlight into sugars. These materials, also selective, were in general much safer for insects and mammals for the obvious reason that only plants photosynthesise.

The best-known of all of them was paraquat, or Gramoxone, which was not selective and achieved wide use as a chemical plough. Scientists and farmers had increasingly asked themselves the question, what is ploughing for? The chief answer was weed control. If chemicals could do that job, why not use them instead of the plough and design a drill to sow directly into the stubble of the preceding crop? Such thinking in the early 1960s combined with the appearance of paraquat to give rise to direct drilling and minimal cultivations.

This marked an important change. John Fryer pointed out that until then herbicides had simply been chemical hoes. They fitted into a husbandry which remained similar in many ways to Tull's horse hoeing. Now, with what he called the herbicide revolution, they were part of a more fundamental change. They allowed farmers not just to drill crops but also to change the productivity of pastures and meadows, all without the time, trouble and expense of ploughing. They could keep orchards permanently clean. They could keep paths and roads weed-free. Weed species might now begin to disappear, and the animals which lived on them to become scarce.

The third generation of herbicides worked by stopping cell-division in plants. Again, many of them were selective, and again the best known, glyphosate, was a total herbicide. Glyphosate, or Roundup, was first discovered during a search for fire-retardant chemicals. For a fire retardant it turned out to be a helluva weedkiller, becoming the best-selling and most profitable herbicide of all. It is widely used for chemical ploughing, but unlike paraquat – which is safe when used correctly but poisonous if swallowed directly – it has very low toxicity. When Monsanto first launched it to a press gathering in this country they 'forgot' to mention this fact. The journalists took the bait and opened with a predictable barrage of questions about toxicity – allowing the company's American representative to drawl that it was 'a good deal less toxic than table salt'. Since that was 'match' to Monsanto it was unnecessary to add 'We think it's pretty safe.'

This means Roundup can be used in ripe crops to control weeds before harvest, a method which offers the most effective form of couch control yet. The chemical is widely used to deal with this all-embracing weed, and has taken the herbicide revolution to a new stage which is still not over.

John Fryer's fears about all this have not proved groundless; nor have they been entirely fulfilled, and we shall come back to the danger of disappearing weeds later. More immediate environmental effects had, however, caused greater concern. As early as 1954, Norman Moore, then a regional officer for the Nature Conservancy, had described: 'reports that hares and game birds had been turned yellow and had been killed by DNOC . . . We tried to measure the effects of spraying by making observations before and after spraying. It was my first encounter with the problems of doing research on the effects of pesticides. I learnt how extraordinarily difficult it was to obtain results . . . pheasants, partridges and hares are large animals, they are not nearly as easy to count as one might assume.'

This was because movements of animals around the countryside could easily mask the effects of any poisoning. If Moore found this the case with yellow hares, the difficulty of counting small birds or insects can be imagined.

These largely unforeseen and unwelcome side effects were to emerge most severely not with the chemical hoes but with the new insecticides, whose story is told in the next chapter. Full control of their use took many years, though the beginnings of the regulatory agencies which were to supervise the sale and use of new pesticides were starting to appear. If there is now a sense of string and sealing wax about these pioneering efforts, it is worth remembering that it was not until 10 years afterwards that Rachel Carson's *Silent Spring* alerted a wider audience to the fact that the pesticidal miracle was neither so unconditional nor so simple as it first seemed.

# CHAPTER TWELVE

# Pest Control Ltd

Weeds need farmers. Insects are farmers. While they eat, they pollinate, so today's consumer sets the seed for next year's food supply. Co-operation and competition between insects and plants has gone on for millions of years. When the first human farmers arrived the insects ignored them. They went on eating, pollinating, and sometimes infecting plants with diseases and there was nothing farmers could do about it.

The war between plants and insects is fought alongside another battle between the insects themselves, which eat each other just as eagerly as they eat plants. Of all the species in nature, plants make up a quarter, insects that eat them another quarter, and insects which eat each other a further quarter again. But, although insects have always been the farmer's main competitors for food crops, plant eating came late to their lives. Early in their evolution, they found it easier to eat each other. When they did at last learn the trick of eating leaves and other vegetables, the plants fought back.

They did so by meanness, keeping their feeding value and particularly their nitrogen content as low as possible. They did so physically with spines, hooks and toughened leaves. They did so chemically by learning to manufacture a weird variety of defensive poisons. Oxalic acid, cyanide, cyanogenic glycosides, alkaloids, toxic lipids, terpenoids, saponins, flavonoids, tannins and lignins . . . the experts come up with an impressive list of horrors. Insects forced plants to make poisons, often very unpleasant ones indeed, for self-defence.

This defence is costly. Energy is needed to keep the plant's insect-repellent factory in good order, and to make and store the chemicals. Some plants put such energy into short-term self-defence that they became less competitive with other plants in the long term. Other plants which chose meanness ran into a different problem when plant-eating animals joined the feast, for the herbivores had to eat a lot more of the lower-quality plant to get the same amount of nourishment. All this time, farmers stayed on the sidelines. Worse, it seemed they could only join the struggle on the wrong side. When they grew higher-yielding crops in more fertile soil, the insects simply enjoyed a bigger feast. Every farming gain meant a heavier pest tax.

Slowly, farmers worked out answers – rotations, or planting dates, or crop varieties – to guard against this inland revenue of insects. Then, about 100 years ago, they turned to chemical defences. Like the natural repellents which plants made for self-protection, these could be very unpleasant. Cyanide was one possibility, arsenic another, but since they offered a way of fighting back against the buzzing, biting hordes, both were used with misplaced confidence.

This quickly forced a search for safer methods, and eventually led to such devices as the Pest Control Ltd nicotine gasser. But it was the discovery of the insect killing properties of DDT which really sparked things off. As the company history observes: 'when DDT became available to agriculture the excitement caused can now hardly be imagined. Contact insecticides, active in ounces per acre instead of pounds and apparently effective for weeks seemed miraculous.

'Apart from their immense value in public health, they solved so many agricultural problems so efficiently, safely and cheaply the farmer could grow notoriously pest-ridden crops without fear of failure and without having to rely on expensive contractors.'

The Pest Control company history does not exaggerate. Churchill called DDT the miraculous white powder. It possessed tremendous insect-killing powers, yet was so safe with human beings it was dusted on them to get rid of lice – which helped control typhoid – or sprayed round houses to kill mosquitoes and control malaria. During and immediately after the war, DDT was very widely used both for human and plant health purposes. Its only drawback seemed to be that it was not selective. As a result, helpful insects were killed along with harmful ones. Also, it was soon recognised that DDT broke down slowly in the environment; indeed, one of the reasons for its ability to kill insects was just this persistence.

DDT, an organochlorine, was a contact insecticide. The sprayed chemical had to touch or hit the insect to kill it. In wartime Germany, scientists had developed organophosphates to kill insects. These were systemic insecticides. They were taken into the sap of the plant, and when an insect fed it would swallow a fatal dose. Dr Ripper saw two obvious advantages in this. The need for the chemical to contact every insect would disappear, and if the chemical was delivered in the sap then only the pests which fed on the sap, and not their natural enemies, would be killed. He became particularly interested in schradan, which Pest Control was soon marketing as Pestox 3.

When James Nott, of Tenbury Wells, allowed the first field trial of this chemical to be held in his hopyard he was so excited by the results he refused to let Pest Control's research department go on with their work on comparative plots, or even to spend a day counting aphids to assess results. The whole hopyard had to be sprayed with Pestox 3 instantly. He was not in the least worried by the possibility that an insecticide which could leave toxic residues inside a plant, where they could not be washed off, might be too dangerous for practical use. Luckily, he was right – but it took 10 years of research to prove it.

These early investigations made clear the need for proper research into toxicity. The company history says: 'it was fortunate the first few organophosphorus insecticides were so intensely poisonous. Had the first discoveries been as "safe" as malathion (introduced in 1950) the detailed biochemical and safety studies, in which Pest Control played so large a part, might have been considered unnecessary'.

Direct human toxicity was not the only worry. In the run-up to the formation of the Nature Conservancy in 1949, the physiologist Dr V.B. Wigglesworth warned that DDT could be 'like a blunderbuss discharging shot in a manner so haphazard that friend and foe alike are killed'. The trouble was ignorance. A government working party reported in 1953 that 'little was known about the extent of pesticide use on specific food crops or about the actual levels of residue in different foodstuffs. The toxicological significance of any residue found was often unknown, and methods of analysis for detecting them were either lacking or could not be adapted for enforcement purposes'.

Ignorance of ecology was much greater. In 1958 the Annual Report of the Nature Conservancy said there was little evidence to prove the new chemicals were reducing bird or mammal populations. It was not until 1960 that the Conservancy set up the Monks Wood Experimental Station to begin a scientific study of the problem, and Dr Norman Moore was appointed head of the section concerned with pesticides and wildlife.

Moore did not look at the most widely used chemicals, the herbicides. The Nature Conservancy could not ask farmers to weed less efficiently in order to protect weeds. Instead, he looked at aldrin, dieldrin, endrin, and heptachlor, the group of organochlorines often referred to as the drins. He soon came to suspect they did not break down easily; the chemicals could build up in the fat of insects and animals, and then accumulate even faster in the animals which ate them. He began to study persistent chemicals, even fairly non-toxic ones like DDT. He felt strongly that it was no use becoming simply anti-farming and anti-chemicals. Food was too important and the chemicals too useful for food production. He wanted farmers to use chemicals so as to minimise any damage.

In 1959 and 1960 dead birds were seen in fields where seed had been treated with the drins to protect against wheat bulb fly. Reports also came in of foxes dying in large numbers. By 1960 the Master of the Fox Hounds Association had reported 1300 deaths. Questions began to be asked in the House of Lords. As Moore points out 'it was particularly fortunate that one of the first casualties of the persistent organochlorine insecticides was an animal whose welfare was so dear to the Establishment of the United Kingdom.'

Soon Moore and his colleague Derek Ratcliffe decided that birds of prey were suffering the same fate. Like foxes, they ate poisons stored in the fat of their prey. But the scientific evidence was either not available or hard to get, which left a gap between what the two scientists believed and their ability to prove it. It was Monks Wood's job to find the proof.

The work was not straightforward. Landowners, asked to send dead animals, often used the post. One person sent a fox the day before a postal strike. On another occasion: 'the first pike which we analysed contained a good deal of pesticide. This rather worried one of my colleagues who had made an excellent meal on those parts of the fish not required for chemical analysis before he had received the results from the chemist. He suffered no ill effects.'

In 1961 a voluntary ban on using the drins for spring sowings of cereals was introduced. Even so, in the mid-1960s these persistent chemicals were spread throughout the country and the surrounding seas. They had very different effects on different species. Herons maintained their numbers despite the pesticides. Peregrines suffered badly; they were killed directly by chemicals, which in addition interrupted the breeding patterns of those which survived. Moore knew the spring ban was not enough. The drins should be further restricted and then banned completely. He describes the difficulties he faced: 'Like most scientists who were new to politics I thought that changes in opinion and action were mainly produced by obtaining facts and arguing logically from them. I was soon disillusioned. I found there were immense obstacles. Facts and logic were only the first phase.

'The obstacles to a ban were formidable. All the persistent organochlorine insecticides were extremely effective agents of insect control. DDT had saved millions of lives by controlling a number of important diseases and all of these pesticides had saved many other lives indirectly by controlling insect pests of crops. In the case of DDT, these miracles had been achieved with the loss of few if any human lives since its toxicity for man was so low.

'The more toxic aldrin and dieldrin had caused a few fatalities, when seed corn was eaten by mistake, but the losses were small compared to the benefits obtained. Few people wanted to hear about the disadvantages when the advantages were so great, least of all those who earned their living by making, selling or using them.'

It took nearly 20 years to achieve the restrictions which the Nature Conservancy felt necessary, but before this happened the limits on use had seen the stricken species beginning to recover. Moore makes the point that pesticides are not inevitably concentrated in food chains. 'Even today I frequently meet people who believe that all pesticides become concentrated in food chains. Fortunately the persistent organochlorine insecticides are exceptional (indeed, highly unusual) in this respect.'

Any chemical can do damage at some level of intake – and living beings differ in the way they deal with different chemicals. Our bodies are very good at dealing with small amounts of very toxic compounds like alkaloids in potatoes, caffeine in coffee, or alcohol. We can also cope with large amounts of less toxic compounds such as sugar. Mark Twain summed up the science of toxicology when he joked that water taken in moderate amounts cannot do you serious harm.

What is safe for one animal or plant can damage another. But, as Moore says: 'the layman, despite all evidence to the contrary, divides substances into "safe" ones and "poisonous" ones. The toxicologist, on the other hand, works on the assumptions that all substances can be poisonous if taken in large enough doses and that animal and human bodies are adapted to deal with intake of poisons in small amounts.

'It is the job of the toxicologist to work out what doses of the substances under review have no effect and what doses are harmful.' So far as the drins are concerned, he believes that, when the final traces of these chemicals disappear, the birds will fly as widely as they did before the sprays were first used.

While these battles were being fought, and while DDT was still at the height of its powerful popularity in the late 1940s, the next generation of insecticides was moving under the microscope. Scientists began to look again at the self-defences which plants had worked out for themselves. Derris, nicotine and pyrethrum had long been used to kill pests in house and garden. All three in their natural state are powerful insect poisons and each, unsurprisingly, can have unpleasant side effects. Persian insect powder, the dried flowers of a chrysanthemum which contained pyrethrum, had been known in Europe for 150 years, and natural pyrethrum is still used today. But supplies are limited, unreliable and of little use to farmers because when exposed to light and air they quickly lose pest-killing efficiency. Any chemical for use in agriculture must persist at least until it meets and penetrates the pest. Pyrethrum did not persist enough.

By the end of the war, Rothamsted Experimental Station already had 20 years' experience of natural pyrethrums. Dr Charles Potter, then Head of the Insecticides Department, saw that safer insecticides might be found by further study of pyrethrum chemistry. This foresight, which anticipated by nearly 20 years the problems of DDT and the drins, was inspired by experience, intuition and common sense. Insects were already developing resistance to DDT, and, quite apart from safety, Potter saw that other insecticides would be needed both for agriculture and public health.

Dr Michael Elliott, a member of his department, set to work. He is a synthetic chemist, a title he dislikes, saying firmly: 'there's nothing synthetic about me.' His task was to understand how the shape of the pyrethrum molecules governed how they worked, then to change the shape to help them work better. He had no way of knowing whether natural pyrethrins could be successfully modified, but he did have a passionate interest in his subject at a time when it was still respectable in agricultural research institutes to study something for its own sake.

Backed by a team of biologists who rapidly told him how successful his latest idea was when it met a pest, Elliott changed the shape of his molecules hundreds of times. It was detailed and devoted work, and it was 13 years before something of such promise came up that others – especially the National Research Development Corporation – began to see that his steadfast optimism had been justified. At that point he was joined by Norman Janes, and in 1970 resmethrin and bioresmethrin became the first insecticides to be marketed from the years of work. Bioresmethrin is not only a more powerful insecticide than natural pyrethrum, it is much safer for mammals and birds. It has by far the best ratio of insect to mammalian toxicity of any known insecticide, natural or synthetic. But, like natural pyrethrum, it was not persistent so was no use to farmers.

Elliott and Janes were joined in 1972 by David Pulman, and together they succeeded in finding the right shape to make the molecules more stable. In 1973 permethrin, cypermethrin and deltamethrin were patented. While these persist for long enough on plant leaves to kill pests, they break down readily in the soil.

Deltamethrin, much more powerful than bioresmethrin, still retains very low mammalian toxicity – though it shares the one drawback of all pyrethrins, natural and synthetic, that they are harmful to water-dwelling life so care has to be taken to stop them getting into drainage ditches and streams.

It took 25 years of work to produce the synthetic pyrethroids. They are immensely valuable and safe chemicals, used worldwide for crop protection and human health, and have sold hundreds of millions of pounds worth – but these days nobody would pay for work that took so long to find the answers, however important and valuable those turned out to be.

Even with the arrival of safer pesticides, however, concerned farmers have learned not to be over-confident. They have learned to check equipment carefully, follow instructions closely, wear protective clothing – and they want to see continuing research on the consequences of using pesticides. They are reluctant to stop using these invaluable tools because of entirely unquantified risks, so they want much better assessment of what the risks might be. In this the lobby against pesticides has been an important, if unacknowledged, ally since it has quite properly helped to make people far more cautious with chemicals.

# CHAPTER THIRTEEN

# The Pig Improvement Company

Today's pig looks like a cut-down bullet train. Its post-war predecessor looked like a barrage balloon. So pigs have turned full circle, for the beast which rooted through medieval woodland after acorns and beechmast was a razor-backed long-nosed animal which looked far more like present porkers than it resembled the barrels of lard which came in between. The change started when this foraging pig with its browny-red bristles, prominent spine and short erect ears met Continental cousins brought across the Channel. The resulting Old English pig had lop ears, a coarse and heavy frame, a coat of many colours and powerful maternal instincts.

This beast existed in a range of types throughout the country up to the early eighteenth century. It took a long time to reach maturity and then rapidly became very fat. It slowly gave way to 'a smaller race of animals – most apt to fatten, less expensive to keep, attaining earlier maturity, and furnishing a far more delicious and delicate meat'.

These new and smaller pigs made up the different breeds now maintained largely by the activities of rare breed societies. They included the Middle White, the Berkshire, the Gloucester Old Spot, the Tamworth, the Saddleback, the Welsh and others. They also included the home-bred beast which still dominates today's pig industry, the Large White. Julian Wiseman, in his *History of the British Pig*, refers to 'many assertions that the Large White pig could be traced back virtually unchanged to the original Old English'. The experts argue about this, but it is at least possible that an unbroken connection exists between those early acorn eaters and the animals which munch their way steadily through today's cereal mountains.

What is not in doubt is that during a long period of petty inter-breed rivalry, British pig breeding completely lost its way. The concerns became colour and shape rather than productive ability. Some pigs grew so fat and rickety their legs had to be splinted to prevent buckling. With others it was not uncommon that 'to prevent accidents from suffocation the pigs were supplied with pillows made from round pieces of wood. These were placed under the snouts of the reclining beauties; whilst the effort to walk out of the pens to be examined by the judges was frequently so great that the attempt was often abandoned.'

In the immediate post-war period, the British pig was still much as it had been for the previous 100 years. There remained a vigorous tradition of cottage pig-keeping, with domestic scraps carefully hoarded to provide the family with pork and home-cured ham. Government policy, faced by the national shortage of meat, encouraged every farmer to keep a few pigs as scavengers in the farmyard. The system was ramshackle and widespread. One feed which kept Home Counties pigs going during the years of rationing was Tottenham pudding, a processed swill brought in from bakers, shops and canteens spread through London, augmented by the contents of bins left at street corners for household wastes. The result, greedily eaten by the sows, was a diet full of diseases.

Tottenham pudding may have been necessary before the end of rationing, but the risks meant that pig owners were happy to see the back of it. While it lasted it had been appreciated by the sowmen as much as it was guzzled by the sows, for many was the farm worker's table where the silver came from the best hotels in town. The sows left the cutlery neatly licked clean on the ground for the sowman to take home to his wife, and the squeal which went up when cereals finally replaced the pudding was all too often, 'But I only need three more teaspoons for a full set.'

At the end of rationing, there was an enormous demand for pork. Everything was eaten, whatever it was and however it was produced. Labour costs were low, feed conversion was poor, pigs were kept in any old corner or shed which could fit them in, weaning took place at eight weeks, overall efficiency was low, and yet a family could make a decent living with 40 sows. There was no recording, so pig keepers neither knew nor cared how soon a sow was served to get back in pig again, nor for how long a sow had been in the herd. All that mattered was the meat.

The health of these animals was dreadful. Pneumonia, rhinitis, dysentery, mange and lice were universal, and were passed on from mother to offspring. Since pigs were profitable, nobody bothered too much about these diseases, but their toll on production was enormous. The worst diseases spread by poor management and Tottenham pudding were foot-and-mouth disease and swine fever. Swine fever was a killer. In some cases it killed half the pigs in a herd, and even when it did not kill it led to poor performance. It spread very readily from pig to pig, especially through markets and dealers' herds, and attempts to stamp it out had been unsuccessful. It also spread from mother to offspring. Howard Reece, until recently chief vet in the Ministry of Agriculture, is convinced that the pig industry could not have developed as it did until swine fever had been controlled: 'It was economically disastrous. There could have been no development into large pig units while swine fever was still prevalent.'

It was not until 1963 that a campaign to stamp out swine fever was finally launched, with slaughter and compensation as the weapons. In the first year of the campaign more than 250 000 pigs were slaughtered. It was ruthless, and it worked; the industry, and above all the vets responsible, amazed themselves by their success. Swine fever was eradicated. It was to be claimed by an accountant that the extra tax paid by pig farmers after the eradication of swine fever more than paid the cost of the compensation and slaughter policy.

Behind this rickety and ramshackle herd of British pigs still stood the sort of breeding mafia which had slowed pre-war development to a standstill. They bought each other's stock at high prices, and the judgment of breeding worth depended entirely on their word. No aspect of piggy performance was measured, and an animal was a first-class breeding boar or sow if a leading breeder said so. But with pigs, as with cattle, you can tell little by eye.

In the mid 1950s, while breeders and diseases together maintained their assault on the national herd, an important newcomer appeared on the scene. This was the Swedish Landrace. Its arrival marked the start of the battle between scientists, and pseudo-scientists, on one side and traditional breeders on the other. The Landrace, above all the Danish Landrace, had taken a very different path to our domestic breeds. Since the beginning of the century the Danes had been recording pig performance and selecting on the basis of these records, rather than muddling about with the irrelevancies of ear shape or coat colour which had so seduced the British. So successful had they been that, when British breeders wanted to buy their blood lines, the Danes refused to sell (one of the few examples, until very recently, of commercial self-interest overriding the generous farming instinct to share gains and advances as well as worries). The British Landrace Pig Society was therefore compelled to buy the Swedish Landrace strain, and immediately enjoyed very high prices for the stock they bred and sold to their rivals. One of the members was Richard Waltham, whom we met earlier introducing some sense to the silage making activities of the time.

The Society, determined to avoid perpetuating the traditional muddle, set up its own testing operation at Stockton on the Forest outside York. It was soon followed by the National Pig Breeders' Association, representing all the British breed societies, which started testing at Selby. These developments gradually reduced the traditionalists to pigeon-fancier or budgie breeder status – people who did it for love and the challenge of the show ring, but with little further relevance to commercial pig production.

In 1962 the first of the modern pig breeding companies, the Pig Improvement Company (PIC), was founded by a group of farmers in the South Midlands. They felt that the new pig testing programmes were not producing the commercial animal which the consumer and the farmer demanded. One of them was Ben Boughton, who now keeps 230 sows just outside Chesham in Buckinghamshire. For much of his life he has kept twice as many, but these days his doctor says 230 are enough.

In the mid 1950s, Boughton was a member of the Wallingford pig discussion group. 'An awful lot of us realised that progress was going on much faster than we were keeping up with it,' he says. The meetings by the Thames at Wallingford were an attempt to stay out of the backwaters. One of the speakers to address the members was the manager of the newly established Selby progeny testing station, but it was the next speaker who did most to stimulate progress by failing to turn up. Left to itself, the group started to slip steadily further into its backwater with a series of soggy criticisms of the previous speaker. 'That was all very well,' says Ben Boughton, 'But it didn't take us far. Then somebody said we'll never get anywhere if we just talk about what they ought to be doing. We'll have to start and do it ourselves.'

Looking back, he says that the basic opportunity which faced them was simple. So it may seem, now. At the time it must have looked slightly different, because the simple task Boughton talks about was that of modernising the British pig industry. The geneticists knew what facts supported sound breeding programmes – but they had no pigs. The breeders had the pigs – but they cared not at all about the facts of genetic merit. Making the pigs meet the facts was the challenge which confronted the Wallingford group.

Their first move was to buy foundation stock from existing breeders. Their second was to decide what they would measure and how, and in that they were advised first by the Animal Breeding Research Organisation in Edinburgh and then by Maurice Bichard. Their third move was to tackle the problem of disease.

The first pigs, 40 Large White and 40 Landrace, came to a newly bought farm at Fyfield Wick in 1963, where specialised accommodation and performance testing quarters had been built. Along with these first pigs came Managing Director Ken Woolley, who Ben Boughton describes as one of those rare characters who works seven days a week, 52 weeks a year, year in year out, without losing his warm and generously outgoing character: 'He knew where he was going and he dragged the rest of us along in his slipstream.'

Total capital of the new group was no more than £50 000, though extended by generous credit from the local merchants Goodenoughs. Shortly, and before the 12 farmers who had set the whole thing up to supply their own herds knew what was happening, others were clamouring for their stock as well. All around the country pig farmers told each other about the marvellous pigs from PIC – stories which often grew briskly in the telling – and before very long the French and Germans had heard about them and were coming over too. Yet genetic improvement, even when scientifically carried out, is a generationally slow business. It was to be seven or eight years before it accumulated enough to become obvious. So why was the word put about so enthusiastically? Because the PIC also confronted the problem of disease.

Vets in Cambridge at that time had found out that healthy piglets, free of all their mother's diseases, could be born if they were removed from the womb just before natural birth. A hysterectomy – an operation to remove the womb – could be performed, and the little pigs were then reared artificially in completely clean buildings which were guarded against the dangers of infection as carefully as laboratories. The minimal disease herd is not uncommon today, but PIC was the first to put together scientific breeding with full-scale disease control.

The results were spectacular. Little difference was seen until weaning, but then the efficiency of feed conversion and speed of growth improved by as much as 25 per cent. That was what other pig farmers saw and wanted, and it was a crucial factor in the tremendous demand which guaranteed the success of the new organisation. Thus was PIC established. Its pigs, which had drawn on the science of Cambridge vets and Edinburgh breeders, were naturally known as Camboroughs.

As Boughton tells the story now, it wasn't long before the PIC had outgrown its founders. 'Farmers are good people at running their own businesses, not so good at running the sort of job the PIC developed into. We were good production men, and we needed to be marketing men.' The rate of growth was so rapid they needed to be something else as well. Within five years the PIC supplied one in 10 of every gilt bought in this country, had joint companies in France, Germany, Italy and Canada and was about to sign a contract to replace the entire pig population of Bulgaria – which in the five years from 1970 to 1975, it did. 'By 1970,' says Ben Boughton, 'some of us began to get cold feet.' Some wanted to double in size and double again, others looked at the debts which were building up and began to wonder. 'I'm not saying the Board was divided. But some were saying this was an opportunity which could not be missed, that we had to keep on going, while others said that one puff of wind could blow us away.'

In the middle of this debate Dalgety, who not long before had bought PIC's first creditor merchant Goodenoughs from Ranks, came along and said they'd like to buy PIC as well. The founder members sold out at an excellent return, and Boughton became a member of the new board. PIC, one of a number of such rapidly-growing British pig breeding companies, was to become the biggest in Europe and to expand rapidly into America. Now there is scarcely a pig-keeping country without its stocks of PIC pigs, and it is the biggest company of its kind in the world.

Today's animal, says Ben Boughton, is a completely different beast from the one he used to keep 25 years ago. Improvements in genetics – which have led to a much leaner animal and one which is much more efficient in feed conversion – have been matched by similar advances in food, health, housing and management. They had to be. A high-performance animal demanded high-quality management, which rapidly drove out cottage industry pig-keepers. As with chickens, commercial pressures led to tighter and tighter controls which eventually provoked questions about welfare – questions which the industry has begun to face.

# CHAPTER FOURTEEN

# Jack Eastwood and Intensive Chickens

The first broiler chickens flew and floated here across the Atlantic. The strains suitable for breeding them did not exist in this country until after the war, when they were smuggled from America in defiance of quarantine, egg by contraband egg, to start the industry on this side of the pond.

These early arrivals established a bridgehead, but the broiler invasion could not begin until the end of feed rationing in 1954, and then it took off. There was no domestic competition. The commentator P. Hewson has described how fattening chickens 'were fed a watery mixture of Sussex ground oats, skimmed milk and mutton fat. After 10 days the birds lost their appetites and so for the next 10 days the same mixture was pumped into the birds' crops with the aid of a cramming machine. The real experts at this job were to be found in Surrey and Sussex – which is why the words Surrey chicken still appear on dinner menus. It is most unlikely that the birds have ever been anywhere near Surrey.' Before the American strains were brought over, these Surrey chickens might take 12 weeks to reach 4 pounds in weight, and poor specimens never got past 3 pounds. The new broilers reached 4 pounds in 11 weeks or less.

Early punters were flamboyant entrepreneurial figures. One was Charlie Wood, the first man to put a branded rabbit into Birmingham under the 'Bunny' label. When myxomatosis destroyed this enterprise, he replaced it with a branded chicken which, inspired by the nursery rhyme, he called 'Chooky'. Another, with whom Wood collaborated, was Lieutenant Colonel Uvedale Corbett. It was not until timber went off rationing and building controls were relaxed that the new hatcheries and broiler houses could be built, so Corbett filled the first floor of a fine early

Georgian mansion with hatching chicks. Now retired, he sits in the panelled study remembering the boxes where those early birds (smuggled American strains every one though the Colonel had confined his own buccaneering imports to turkey eggs) cheeped cheerfully through the first two years of the business which was to grow into Sun Valley – the name inspired not by a nursery rhyme but by Housman's:

> In valleys of springs of rivers
> By Ony and Teme and Clun
> The country for easy livers
> The quietest under the sun, . . .

Corbett began by supplying poultry and hatching eggs to a leading commercial broiler company. He then suggested to some of his fellow Herefordshire farmers that they should form their own company, which they successfully did in 1960. Within two years Sun Valley had grown big enough to be approached by Marks and Spencer, whose food interests were then being run by Marcus Sieff, to see whether they would produce fresh chickens instead of the frozen birds which were still commonly supplied. Until then, says Corbett, everyone had been scared stiff of the idea of supplying tens of thousands of fresh chickens. It proved, he says, a very testing operation to get the new arrangements to work. In fact, FMC Poultry had supplied Marks and Spencer with chilled chickens at the very end of the 1950s; and soon Marshall's joined in to give a fresh boost to the industry.

Broiler chickens rose with the rise of supermarkets. Lloyd Maunder, the Western Chicken Company and Buxteds were others competing in an industry which, from the start, has been driven by the demands of the consumer as interpreted by the supermarket buyers. The birds which filled their broiler houses came from increasingly specialised breeding companies. Biggest of all the suppliers of the new birds in the end was to be Ross Breeders, which started life as Chunky Chicks at Ingliston, Midlothian. Rupert Chalmers-Watson, a tough cheerful Scot had first brought in American birds in the late 1940s, well ahead of the burst of 'broiler awareness' stimulated by other breeders visiting America. He and his colleagues launched Chunky Chicks in 1956, to build on their previous experience and offer a highly specialised approach to broiler breeding.

Over the next 30 years the industry was to see continuous expansion. In the early 1950s, under 5 million table chickens were sold; by 1957 that had risen to 45 million, by 1959 to 75 million and by 1960 to 100 million, produced by well over 1000 independent growers. The rocketing expansion was to see a series of company takeovers which ended up with Chunky Chicks as part of the Ross Group Poultry Division, covering all aspects of the chicken business and, increasingly, all parts of the world. That was to lead to Chalmers-Watson's original Chunky broiler becoming world number one under its new name of Ross 1.

The 1960s saw a further inrush of modern technology and mechanisation; by its end broiler production was up to 260 million and the number of growers was falling towards 500. Many of these changes were stimulated by the 'think big, drive hard' attitudes of John Eastwood, and his company's pioneering approach to vertical integration in the industry. As the company history *The Eastwood Story* puts it, the organisation had rapidly reached the position where 'every stage in the chain, from raw material to the delivery of the final product to the retailer, is carried out by the Company.

'This means that the Company constructs its own buildings, mills all its own food, breeds all its own hatching egg requirements for both poultry-meat and egg-laying strains, rears all its own poultry, packs and freezes them, packs its own eggs, and then sells and distributes the finished products, country-wide, through its own distribution network.' Before long, other poultry businesses had been driven to follow Eastwood down this route and poultry production moved further and further away from farming towards what became known as agri-business.

If all this was in sharp contrast to the Surrey poultry crammers, it was also astonishingly different from traditional egg production. Just before the first broiler eggs were smuggled in across the Atlantic, Bill Martin met his first laying hen on the family farm in Surrey in the spring of 1946. His grandfather bought 500 day-old chicks, which were brooded in the stables left empty by the disappearance of the farm horses. The pullets went into three arks in the orchard and started laying eggs. But, says Bill, they never laid many. Disease and his own inexperience didn't help, but winter was the killer. By April 1947 – while the sheep in the west and north still struggled against death in the snowdrifts – there were only 38 layers left.

Just on 40 years later, in October 1987, natural disaster again struck when one of Bill's free-range flocks was blown away by the hurricane. By then he was in charge of millions of chickens at Stonegate Farmers Limited, had learnt a lot more about egg-laying and was better able to withstand the blow.

Stonegate began life in the Sussex village of that name in 1926 when three farmers, fed up with selling their eggs in the local markets, formed an egg packing co-op. Development was suspended through the war, when the whole industry of egg packing and marketing was taken over by the men from the Ministry, but with the end of rationing Stonegate started operating again.

Those were the days when domestic egg supply was still largely seasonal. Hens laid best in the summer, and the glut was preserved by putting eggs in water glass. This alchemical liquid was poured into great stoneware pots which were filled with shell eggs rather as hard-boiled eggs are still put in pickle jars in proper old-fashioned pubs. The eggs came out sheathed in a rubbery seal which kept them edible, if not exactly fresh.

The problem facing those who wanted to extend the season lay in the origin of the farmyard hen. She had come from the jungles of South-east Asia, where it was warm and humid all year round and days and nights were of equal length. The British chickens which Bill Martin bought had adapted admirably to the very different climate of Surrey, but they hated winter and refused to lay when the days were short. They were also exposed to diseases, some of which they had known in Malaysia, others of which were new.

The consequence was very high mortality. Our hen population just before the war was over 100 million, and getting on for 20 million of these died each year from disease, predation or hard weather. Today, in a flock of around 35 million, fewer than 2 million die from disease or other causes. 'Death in production', as the industry puts it, has therefore been reduced by some 15 million birds each year.

Egg production in the early 1950s was in the hands of 350 000 producers. A flock of at least 1000 birds was needed to make some sort of living, but the average size was well below that. Some producers used movable houses so that the birds could fit the farm rotation. To avoid the build up of disease these houses needed daily shifting, and as Hewson remarks 'unless land was fairly level and well drained, enthusiasm for moving this heavy equipment on the necessary daily basis was soon lost.' Others, desperate to reduce mortality and to get away from imports and preserved eggs in winter, started to experiment with batteries. The first battery cages had appeared before the war, but in those days they were single bird cages, the point being to find out which chickens laid what amount of eggs. Others again were trying deep litter. As Bill Martin puts it: 'the only way we understood was to get them indoors, because at least then we thought we had a chance.'

The move to deep litter and straw yards meant that no one had to shut the birds in every evening and that winter lighting could be introduced to stimulate birds to laying all year round. Control of lighting altered egg production. Poultry farmers had long known that the time of year when a chick hatched influenced its behaviour. January chicks laid large numbers of small eggs within four months of emergence; September hatchlings took longer to lay and then produced larger eggs. By the mid-1950s, understanding of all this meant recognition of the need for adult birds to stick to the light pattern they'd grown up with. That meant windowless housing with controlled lighting, and that in turn meant efficient venti-lation. But early ventilation systems were often inadequate, insulation was poorly understood, and that led to outbreaks of respiratory disease.

These changes occurred slowly. Most of the 350 000 flock owners weren't interested. Early in the 1950s, less than 10 per cent of laying birds were in batteries, just over 10 per cent were on deep litter, and the remaining 80 per cent were free-range. It was then discovered that three birds in the same battery cage performed just as well as one, and this brought the capital cost down below that for deep litter. The switch was not immediate. Ten years later, battery birds were still well under 30 per cent of all layers while deep litter had gone up to over 50 per cent, with free-range down to about 15 per cent. Increasingly, however, these developments interested the businessmen and accountants who had moved into broilers. When the sudden acceleration of battery cages came it was catalysed by the integration and expansion undertaken by the Eastwood organisation. In 1965 50 per cent of all laying birds were in batteries, by 1966 it was 75 per cent.

According to *The Eastwood Story*: 'It was only in 1964 that the Company decided to extend its application of intensive livestock production expertise into the field of egg production. In the space of only 10 years the Company has grown to be the largest single producer of eggs in the world and production has increased from zero to 50 000 cases (of 360 eggs each) by 1975.

'The principle of integration is carried through to egg production. Day-old chicks are produced from the Company's bought-in breeding stock and hatched in Company hatcheries. Egg laying birds commence producing at something over 20 weeks of age and thus have to be reared from day old to 20 weeks, this again being done in the Company's own buildings.

'At 18 weeks of age the birds are transferred to the Company's laying houses, and as they have been reared from Company-produced chicks on Company-produced feed in Company buildings they do, of course, cost considerably less than the equivalent point of lay pullets that the vast majority of egg producing farmers would buy.

'Egg production is in standard 250-foot long and 60-foot wide houses, and the birds were originally in Company produced wood and wire stepped cages where some 33 000 birds a shed were housed. Using this system, feeding and egg collection were by hand.

'Over the last year or so, the Company has commenced a replacement programme for cages where, using the perfectly adequate existing housing, the old cages are being replaced by metal cages with automatic feeding, manure removal and egg collection, which has led to an improvement in the efficiency of egg production.

'Tight control is kept on the health status of the birds, carried out by means of monthly representative blood samples. The quality of Eastwood eggs is rigorously controlled, and the eggs are produced without the aid of antibiotics or artificial colorants.

Vitamin content, egg quality and yolk colour are assured by the inclusion of the Company's own production of dried grass meal.'

Those were the days when we went to work on an egg, and when happiness first became egg-shaped. The thinking behind this new world was summed up in the entrepreneurial comment: 'You tell me how many birds I can put in a cage; I'll tell you the price of eggs', and once big producers took that attitude small producers had to follow or get out. The result was intense competition, and the end of the British Egg Marketing Board and the managed market in eggs. The free market was to have important consequences for producers, consumers and chickens.

The one thing Eastwoods did not do was produce the original breeding stock. This remained a highly specialised activity, demanding an increasing expertise in genetics to keep both broilers and egg layers outperforming their rivals. By 1970, Ross broilers were weighing more than 4 pounds in 57 days. There was, however, more to the business than expertise. According to Robin Pooley, another of the poultry entrepreneurs, the geneticists themselves were not very good at dreaming up world-beating combinations.

Pooley alleges that the combination of traits and genes which went into the Ross 1 strain struck Rupert Chalmers-Watson forcibly one evening while under the helpful stimulation of a dram. This combination of whisky and entrepreneurial talent, says Pooley, is an excellent mix in the search for 'nickability'.

'To get a good new strain you've got to nick a bit of this and nick a bit of that. What you need is the entrepreneur to come up with the cocktail that works. Then you bring in the geneticists to trap the characteristics and refine them.' When – as with the Ross 1 – entrepreneur, whisky and breeder between them get it right, they also get nearly 40 per cent of the male line for the world broiler market.

Poultry genetics is full of surprises, as anyone who has ever seen the range of ornamental chickens at a poultry show will know. In the world of turkeys it has led to what Pooley describes as the King Farouk problem, or as Hewson expresses it more delicately: 'in the early 1950s broad-breasted strains found their way to this country from America and with the multiplication of this material it soon became clear that, as the broad-breasted conformation became more pronounced, stags experienced increasing difficulty in mating naturally.' The answer was AI, which has been widely used in turkey breeding ever since.

The genetic potential for broad-breastedness in turkeys seems to be almost limitless. At one stage the breeders had taken it so far that the central muscle – which raises the bird's wing as the much larger external muscle lowers it – became redundant, and died. When it did so it went green. Oregon green muscle syndrome was not toxic but it ruined the Thanksgiving dinner, so the geneticists had to breed the broad-breastedness down again.

Despite these drawbacks, entrepreneurs and geneticists have been unrelenting in their search for nickability. But it was not every new wheeze in this chicken bonanza which disappeared in larger quantities and with bigger profits down the public throat. Here, for example, is the tale of the origins and brief history of the Churkey, as told by its creator Robin Pooley.

Pooley is a most ebullient and energetic man, bearded and beaming like a slightly punk Father Christmas. A past Master of the Worshipful Company of Butchers and once chief executive of the Potato Marketing Board, he now runs Anglian Produce. These days he belies his early nickname of Drainrod, earned as a slaughterman's apprentice when his arms were so thin he could tackle the blockages more conventional tools could not reach. He cheerfully admits that when he left British rationing in the late 1940s and arrived in a New Zealand full of cream and butter his weight went from 8 stone to 20 within a very few months. When it comes to food, he knows his onions.

His family has long connections with food and farming – indeed, it was his father Melville whom we met placing the world's first Woolton pie in front of Winston Churchill. In the early 1970s, Pooley went to work for Buxteds, where he was responsible among other things for attempting to raise the Buxted share of the turkey market. He liked the business of that period. 'The birds were reared in deep litter, they had the NHS coming down the water pipes – more prophylactically correct than the human NHS – air conditioning and excellent food. It was a merry life but not a very long one.'

In the 1950s the bird appeared on Christmas dinner tables, then vanished for the next 364 days. We ate less than a million in a year.

Now we eat more than 25 million of them, partly according to Pooley because they are much better entertainment than a chicken. In an age increasingly aware of the theatrical appearance of food, a turkey makes a striking centrepiece.

Buxteds had three strains of turkey, maxi for catering, midi for Christmas and mini for the rest of the year. Pooley saw the chance for a micro, a bird the size of a chicken but retaining the turkey's higher theatrical value. For the geneticist, the blend was fairly straightforward, and before long a micro turkey was putting on weight in the deep litter house. It put on flesh in all the right places at all the right times. It looked a beauty, plumper than a partridge, but it tasted of nothing. It was ready for the table so quickly that it had no time to develop any flavour. The project was sadly vacuum-packed away.

Shortly afterwards, a new development occurred in the poultry world. A clever chemist discovered how to make synthetic chicken flavouring which tasted like – well, somewhat like – the real thing. Until then, chicken soup canners had bought a rich broth made by Buxteds and others by boiling down tens of thousands of old laying hens. This traditional material was delicious but was variable in flavour and needed careful handling to preserve its qualities in a hygienic state. Even then, it was not an easy ingredient in a mass production soup, so when the chemical taste turned up, the stock became yet another product sidelined by technical development. Pooley was faced with tens of thousands of gallons of unwanted chicken soup. This immediately offered an opportunity. On the one hand, a magnificent-looking but flavourless bird; on the other, a quantity of richly flavoured broth. A marriage could do nothing but advance the prospects of both parties: soup and a bird on the same plate – feed it enough fishmeal and you might even end up with the ultimate convenience meal of soup, fish and a bird in one. The shotgun for such a marriage was to hand in the multiple injection head used to force brine into hams and bacon. All that was needed was to fill the brine vats with chicken stock.

It didn't work. When the bird was cooked, the soup separated out into yellowish globules of fat, distressingly diseased in appearance. Once again, it was back to the vacuum pack. Not long after that, Pooley had his annual flu jab. He'd been putting it off.

He always put it off. He rolled up his sleeve, looked away, gritted his teeth and waited. Go on, he said, just get it over with. The nurse told him she'd already done it. The new vaccination was a blast of compressed air containing the vaccine which immediately dispersed into the muscle tissue. Pooley was heading for the telephone thinking of chicken soup before he had his sleeve rolled down again. A development programme soon adapted the vaccine gun to the requirements of chicken soup – which among other things involved upgrading the medical implement to meet the particular hygienic requirements of the food industry. And it worked. Vaporised soup shooting through the skin of the bird spread in a mist of flavour through the flesh to produce the ideal marriage of succulence and taste.

What should the new product be called? Opinion was split between Churkey and the Golden Roaster and, after energetic debate, came down in favour of the former, for the worst of reasons: the Chairman liked it! Preceded by a fanfare from the trumpeters of Pooley's old regiment, the Churkey was launched at the Savoy. Yet another innovation in the poultry market was about to hit the shelves. Alas, the genetic work on the bird, the upgraded vaccine gun, the soup, the entrepreneurial flare, the name, all were to collapse: the great British consumer just wouldn't live with so much muckin' about with nature. Pooley was to leave Buxted and the new management decided to develop other products. But, if the Churkey failed, other bright ideas did not, so the rapid onward trot of the poultry industry continued.

In the early days of the broiler industry, chicken soup was not the only thing which some people thought of injecting into carcases. Unscrupulous operators pumped in extra water, then later substituted polyphosphates for the water. Rogues have always been willing to contaminate food and there were bound to be some in an industry developing as fast and competitively as the broiler industry of the late 1950s and 1960s. But the regulations steadily tightened, the quality demands of the supermarkets equally steadily increased, and as they did so the ability to sell large amounts of water or polyphosphates as chicken fell away. Nothing, it seemed, could inhibit the unbounded public taste for chicken meat.

# CHAPTER FIFTEEN

# Mules and Other Crossbreds

Four million ewes died in the arctic blizzards of 1947. Many died in the deep drifts, but even those in the open starved since it was fiercely hard to reach them with fodder. When it was possible to get small quantities of high-energy cake to them they ignored the unfamiliar stuff scattered on the snow in front of them, for nobody fed cake to ewes then and they did not recognise it as food. Patches of windblown frozen grass were their only nourishment.

Sheep numbers had fallen before this disaster struck. Through the 1930s huge amounts of New Zealand lamb came on the home market, and during the worst of the resulting slump the hill shepherds – whose streak of the stubborn, solitary single-mindedness needed to work with sheep is at its strongest – almost gave up. When lambs sold for as little as 5 shillings each, the arts and exhaustions of shepherding no longer seemed worthwhile. Often too weak to lamb, ewes and their meagre offspring died in dozens even in the mildest winters and balmiest springs, since the effort of saving them met with so little reward.

That effort is greatest at lambing. Shepherds say that the first three weeks are half a sheep's life; in that time it finds as many ways to die as in the rest of its days put together. Horribly often it can be born dead, for twin lambs can get intimately entwined after five months inside their mother, and then the ewe tries the impossible which is to lamb them both at once. Deep in the hidden womb the shepherd's work-hardened hand must delicately disentangle the legs and bodies, pulling one lamb forward, pushing the other back – all the while resisting the muscular contractions of the uterus which powerfully squeeze everything in the womb towards him, all the while asking numbed fingers to say if there might be triplets rather than twins. A stillbirth is the most depressing sight a shepherd sees, though nearly as bad is when a live lamb emerges with all the vitality of a wet sock from a washing machine. Its tongue, instead of vigorously sucking the life-giving milk, fumbles uselessly even when the teat is held directly in its mouth, and the shepherd must delicately thread a tube down the cold throat and dribble colostrum directly into the tiny stomach.

Even when safely born, lambs must be closely watched to make sure they get enough milk, resist the wet, avoid the raven and the fox, and throughout the exhausting weeks of lambing the same patient attention must be paid night and day. Some breeds of sheep are hardier and more self-sufficient than others, but caring for ewes was enough to explain the shepherd's reputation for cussed independence and rudeness to farmers, families, bureaucrats and bank managers alike.

For a brief moment when lambing is done the shepherd can relax as lamb derbies, king of the castle, head-butting contests and stiff four-legged high-jump competitions divert the young from the endless calling of their mothers. Then the work goes on. The sheep must be shorn; they must be dipped to protect against flies, which even then find the fleece a haven for their eggs; healthy feet should be as sharply outlined as halved hard-boiled eggs but are often more like pickled walnuts, and must be constantly trimmed and treated to prevent lameness. The flock must also be drenched and injected against parasites and diseases. Neglect of any of this leads to unthriftiness or death.

As that neglect developed through the 1930s, flock numbers fell. When during the war upland sheep became too valuable to ignore, the Ministry finally set about improving conditions for the hill ewe. It approached the task with extreme nervousness. As one official history expressed these fears: 'Hill farmers were known to be ruggedly independent. A tactless approach to the first few of these isolated hill farms could have caused the scheme to founder as it left the slipway, and it might have taken years to repair such a blunder'. The natives were dangerous, and quite likely to resist interference from bureaucratic busybodies. With a flexibility not always shown by civil servants, the local pub was often chosen as the meeting ground and there, with ruggedness softened by an infusion of ale, the hill shepherds were smartened up on husbandry and management. Unnecessary afflictions like braxy, fluke, dysentery, swayback, louping-ill and pulpy kidney could be readily treated, and with encouragement and hypodermics the survival rates in hill flocks rose rapidly.

The lambs which New Zealand sent in frozen boatloads drove the hill shepherds into this defended misery; they also drove the golden hoof from the lowlands. For centuries sheep had fertilised downland and arable Britain, but they could not be kept for their manure if that meant large cash losses. So New Zealand lamb and Argentinian beef made bagged fertilisers necessary. When Ploughing for Victory saw downland chalk and breckland sands – along with Hyde Park and Wimbledon – again growing corn and potatoes, the sheep had gone and artificial fertilisers fed the plants.

Then came the 1947 Agriculture Act. It supported cereals and milk but passed over the claims of sheep. Next year the great southern sheep fairs which had dwindled in importance through the decades of neglect were again overflowing with sheep as farmers desperately tried to sell out. The old corn and sheep systems were gone, it seemed for ever. The only people who wanted to keep their sheep were those whose land was too steep to plough – and a few strange folk who actually liked the beasts.

One man who did like sheep was Oscar Colburn, just out of the RAF when he came back to Crickley Barrow in the Cotswolds. The brashy soils could grow corn and grass, and the question was what to do with the grass. The way to improve output from it was through better management, with more productive animals stocked at higher rates. He decided to go for more productive sheep. Today, looking at a shedful of Colbred ewes, he says about those early days: 'the fascinating thing in the sheep industry was people were much less ready to use new developments than any other branch of farming'. A sheep's worst enemy is another sheep. With a stocking rate of two ewes or less an acre the enemies seldom met. Higher productivity meant higher stocking rates, and it became important to sort out good from poor performers. Sheep offered a great opportunity to anyone willing to take on the challenge. Colburn decided to try.

'Then and now, most farmers were using crossbred ewes and their performance depended on the sire. That was almost universally a Border Leicester, and in the early 1950s Border Leicester breeders were selecting from the biggest singles, to make the biggest prices at Kelso.

'The average pedigree Border Leicester flock had 12 ewes. There were three flocks with 300, and a small number with more than 100. So breeding for weakly inherited characteristics was impossible.' In short, sheep breeding suffered from all the problems which then afflicted cattle breeding, and more. The rivalry was intense, and accusations of sharp practice abounded. They were colourfully expressed: one breeder described another as a man so crooked he could pass up through a corkscrew with a bowler hat on. The arts of the hairdresser were devoted neither to the shepherds nor to their wives but to their ewes and rams, which were endlessly shampooed, trimmed and brushed for the sake of appearance. Skilfully wielded shears do more to embellish poorly-shaped frames than scissors to shape haircuts – and in those days appearance mattered far more than performance. Too often, it still does.

Colburn saw that the quickest way to improve the perfor-mance of the whole industry was to improve the performance of the crossbred ewe, and the quickest way to do that was to produce a better sire than the Border Leicester. That meant keeping proper records. In 1948, well before pig keepers started truffling in the same country, Oscar Colburn was recording and progeny testing his flock of Cluns. He wanted to improve fertility, milking ability and growth rate, and knew it would take many years to make progress with all three.

This drove him towards a new breeding programme. He began by crossing his Cluns with Border Leicesters, Frieslands and Dorset Horns. For 10 generations he inbred the hybrids he had created. He ended up with the Colbred. This animal would produce half as many lambs again as was common at the time, it was milky, a good mother and its offspring grew fast. The sheep industry rewarded his patience and his improvements by sticking to Border and Bluefaced Leicesters, and the crossbreds they produced.

Other ideas were pioneered at Crickley Barrow. In 1956, the sheep came indoors for the winter for the first time. The aim was not to make life easier for the ewes, though it did that; it was to get them off the grass so it could grow away early in the spring. 'When we discussed this, others thought we were potty. We've been doing it now for more than 30 years, and look how its spread'.

The farm began to grow catch crops for the flock – turnips drilled after the corn had been harvested. When the ewes came in to their new winter housing their forage was straw. The combination of good grassland management, catch cropping, straw feeding and winter housing raised the pressure on the flock. It gave a system which allowed Colburn to select for higher performance and breed a sire capable of helping to raise the output of the national flock. But for every crossbred ewe with Colbred blood in her today, there are at least 500 without. The same has happened with the other new breeds created since the war. The Cambridge, the Meatlink, the British Milksheep, all have their admirers, none has fully satisfied the ambitions of its creator. All demand better management, and many shepherds are happy to stick with breeds and methods they know and trust. But Oscar Colburn, who was to reduce his own interest in sheep breeding and concentrate on cattle, is still cheerful. 'If you look at the formation of new breeds in the nineteenth century, they took at least 20 years to take off. So we are quite encouraged.'

A few years after the Colbred breeding programme started, a father and son team set out from the plains of North Hampshire, close to the heartland of the traditional southern sheep industry. They were travelling to Builth Wells to buy a bunch of crossbred ewe lambs. The father had kept a flock of sheep 'from the time deficiency payments came in at a suitable level. Demand for meat meant they had to start supporting sheep, and they brought in a good system for 18-month-old mutton'. The speaker is Rowan Cherrington, then a lad on his way to Wales to learn how to buy sheep. His father John was a regular visitor to the borders where he bought sheep to take back to Hampshire and fatten up as mutton. When the subsidies swung to support production of fat lambs, his father decided to buy a breeding flock. He started with draft Welsh ewes – old sheep, but ones with two or three crops of lambs left in them. 'That was the cheapest way to buy sheep then. But they died in Hampshire as fast as they died in Wales. Father bought 400 one October, we had 280 left by lambing, then we lost more to magnesium deficiency. I've still got a photo of a ewe lying dead on a block of magnesium from magnesium deficiency.

'So father thought he'd try the halfbreds. When we got to Builth he said they were too dear. Right, he said, we'll go to Lazenby, get some Cumberland greyface. We drove to Lazenby, the rain came down as it only can in Cumberland and in the middle of a ring of steaming farmers father bought 200 ewe lambs.'

Today, the Cumberland greyface is called a Mule. It is the most widely-used crossbred ewe in lowland sheep farming, and its parentage is strictly traditional. It is a cross between a Bluefaced Leicester tup and a Swaledale ewe, and on the face of it neither would be first choice for producing a quality crossbred – Cherrington when in relaxed mood describes one parent as a great gaunt donkey of a thing and the other as three parts of a jack rabbit, and the virtues of this combination were not widely appreciated in the late 1950s. Other crossbreds, Scotch or Welsh or Suffolk or Masham – then as now there were plenty to choose from among the 40 or more native sheep breeds – were as popular or more so, and when Cherrington bought sheep in those days the northern marts might hold 10 Mashams for each Mule on offer. He says the change was due to two men, Norman Little and Harry Ridley. 'If anyone can be called the father of the north country Mule, it's Norman Little.' As auctioneer he made sure the right sheep were offered at the right price, and kept buyers and sellers happy to renew business every season.

A year or two before the two Cherringtons first went to Lazenby, another trade was developing in markets, pubs and farmyards across the country. It was in rabbits, which changed hands for far more than a greyface ewe. But they were not going to breeders and if they had they would not have bred. They were going to farmers, who would pay handsomely for a well-myxomatosed rabbit – for the damage they did as pests cost farmers and foresters around £50 million a year.

Myxomatosis was first reported in Edenbridge in Kent in October of 1953. This was some 3 years after the disease was introduced into Australia as an official control measure, and 15 months after its unauthorised liberation in France by a Dr Armand Delille. No one knows whether myxomatosis reached Edenbridge by accident or not. It was probably deliberate. Whatever the truth the outbreak could not be stopped, and on the second anniversary of the introduction the Ministry of Agriculture told a press conference: 'It is no exaggeration to say that as a result of myxomatosis we may well be approaching a new phase in British agriculture.' By 1955 the Advisory Committee on Myxomatosis was trying to help occupiers in eliminating rabbits that survived.

One farm to cash in was Chilbolton Down, close to the Cherrrington spread in north Hampshire. When Harry Ridley went there in the late 1950s, he brought a belief that the golden hoof still had a place on the light chalk. The farm had been a rabbit warren, but after myxomatosis Ridley could put down some of Stapledon's new leys and stock them with sheep. At first they were bought for him by the managing agents, Strutt and Parker, but eventually he asked his neighbour Rowan Cherrington to buy him some Mules. Visitors to Chilbolton Down, especially when Strutts organised an open day, admired the system and the sheep, and before long Cherrington was buying thousands of Mules each year for farmers in the south. Today he says: 'What we liked was the sheer adaptability of the sheep itself. You could look after it superbly as at Chilbolton Down, or harshly as father did, and it was always prolific, they were superb mothers, they milked well and they fattened their lambs.'

They were also cheap. Cherrington paid £8/2/6 for his Mule ewes in 1958, and didn't pay a penny more throughout the 1960s, which reflected the fact that the sheep industry was pretty much static through those years. 'We did begin to learn some things – especially that a large flock didn't need a lot of shepherds. As wages went up and the price of sheep didn't, shepherds got a bit expensive, so one man started looking after 1500 ewes, plus help at lambing. The fencing changed. The sheep's ability to look after itself changed. Otherwise, things stayed the same.'

What eventually changed was going into Europe. Improvement still came slowly until support systems altered in the early 1980s, flock numbers throughout the country began to rise again, and sheep achieved a popularity they had not known for 100 years. Even so, the British appetite for eating them declined, and despite a noisy insistence on the virtues of natural food our consumption of lamb (the most naturally reared and farmed of all our red meats) has fallen steadily – while that of broiler chickens has rocketed. Luckily, tastes in France have gone the other way, and British lambs now cross the Channel to supply the deliciously garlicky, lightly-cooked gigots which emerge more and more often from French ovens.

Haber's pressure cooker, designed to
produce bagged nitrogen fertiliser, is at the heavy end of the
chemical industry – in this case in a plant run by ICI.

Old muck in new wagons. Machines have
taken nearly all of the backache out of the age-old task
of adding fertility to the soil by spreading dung.

*Above* Early mechanisation in an example
which, while it relieved the muscles of the horse, did little
to help these two dust-shrouded spreaders of lime.

*Opposite* Keeping the crops clean – then and now. Luckily
for the driver of the ancient Fergie, the wind was blowing in the right
direction. The modern method not only secures greatly improved crop
health, it does so while using much less of the spray chemical.

There's more than one way for the farmer – if not
perhaps the flyer – to gain peace of mind without the wheels
of the tractor crunching through the ripening crop.

Putting it just where you want it. The down-draught
from the rotors thrusts the spray into the crop and so
increases the coverage of the protective chemical.

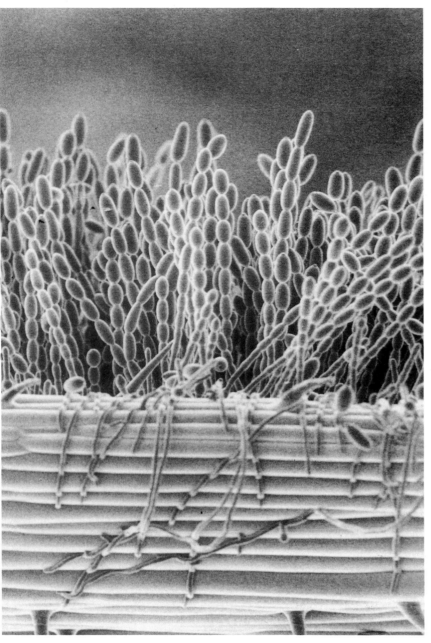

Why sprays are needed . . . the fungus growing here is mildew,
getting its fingers round the throat of a wheat plant, and clearly shows the
choking infection which can develop when disease is left uncontrolled.

Newly-mown grass being picked up by a forage harvester,
which then blows the crop into a wagon trailed behind the tractor – a
technique which allows one man to do all the field work on his own.

The traditional method, in this case with a team of
six men armed with pitchforks – and helped by two horses
and an early elevator – labouring to save the hay crop.

Stooking cereals – on this occasion in a good crop of oats –
demanded much muscle power, first to set the stooks up to dry, then
to pitch them on to a cart to be hauled away for storing in a rick.

There is an enviable spring in the stride of the two nearest
women, part of a large gang hard at work lifting a crop of potatoes
on a farm which had not yet bought a modern harvester.

*Opposite, top* A threshing machine flails the grain from the
corn previously stored in ricks, and loads it into two and a quarter hundredweight sacks – which stand half as high as the men who move them.

*Opposite, below* Now that one man can cut
and thresh the corn with the aid of a combine, the rest of the
harvest gang can fly off on holiday to the Mediterranean.

*Above* There was a time when bringing new land
into production was looked on favourably by the highest in the
land. Winston Churchill, Anthony Eden and Christopher Soames
admire the work of Harry Ferguson's little tractor.

The essential preliminaries to the oldest festival of all, the
harvest, being carried out by two men and their machines under the
peaceful protection of the church tower near Upton in Worcestershire.

An early answer to mechanising the same
activity, with the grain being delivered straight into a sack
and the straw left in a swath on the cut stubble.

The struggle to get the land ready for sowing demanded long
hours as well as a prayer for the weather to hold – and between man, horse
and prayer, it was a rare spring when the job did not get done.

An immediate harvest greets the Ayrshire seagulls
as two tractors take advantage of a break in the snow
to prepare the ground for the following seed drill.

Hand-milking required one milker for every eight or ten cows in the herd. It was hard on the hands and arms – and the cow-shed wasn't always clean enough to make boots unnecessary.

A modern rotary milking parlour offers a technology which can allow one milker to cope with more than 100 cows an hour.

Although the similarity to a barrage balloon is clear
enough there was never any real danger of this Large White
flying, even without the three helpers hanging on at the back.

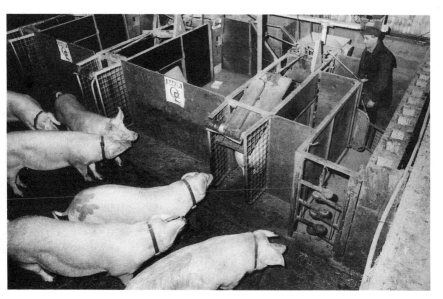

The transponders which these sows wear round their necks allow
them to eat their food without a punch-up at the trough. It is a technology
aimed at giving much more freedom to sows when they are kept indoors.

*Above* Isabel and her 19 calves, all of which came
from one embryo collection and were then transplanted and born to
foster mums. The admirer in the middle is Geoff Mahon.

*Opposite, top* Chris Polge in his laboratory in Cambridge.

*Opposite, below left* Bobby Boutflour, in a
photograph taken shortly before the war.

*Opposite, below right* The portrait of George Stapledon which
hangs in the Welsh Plant Breeding Station in Aberystwyth.

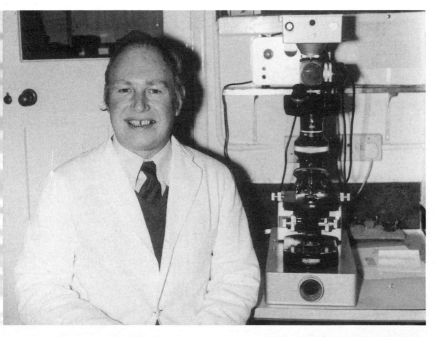

Harry Ferguson (left) talking turkey with Henry Ford.

Dan Bullen (left) helping with the barley
harvest during his 103rd year and Richard Waltham
(right) off duty and so off his silage clamp.

CHAPTER SIXTEEN

# Food Security Threatens Farmers

In 1946 A.G. Street wrote in his column in the *Farmers Weekly* about a serviceman friend of his whose fellow squaddies, waiting to be demobbed, kept in touch with their future jobs by reading the *Steel Worker*, *Flight*, or the *Autocar*. When *Farmers Weekly* arrived for Street's young friend it was greeted with loud cheers, jeers, guffaws, grunts and other animal noises. Street commented that this happened because most people had been taught to despise farming and those engaged in it.

Others have echoed this. The schoolboy who said he was going on the land could rely on at least one of his teachers to ask 'What as, lad, manure?' Some considered the subject adequately covered by intoning 'ooh aah'. The author and journalist Tristram Beresford, writing in the mid-1970s, said it was as though the drift from the land was not just a social migration but an intellectual aversion; as though urban society had chosen to disclaim its roots. He describes this as a failure to connect, a defect of vision leading to condescension.

It was not surprising. The agricultural collapse of the 1930s had seen farmers considered inferior to professional and commercial men and farm workers despised by the masses toiling in industry. Both were thought to live in ignorance; both certainly did live in damp houses, often with little plumbing and no electricity, surrounded by hungry animals and derelict pastures. Ashley Cooper says these circumstances marked the men concerned for life: 'Just as the depression has left an indelibly bitter scar on the mentality of the Jarrow marcher and his generation of industrial England, so too a complex of fear and ruthlessness developed in the farmers of East Anglia. The excessive removal of hedgerow and woodland which occurred in some villages during the '50s and '60s can in part be traced back to the memories of those times.'

In 1945 it could still be written that 'thousands of cottages have no piped water supply, no gas, no electric light, no third bedroom and often only one living room with no separate cooking and scullery accommodation. For the great majority of rural workers a bathroom is a rare luxury.' That is from a government report on how farm workers lived at the end of the war. Above all, the lack of electricity counted hard; no lighting, heating, water-pumping, washing or ironing; the standard of living needed to rise sharply and no one was more aware of it than those who suffered, the farm workers and their families. The change in 30 years was revolutionary. Howard Newby, who quotes the report referred to above, goes on to say that by the 1970s the English village as an occupational community had virtually disappeared. Before the war it might have held 'a pub, two off-licences, two bakers, two shops, a post office, a school, a bicycle repair shop, a blacksmith, a carpenter, a wheelwright, a cobbler, a foundry, a brickmaker, pottery works and also an undertaker'. The list is Ashley Cooper's, and he adds that the farms surrounding such a village would grow as many as 20 different crops and rear five species of livestock.

Now the shops and services, many of the crops, much of the livestock, and a great number of farmers and farm workers have gone. In 1945, more than 1 million of us worked in farming, of whom nearly 1 million were employed as workers. By the mid 1970s there were fewer than 300 000 farms and 375 000 workers – but to make up the loss there were by then more tractors than farm workers. The farm workers had disappeared because they saw more opportunity and more money elsewhere. Low wages were the chief reason for going. Long, uncertain hours, health, redundancy and bad employers, the tied-cottage system and lack of prospects have also been quoted as reasons for changing jobs. But, although low wages pulled people out of farming into better-paid jobs elsewhere, it was also true that food could be grown more cheaply with fewer people, however well or poorly paid they were. So they were also pushed out of farming by capital investment in new machinery, new buildings and new technology.

The reasons for the decline in the workforce seem clear enough; but where were the farmers going? Small dairy farmers, for example, never expected to make a fortune from their labours, indeed were never very far from need; but 30 years earlier they had still been men of some property and a small independence. Now they too were following the farm workers out of farming.

They had been caught in a squeeze. The government had asked them to expand and had given them the support and confidence to do so. Expansion was welcome when it meant more income, but this was not all it meant. It also meant higher land values and therefore higher rents; it meant taking on some labour, which led to a wage bill; it meant new investment and borrowing which led to doing more work for the bank. Before long, such folk found themselves spending more on rent, labour and borrowing charges than on their cows, themselves and their families. A few refused to change; they went on milking their own cows by hand, they never borrowed money to buy a bigger tractor, they stayed true to the old ways and ignored the consumerism of modern life. But the vast majority moved with the times; when they could no longer keep up, they sold up. Their places were taken by neighbours or newcomers expanding to meet the demands of modern food production. Where 10 cows had once given a modest living, it became 20, then 30, 40 and 50. If there seemed no end in sight to these increases, there was still a thriving future for those with the spirit for it.

The underlying reality behind this process was, and still is, twofold. One part, the continuing acceleration as farming moved inevitably from the amble of a craft-based inheritance to the sprint of a science-based industry, was too much for many small farmers. The other part was that, run as fast as it might, farming could never catch up with the rest of the working world. This point explains so much of what has happened in farming, and even more of what has been misunderstood, that we must dwell on it.

In 1947 it took someone on the average wage – which was then 23p an hour – over eight minutes work to buy a pint of milk; in 1973 it took four minutes, and today it takes less than three minutes. A dozen eggs meant an hour's work as recently as 1955; 20 years later it meant less than 15 minutes, while today anyone who wants 12 eggs to throw at a politician can buy them by clocking on for just over ten minutes. The same story is true for everything we eat which we grow in this country, except beef. That took 36 minutes of effort for an expensive 1-pound cut in 1947 while today it takes over 40 minutes.

Those numbers work the opposite way round for the farmer. In 1947, I as farmer could buy over eight minutes of your work with a pint of my milk. By 1973, I could only buy four minutes. Now, I can buy less than three minutes with the same pint – so to buy the original eight minutes now costs me three pints. I must now produce 144 eggs to buy as much of your work as 12 eggs used to buy me. Whatever I grow, I must work harder to earn the same amount of your money; the more I produce, the less I get for it.

What is true for each individual farmer is true for farmers as a whole. In 1947, of every £4 we spent altogether, £1 went on feeding ourselves and our families. In 1973 we spent less than £1 on food in each £5 we spent altogether, and today that proportion has fallen to little more than £1 in each £10. As time passes, farmers get less and less of our total income. That unavoidable decline is made worse because, of the money that is spent on food, more and more goes to processors, manufacturers, wholesalers, retailers and others in the supply chain, and less to those who grow the food.

The result of all this is that a larger amount of agricultural output buys a steadily smaller amount of other things. The gap between living costs and agricultural prices widens. It widens faster when living standards overall are rising, when inflation is high and when efficient farming is bringing down the price of food. Since all three things have been happening for most of the last 40 years, the gap has widened fast, and farming incomes have fallen.

To live with this, farmers have responded by producing more. When each pint, or egg, or tonne of wheat buys less, you must produce more milk and eggs and wheat. This means farming more efficiently on the same land, or getting more land, or both. And while it is certainly true that subsidies have prevented prices falling as fast as they might have done, they have still fallen. So despite more efficiency, bigger farms and subsidies, farming faces a falling income.

In some ways the problem seems quite intractable. The industry had got nearly everything it asked for, and the troubles seemed to get worse. Writing about developments since the war Tristram Beresford put it like this: 'A great deal had been stuffed away. Farmers had asked for Marketing Boards – they had them. They had asked for a long-term policy – they had the nearest thing. They had asked for credit – they had a Credit Corporation. They had the Farm Improvement, the Horticultural Improvement, the Small Farm Improvement Schemes. They had wanted a working part-nership with the Agricultural Cooperative Association – that had been arranged for them. They had wanted an agency to sell meat – they had got one, the Fatstock Marketing Corporation. They had wanted technical and economic advice – they had a state-financed independent advisory service that was free to all. They had wanted influence in high places – the Minister of Agriculture had a seat in the Cabinet, and the Ministry of Agriculture scarcely made a move without consultation with the Union.'

All of this helped farmers greatly. The technical revolution, the political and public support, had undoubtedly led to much higher productivity and far greater efficiency. The pressures which the hard realities of economics had put on prices had indeed been held in check at first by price support and then by grants towards farm modernisation. But the process, far from stopping, simply went faster. There was more new technology, more buildings, more machinery, more borrowing, fewer workers, larger farms, fewer farmers and higher rents – and in the long run, steadily lower prices for the food which farmers grew. The pressures kept on mounting, and not everyone wanted to live with them.

In the good times – and there had been many good times since the war – most farmers made money. In the bad times, large, efficient farmers went on making money. The largest and most efficient made a lot of money, so much that they slowly worked themselves into a position where, whether they went on getting price supports or not, they could survive in a competitive agriculture. The Common Agricultural Policy (CAP) which was about to take over the political direction of their lives would in fact bring them both more protection and higher prices – for the time being.

It was the small farmers who had suffered. They had not been able to increase output as much as large farmers, and smaller output meant less subsidy. But small farmers could also look forward to joining Europe and the CAP, because the CAP had been designed with small farmers in mind. Where British policy had concentrated on making farming more efficient, more able to take care of itself, while nodding occasionally in the direction of small farmers, the CAP had been designed with the family farm firmly in the middle to sustain social and economic growth in the countryside.

So in spite of its problems the agriculture which prepared to enter Europe in 1973 could feel reasonably confident. It had lived through the excitement and turmoil of a quarter of a century of technical development and political support, and in meeting Churchill's instruction 'take it away and bring me beef' it had modernised itself to become one of the most efficient industries in the country.

Labour productivity had risen at twice the national average rate. Output had risen at between 3 and 4 per cent each year, again around twice the national average, so that yields had doubled. Much more of the diet of a larger population thus came from home-grown food, including all our milk, pork, eggs and table chickens and most, if not all, of our beef. Cabbages and Brussels sprouts, maincrop potatoes, carrots and other root vegetables, peas and mushrooms were all home-grown. The farmers who had achieved all this had much to be proud of.

What they had never been good at was explaining these achievements, this pride, to their fellow citizens. This was perhaps understandable in the days when food was desperately needed, but by the time those days were over this habit of independence, reinforced by the natural isolation of daily work with stock or crops, had become hard to shift. It was not encouraged to do so by the intellectual aversion referred to by Tristram Beresford, which led the public to fit all the complications – all the different types of farming – into the single category of moaning Volvo driver. The moaner and the Volvo driver were not always united in the same farmer; both existed alongside many other farming types.

This blame for this failure of communication must lie with farming's leaders. The NFU's reputation as an efficient political lobby was fully justified in Whitehall and Westminster, but its successes there blinded it to the need for wider lobbying skills. The blindness cost little while the country clamoured for more, but it became a weakness as surplus loomed. This did not concern James Turner, widely recognised as a big man in every way, who led the post-war NFU almost as an ex-officio Cabinet Minister. It started to weaken Harold Woolley when debate about joining Europe first occurred, and could have wrecked Henry Plumb who at first opposed entry. The extent of his political skills can be judged from his present position as President of the European Parliament – but even his skills might not have been enough to soften the bout of farmer-bashing which broke out in the early 1980s.

Perhaps there was little that Plumb and others could have done, even with the aid and advice of the ultimate back-room boy, Asher Winegarten. The NFU Council meeting did not exist which the one-time economic adviser, and then Director General, could not manipulate. As one council member explained, 'He never fails to put a new complexity on the matter.' Such complexities were a boon to Plumb, but Winegarten's line of economic argument was aimed at members, not the public. Too often, as the public grew more concerned, the NFU found its guns pointing the wrong way.

Neither the underlying economic realities which faced farming nor the fact that the CAP was ill-designed to succeed in its aims made much difference to public reaction in this country. As we followed Ted Heath into Europe, many more consumers were now ready to echo the view of Alderman Roberts that the chief business of farmers was banking government subsidy cheques.

# CHAPTER SEVENTEEN

# Shifting the Scenery

When farmers threw off the bedclothes on 1 January 1973 to get up into the bright new dawn of the Common Agricultural Policy, the view across the fields – as the mists quickly dispersed under the rising sun of European subsidy – seemed reassuringly familiar. But something new was happening out there, as the comparatively closed world in which agriculture had worked for 25 years began to open up. A close look through the window that New Year's morning would have shown various groups pushing forward into the scenery arguing as they came. Each had different things to say and each proclaimed that farming was too important to be left to farmers.

These groups concerned themselves with preserving birds or protecting rural England, with rambling or rural access, with food prices and subsidies, with diet and nutrition, with welfare, or wildlife, or the environment. To begin with they did not make common cause, and some of them were dismissed as cranks, which led to sharp skirmishes between farming and its critics, most of which the farmers won as they went on with their business of growing more food. They might have gone on winning. But the more food they grew, the more they fashioned a flail with which their critics could thrash them. That flail was surpluses.

The post-war argument had been all about shortages. Farmers had been passionately supported while people were poor and hungry. When surplus replaced shortage and people grew fat, the argument turned inside out as consumers replaced producers in the middle of the landscape. So long as surpluses lasted, it was producers who were the more likely to feel poor and hungry. So it was not surprising that one part of the debate about farming began with fat.

Philip James knows a lot about fat. When he first announced that he meant to study it, his friends told him not to waste his time. He didn't. As a result he says there are now those in the worlds of farming and food who look on him as the godfather of a terrible nutritional mafia, producing reports on diet which have to be suppressed before they destroy great chunks of those industries. Though he says this with a laugh, it is the slightly Machiavellian laugh of a man who enjoys the politics of food almost as much as he enjoys eating.

In 1970, James – now Director of the Rowett Research Institute outside Aberdeen – came back from the tropics and wondered what on earth he was going to do. Human nutritional science was in the doldrums. For 25 years, quantity had counted. The science of food, still directed by those with aching memories of how nearly we had starved, had been aimed at production, not consumption. At least until the mid-1970s, animal nutritionists looked with what James describes as withering scorn on human nutritionists, who did little more than tell people to mind their vitamins and eat enough protein. As a result it is still true today that we know more about livestock than human dietary needs – which lessens the force of a number of claims about what's good for us.

In 1974, James started to wonder whether there was anything to be done about obesity: 'No one did any work on it. It was thought to be the death knell of any respectable scientist. Obesity was about stupidity and will power, not science.' When in 1976 the Royal College of Physicians produced a report saying the national diet must change, nobody tried to suppress it as they tried to suppress later reports because, apart from the authors, nobody believed it. 'Doctors knew it was tommy rot. What's cholesterol got to do with heart disease? Don't give me that claptrap about prevention.'

Those attitudes took some shifting. When at that time James did some programmes on nutrition education for the BBC, the academic world was outraged. 'It was when dietary fibre was first talked about. I said if only everyone ate enough bread and lettuce everything would be fine. There wasn't the evidence for it, only anecdotes. Academics thought I was an ego tripping hoodlum who should be sent off to some polytechnic to produce videos for nurses.' Battle was joined over whether nutrition had anything to do with obesity, with James continuing to argue that they were related. The outcome was to have a direct influence on agriculture.

James came to the Rowett from the leading human nutritional centre, the Dunn Clinical Nutrition Centre at Cambridge, originally housed in a couple of Portacabins. When he first saw the range of granite mansions outside Aberdeen his first reaction was that they couldn't possibly be the Rowett: 'The buildings went on and on. We walked around for four continuous hours, through laboratories, facilities, farm buildings. I'd never been anywhere like it.' In Cambridge, he had just established the first unit where feeding trials on humans could be carried out, for as much as six weeks at a time; at the Rowett he found that animal trials lasting for weeks and months with as many animals as necessary had been going on for years. It was, as he says, mind-boggling. And it was all about to change.

When Sir David Cuthbertson had moved from the Medical Research Council to the Rowett 30 years earlier, his brief had been 'forget about human nutrition'. Wartime rationing had succeeded well enough for the population to be better fed than it had been six years earlier. For the first time in our history the offspring of different social classes grew to a similar height as adults; before the war, richer children grew taller – as they do again today. Evidence like that linked with the experience of rationing to suggest that we knew all we needed to know about feeding ourselves. Now the task was to learn to produce milk and meat so we never went hungry again.

Under Cuthbertson, the Rowett learnt fast. While Lord Boyd Orr left to set up the United Nation's Food and Agriculture Organisation to grapple with similar problems worldwide, back in Aberdeen the scientists studied dairy, beef, sheep and poultry. The work was so important that it went on well beyond the Rowett. A second institute completely devoted to poultry was set up at Roslin and the Rowett's work transferred to it. The Hannah Institute studied dairying, as did the National Institute for Research in Dairying outside Reading, and the Grassland Research Institute nearby.

Blaxter, James's immediate predecessor, sorted out the science of the energy content of animal feeds; Ørskov unravelled the importance of protein needs, to put the subject on a scientific basis:

each was an immense achievement. The money poured in, especially during the Wilson years in the 1960s – and while the scientists found out more and more about animal nutrition, 300 miles further south the Dunn Nutrition Centre in Cambridge, on a fraction of the cash, was doing some work on Vitamin D.

When Blaxter handed over to James in 1982, he wished him luck, thanked heaven he was getting out just in time and, after nearly 20 years of expansion and continuous success, told his successor he didn't envy him the job. A week earlier, James had been handed a policy document by the Scottish Office which told him the world was to be turned upside down. Farming had been mollycoddled for years, now everything had to change. From then on, says James, a similar document came out about every three months. 'I suddenly realised it was going to be exciting, as this unbelievably well-funded and resourced series of institutes had to go into a completely new world.'

The thrust was to swing from farming to food, from quantity to quality, from animal to human nutrition, from producer to consumer. James says bluntly that 'human nutrition and public health started influencing agriculture for the first time since the war'. The impact was to be felt throughout the livestock industries, as the call went out to cut the fat. Once started, the debate spread to all farm produce as worries, justified or otherwise, developed about food additives, pesticide residues and other alleged dangers of chemical food production.

As James puts it, animal nutrition research had to change. It could no longer be 'teams of scientists who fed and weighed groups of 100 cattle on turnips, straw, or whisky wastes. We had to go for the big breaks, not do work like that. But nobody has left the Applied Nutrition Department, bar one, and everyone is now integrated with basic science.' The basic science is biotechnology. It is of course the go-go area, and as we shall see the Rowett scientists are as good at it as they were at working with turnips and whisky waste.

The dietary revolution was not the only one rattling at the bars. A social revolution was at work as well in the countryside. The vacuum left by disappearing small farmers and farm workers was filled by retired folk, weekenders and daily commuters. These newcomers, as Howard Newby has pointed out in his book *Green and Pleasant Land?*, looked at the countryside not in agricultural but in aesthetic or recreational terms. Beyond the double glazing, they wanted something which was beautiful to look at and did not smell. Thus the agricultural revolution of efficiency came face to face with the social revolution in the English village, and the battleground became the environment.

The conflict was slow to develop. When the Donaldsons wrote their book *Farming in Britain Today* in 1972, they could quote Evelyn Waugh's observation, 'to have been born into a world of beauty, to die in ugliness, is a common fate of all us exiles', and then write, 'when applied to our cities and towns this is a melancholy and irreversible truth, but the countryside is quite a different case'. As time passed fewer people would agree with that, for Newby has pointed out that as the newcomers peered through their double glazing they confronted another and much more ancient truth. Two hundred years previously, William Gilpin had said 'land which is merely fertile is a barren prospect'. He meant the same thing as the famous landscape gardener Humphrey Repton who commented that 'the beauty of pleasure-ground and the profit of farm are incompatible'.

Neither man was thinking of environment or wildlife in today's sense, but that too is incompatible with profit and efficiency. In their book *Farming and Birds* O'Connor and Shrubb write, 'in every type of farming system, no matter how traditional, wildlife thrives on inefficiency. Overgrown hedges, weedy fields, undrained pastures – all of which improve the feeding resources available to birds – are simply symptoms of inefficient management'.

At first, therefore, the communication gap between farmers and newcomers was wide. The disagreements directed at the former were often enough the guffaws described by Street. Sometimes, though, the jeers were aimed at a different image – that of a subsidy-profiteering countryside-flattening agri-business run by a mafia of rural razormen. There were ruthlessly opportunistic operators, of course; but the vast bulk of the industry, then and now, was made up of small family farms which had benefited from the good times only to the extent of staying more or less confidently in business.

This is clear from the fact that farming enjoyed two opportunities of profiteering, and rejected both. The first came just after the war when a black-market bonanza was there for the taking – but the vast majority of farmers stuck to their agreement to produce more food at negotiated prices. Then in the run-up to Europe, during the early 1970s, land values boomed. In any other industry there would have been a lot of profit takers when a 500-acre farm suddenly became worth £1 million; but few farmers swapped the cowshed in Loamshire for the chateau on the Côte d'Azure.

For all these reasons, the big world outside was now looking at farming much more closely albeit with a squint and through rose-tinted double glazing. The implications of this were scarcely seen in 1973, as the Donaldsons make clear, but with hindsight, the change of emphasis was inevitable. There were two reasons for this early haziness. One was the CAP itself, which was devoted to the struggle to keep small farmers in business throughout Europe by keeping food prices up. The other was the global market for food, where shortages and what became known as the Great (Russian) Grain Robbery, saw prices rising rapidly. This was so much the case that prices within the CAP reversed their normal pattern and fell below those on world markets. The familiar threat of famine was sufficient to persuade politicians and the public that food supplies were once again at risk, so the old message went out to accelerate production.

Farmers in Britain responded with skills gained from 25 years of crisis. In 1976 the Labour government issued a White Paper 'Food From Our Own Resources' which urged output higher still and higher; and as late as 1981 the succeeding Conservative administration followed a similar course with 'Farming and the Nation'. But if it felt like more of the same, it was not. The landscape altered visibly as the surpluses piled up into the notorious lakes and mountains. The more it changed, the more it united the critics. Where fat led, greens followed. Farming became noisily public, politicised as it had not been since the year before Dan Bullen's birth when the Repeal of the Corn Laws sent it into 100 years of silence. The ensuing arguments have rattled to and fro for 15 years – and are still not fully answered.

# CHAPTER EIGHTEEN

# Milking Politics

Dairy cows went into politics in 1973. A corner of the Ministry of Agriculture (MAFF) had long been reserved for them but as the tide of milk throughout Europe rose higher so they occupied more of Whitehall, Westminster and Brussels. They also got jammed into the mainframe computers of the agricultural economists – as early as 1964 Barbara Castle was complaining that the Milk Marketing Board (MMB) at Thames Ditton employed more economists than the government – and into the PCs in with-it farm offices.

Although there are five MMBs in Britain, the Board for England and Wales is much the largest, and for a 30-year period from the late 1950s to the late 1980s it was run by two men. While they could scarcely have been more different in outlook and temperament, each in his own way was a skilled political and commercial operator. Richard Trehane, tall and urbane, ran the Board with the polish of a diplomat from 1958 to 1977. In that time the number of producers halved, while herd size doubled and milk output rose by more than 50 per cent; the number of commercial dairies which bottled and sold the milk to the housewife fell from over 2000 to under 500. These economies of scale were sharply forced on the whole industry. Dairy farmers' costs went up by more than 50 per cent while the price paid for their milk rose by 10 per cent, and the only way the survivors could manage was by producing more milk more efficiently. Man hours per cow were halved; by the end of the 1970s one man could look after 80 cows and more, a feat achieved by more efficient milking as parlours replaced cowsheds and bulk collection took over from churns.

Over-production was a constant threat – even though by the end of Trehane's time we produced no more than 50 per cent of the cheese we ate and less than 10 per cent of the butter. In those days milk went for manufacturing in this country for one reason: a guaranteed 365-day supply of milk meant unavoidable spring and early summer surpluses; these were made into butter and cheese. We imported all the rest, with the comfortable feeling that New Zealand was a domestic supplier a little to the south of the Isle of Wight. This outlook led the Ministry to sound warnings as early as the 1954 price review; by 1958 the Minister spoke of production 'substantially above current requirements', and by 1961 Christopher Soames wanted quotas. The idea was rejected both by the MMB and the NFU, and in response Soames promised years of falling prices.

All that was to change – temporarily – when we joined the Common Market. The Wilson administration which replaced Ted Heath's Tories promptly called on farmers to respond to the challenge of the Common Agricultural Policy by pushing up output. The CAP dominated Brussels' spending and, since it benefited countries with large farm sectors, it made political and budgetary sense to enlarge our agriculture.

Towards the end of the five-year transition period to full membership, Trehane finally retired as Chairman of the Board. He was replaced by tough, combative, jovial Steve Roberts on 14 July 1977 – or as the new chairman put it with the harshly jocular chuckle which often rattles through his conversation, 'on Bastille Day'. In his very different way Roberts was also a clever politician and businessman, but one with more of the instincts of a street-fighter than a diplomat, a man who loved a scrap and who led with his chuckle and his chin.

Roberts faced two problems: he was determined to grab more of the butterfat market for domestic producers; and he had to be sure that the Board was not split by the political axes swinging in Brussels and elsewhere. His response was to push up domestic output while also pursuing a well-kept secret defensive strategy to benefit producers should the axe fall. When it didn't, he went ahead with his defensive strategy regardless, buying from Unigate a number of the creameries where it manufactured cheese and butter. It was a bold move, which took the MMB deep into the marketplace. It both committed dairy farmers more closely to dealing with production surplus to liquid needs, and gave them the chance to enlarge that surplus by selling more milk products directly to consumers. The fact that Unigate shares rose after the deal was announced suggests that, at least in the short term, the disadvantages of the first were thought to outweigh the benefits of the second.

Roberts, with the light of a good scrap bright in his eye, told farmers the Board would market every drop of extra milk they produced. He saw little reason to hold back before we could produce not just all the milk we drank, but all the cheese, butter, cream, yoghurt or ice-cream we ate. He argued that the butter mountain he was climbing was not of our making and he was determined to lead his forces to the top of it.

All over the country the bulk tanks got fuller and fuller to pay for higher wages and more expensive tractors, fuel and fertiliser. The price of the pinta on doorstep, shop and supermarket counter rose more slowly – and as we have seen less of the money ended up in the farmer's pocket. Worse still, fewer of those pintas were being bought. In the 1950s, at the top of the post-war binge, we sank over five bottles a week each; by 1980 that was under four and falling.

But there was more to the market than liquid milk. In 1975 we ate 520 000 tonnes of butter, of which we made 50 000 tonnes and imported nearly half a million. By 1983, a combination of cost and the fatty fears of people like Philip James meant that butter had become something of a yellow peril and no more than 300 000 tonnes slipped down the national throat: by then we were making nearly quarter of a million, and importing less than 200 000 tonnes. Although we exported as much as we had made altogether 10 years earlier, stocks rose by 100 000 tonnes in 1983 alone. Still Roberts urged his men on.

The extra milk which came from the hard work of thousands of dairy farmers had been demanded by the politicians. Mrs Thatcher's Conservative government, with Peter Walker as Minister of Agriculture, backed the expansion of farm output at least as vigorously as the outgoing Labour administration. The White Paper 'Farming and the Nation' wanted output boosted by as much as 20 per cent over five years, using more investment and higher technology; milk production was not excepted. Though liquid milk consumption might be falling along with butter we were producing nearly 70 per cent of our cheese and diverting vast amounts of butter into intervention when the change Soames had suggested more than 20 years before at last placed a flood barrier round the European milk lake. On April Fools' Day 1984, milk quotas were imposed by Brussels.

Roberts fought them to the last midnight in March. He continued to argue that dairy farmers had every right to compete in the domestic market, that price must be the weapon of supply control and that quotas would be unworkable. The NFU ducked and weaved but, with the exception of the then Deputy President Simon Gourlay, was largely jollied into following the Roberts line. The Ministry, where Jopling had replaced Walker, was in the process of changing its tune and the melody it now choruses sounded threatening to traditional ears. One civil servant observed of the new Minister: 'He's not terribly bright but is very stubborn and, unlike Walker, he will do what Maggie tells him. Maggie has given him an axe and told him to cut us down to size'. Other apparently government-inspired criticisms of farming appeared in the Press in the early months of 1984, and it was clear that the spirit of 'Farming and the Nation' had withered in Whitehall and Westminster, if not yet in the field. By then Roberts was well on up the mountain, still chuckling as he went, convinced among other things that the French would never allow quotas to be introduced. But they did.

At first, he and his Board members believed the scheme would fail. One member said at the time: 'It's not our fault we've got lumbered with this disaster and we want to stay as distant from it as possible. Then, when the scheme collapses in a year or two, we will have been proved right.' Today, it would not be easy to find a dairy farmer willing to give up quotas for another means of supply control. Individual farmers may have suffered because of them, and they have not stopped the slow decline of numbers in the industry, but to the large majority they have given a security not enjoyed by other sectors of farming.

The biggest single cost of quotas has been that of closing down five of the creameries bought from Unigate. They had been upgraded at considerable capital expense, only to run dry of milk when quotas came. The Board may have had little choice about buying them, but it is dairy farmers who have met the bills in both directions – so the profits which finally started to emerge some 10 years after the original investment have been most welcome.

The claim that quotas would push up milk prices has not yet been sustained, though recent increases ave at least matched the rate of inflation. For those already inside the quota ring they have been a windfall capital asset, for those outside a liability: it costs between two and three times as much to buy the quota for a cow as to buy the cow. And they have worked. Lakes have dried up, mountains melted, and the occasional rift has appeared as milk has been briefly in short supply.

The claim that they would mean inefficiency has not so far been sustained either. On the contrary, they have helped to achieve what George Stapledon argued for all those years earlier. Because they blocked expansion, they made low-cost milk the target; to hit it, farmers had to feed their cows more grass. Cake sales fell sharply. Profits from milking rose and Gordon Newman suddenly found himself surrounded by admirers sharing his lifelong love affair with silage. New feeds like maize silage and treated straw also clamoured for his affection. Cows had long been fed on such home-grown forages; quotas persuaded a lot more farmers to try them. They did not abandon the cake bag; they used it with less abandon, and concentrated instead on forage feeds, especially grass.

This was a profound change. When, through the 1970s, average output rose by 1000 litres a cow, 900 came from more cake, just 100 from better use of grass. High stocking rates and well-managed grass might give cheaper and more profitable milk but they were a hassle, and the widespread attitude was, 'Why bother?' Living standards could be maintained by pushing up yields with the cake bag. Even if the profits were smaller, they were more certain.

Few knew this better than the scientists at the Grassland Research Institute, where Stapledon's ideas of marrying farmer, beast and grass had continued to dominate the research. The marriage seemed to have succeeded when, at the silver jubilee in 1974, the Director Professor Woodford said, 'from the start, grassland research was to be interpreted in its broadest sense as the study by scientific methods of the problems of the men and women who farm 34 million acres of sown and natural grassland in the United Kingdom.' He went on to claim that research had been bio-economic, multi-disciplinary, and holistic. He spoke of the tremendous improvements in grassland husbandry and animal production since 1949 though reluctantly admitting that changes in grassland productivity had not been as spectacular as those for other crops.

A silver jubilee is no time to mention divorce, but the Director may not have persuaded all who heard him. No more than six years later, his successor Professor Lazenby apologised to a different audience: 'We have succeeded in separating, rather than bringing together, the plant and the animal; the credibility of our grassland research has suffered in the eyes of many farmers.'

By the time quotas came in, however, there was confidence that the scientists now knew the secret of grassland management: it was eternal youth. To achieve it, they suggested three methods: cut off its head, cut off its head, and cut off its head. The reasons lie in the natural behaviour of productive pasture grasses. The aim of a ryegrass plant is to set as many seeds as possible. To do this it puts out tillers each of which, if unmolested, will end up as a seed head. Each tiller carries three leaves. It grows a new leaf every 11 days, and as the young leaf appears so the oldest one dies. This process continues as the seedhead forms and emerges on its stem, and as it does the plant puts more of its resources into the seeds and less into the sweet young leaf. This makes it less palatable to livestock. But when a passing beast bites off the seedhead-bearing tiller, the whole process must begin again, and the plant puts out new tillers supported by more sweet young leaves.

It is this which gives the grazier his chance. To keep up the supply of young leaves, he must arrange for his beasts to keep biting off the tillers so that the plant constantly puts out more. They must not bite so often they set the plant back too severely, nor so seldom they let the tillers put out seedheads – though when that threatens there is always the mower to use as an artificial mouth, its action shaving the sward back to where it was before spring growth started. These tightly grazed swards remain dense, leafy and green throughout the season, with a high production of sweet new leaves – and there is even a grassland ruler called a swardstick to keep a check on the trimness of the designer stubble.

If this sounds easy, it is not. Keeping three lanes of a motorway safely surfaced and open to traffic all the year round is straightforward compared with keeping a grazing field at a level 3 inches of growth throughout the season. To achieve the latter demands high stocking rates, which in itself increases the risk of the grass going short. What the animals want and what the grass provides do not readily match. A beef animal, for example, needs more and better grass to eat as it grows bigger through the grazing season, which is the opposite of the natural pattern of grass growth. A high-yielding dairy cow needs a similar amount of quality feed every day, and grass cannot be relied on to produce this. Clever juggling of grazing and mowing helps keep milk production up, but it needs art as well as science to match grass and cow through every day of every season.

At these very high rates of livestock output, large amounts of nitrogen are needed to keep the grass growing, and high-output dairy cows will continue to eat heavily fertilised pastures. But for beef and sheep, or for lower-output dairy cows, clover is becoming a real alternative and will in future be much more widely grown. It can produce as much grazing on a hectare of ground as around 200 kg of nitrogen, which is half the top rate of use for intensive grass growing. It is also a very palatable feed which, unlike grass, does not grow rank and stemmy as the season passes. This palatability means that well-managed grass clover swards grow good silage as well as good grazing, and that stock do very well on both. The drawbacks are that clover adds some snags which are all its own. The most threatening is bloat, a condition in which rumen gases are unable to escape and inflate that organ like a balloon. The pressure, unless rapidly relieved, leads to heart failure.

Now, clover breeding is challenging the doubters and overcoming the difficulties. Cold-tolerant varieties have been found in the Swiss Alps; these, and other new varieties with greater persistence, are bringing more reliable season-long growth. The risk of bloat will go; the clover plants themselves will be higher-yielding, and they will be sold with improved strains of Rhizobium to increase their nitrogen fixing abilities. As Dr D. Wilson, following in Stapledon's footsteps at the Welsh Plant Breeding Station, put it recently: 'white clover is currently the subject of a very large research effort yet even five or ten years ago it was considered by many to be a weed'. The pressure for low-cost systems is growing, and clover is the pump.

Grass breeding will also contribute. The new varieties are more palatable and digestible, more cold-tolerant, better at using nitrogen, and higher-yielding. Cows grazing one new Italian ryegrass gave 730 litres more than their sisters because of the greater digestibility of the new variety. And a new cross, between ryegrass and giant fescue, offers a hybrid with very high yield, excellent winter hardiness, drought-tolerance, persistency and productivity at low levels of nitrogen fertilising.

Such changes could affect cattle breeding as well as feeding. When Bob Ørskov was working in Bangladesh, he realised their cattle ate twice as much straw as ours. At first he thought that was because of poverty, or simply because the weights were being wrongly recorded. Then he realised it was because their gut volume was proportionately twice the size of ours. They were able to digest more straw. 'Their cattle would grow slowly on a diet where our cattle would die.' He realised that selection for high levels of milk production had also selected against gut volume. Now he argues that, as we move towards a future of renewable resources, so we must tailor our wastes to fit our animals and our animals to fit our wastes. In effect, he is offering Bobby Boutflour's bet, but in reverse. He will produce large amounts of milk on grass, straw and protein supplements like maize gluten or fishmeal.

Ørskov describes the triumph of cereal production as an artificial success story, because we only use half the crop. 'Farmers have been able to expand through profits made from the seed alone. They have been able totally to ignore the rest of the crop. We have got into a skewed situation. The main effect has been that livestock have been ignored and the countryside is full of excess by-products. It hasn't paid to use the straw, so like any other waste we burn or bury it.'

Using small nylon bags, he has studied straw as a feed; each bag is filled with straw from different cereals, and put in the cow's stomach. At intervals the bags are taken out again, to see how well the contents have been digested. He has not only found large differences in food value between different straws, he has found how to pre-treat them to improve digestibility. And he has found that, while the leaves from wheat straw are as nourishing as good hay, barley leaves are almost as good a feed as the cereal-based concentrates themselves. The straw which comes out of the back of a combine is 50 per cent stems, around 40 per cent leaves, and the remaining 10 per cent chaff and stem nodes. What's needed, he suggests, is a machine which separates leaf from stem, as seed is separated from straw in the threshing mechanism of the combine.

Whether we shall see cows bred to fulfil such aims is uncertain. If so, genetic engineering will help by producing super-efficient enzymes to speed the digestion of these fibrous feeds in the rumen. Meanwhile the possibility offers another approach to some of the problems of pollution linked to intensive farming, while the improvements in clover have renewed interest in ley farming both for organic farming and for more efficient use of nitrogen in conventional farming. Environmental concerns about slurry and silage effluent have also led to much new research at the Institute of Grassland and Animal Production – as the old GRI is now called.

None of these changes, actual or possible, has backed the cow out of politics however, and the latest issue to come in for vigorous debate well beyond the parlour is bovine somatotrophin (BST).

BST is a naturally occurring growth hormone. The work in and around Cambridge which led first to AI, then to embryo transplants, identified BST many years ago. Further work showed that all cows produce it in small quantities, that it could be extracted, and that when it was injected back into a dairy cow it stimulated more milk production. But there for years the matter rested. The extract was too expensive to use. When biotechnologists discovered how to produce BST cheaply, detailed studies of the consequences began. They showed that BST can increase milk output by as much as 20 per cent: short term, neither milk-producing cows nor milk-drinking people suffer ill effects from using it; long term, the same is true for drinkers and looks to be true for the cows too, though the evidence here is not yet complete. The argument about BST has concerned neither its safety nor its efficacy, both of which seem to be fully established; instead it confronts the political question, 'Who needs it?'

Two answers have been given, which do not overlap: one is everybody, and the other nobody. The first says you can stop neither technological progress nor economics; more efficient milk production is cheaper milk production and the world needs both. The second says we are awash with milk, that dairy farmers are a threatened species in need of conservation, and that we need more milk like we need a hole in the bucket. History suggests that the first answer will win – and in this case it is backed by technology both old and new.

The stately black and white British Friesian has recently met competition from her own black and white cousin, the slimline North American Holstein. Both started out as sisters on the North German plain around 1910, and the difference in the two since then has been due to breeding. The North Americans were better than the British at breeding an out-and-out dairy type, a gaunt, lean animal with higher milk yields than the rather beefier British Friesian. As they selected for higher milk yields, they were also unconsciously selecting for higher BST production, and when the techniques of AI and embryo transplant brought the Holstein genes rapidly across the Atlantic, they carried more BST with them. These genes are now spreading fast through the British black and white herd.

Bio-engineered BST has been described as 20 years of breeding in a syringe. But before long the genetic engineers will have worked out how to insert the relevant genes directly into breeding animals. This will accelerate conventional breeding programmes along the paths they are already following and shrink the influence of the syringe to a much shorter period. Therefore, whatever the decision about injecting BST, it can only briefly influence the rising graph of yield per cow, stimulated by BST in one form or another – and BST is only part of a widespread research programme on efficient milk production, and the hormones and ultimately the genes which control it. In fact BST itself is not all that important. What is important is that both sides have seen it as a test case for the commercial application of biotechnology.

These essentially political arguments have also reached into the field of animal welfare. Some say that the modern dairy cow is a miserably put-upon beast, suffering from mastitis, lameness, acidosis and a range of other discomforts, and that BST is yet another case of more means worse. High-yielding dairy cows certainly need good management to keep them happy, and for every critic there are hundreds of dairy farmers patting the necks of their zero-flight-distance cows – free from the old plagues of TB, brucellosis and foot-and-mouth – to confirm they get it. The skills of good livestock management are increasingly demanding, however, and not every dairy farmer has the temperament and training to meet them. Now the engineers are working towards a solution which they argue will take us back to the days when every animal got close individual attention. Then, there was an affliction called smallholders' disease, which arose from overfeeding; now, the claim is that robotic milking will provide an electronic intimacy between cow and computer, without the complication of smallholders' disease.

John Bramley based at the AFRC Institute for Animal Health at Compton has been working with the engineers from the Institute of Engineering Research at Silsoe. 'Robotic milking is no longer sci-fi,' he says, 'and some major benefits will be seen in terms of health. It will almost be like going back to the original system of a cow being sucked by her calf.'

He describes a future in which the cow can wander up whenever she likes to an intelligent robot working round the clock. The machine will know her history – of calving and the present stage in her reproductive cycle, of yield and health, of diet – as well as the shape and size not just of her udder but of each teat and quarter. 'Patterns of milk flow from different quarters are different. Determine the flow by sensors, and what the flow does to vacuum fluctuations and pressure changes and the consequences for disease may be considerable.' As an obvious example, says Bramley, it has long been known that because front and hind quarters give different quantities of milk, and hind quarters take longer to milk, so front quarters are often over-milked. 'Instead of the liner banging away on an empty front quarter, damaging the teat and risking infection, an intelligent robot could balance the timing.'

The udder infection mastitis is not caused by machine-milking – it also occurs with hand milking, when a cow is sucked by a calf, and when she is dry and not being milked at all – but machines do contribute to it. High-yielding cows are more susceptible, cross-infection is more likely in large herds, and poorly maintained machines do undoubted damage. Obviously the udder's natural defences evolved to cope with the stresses of suckling a single calf, not to feed people economically through mass mechanical milking. Machine-milking is therefore an important factor in mastitis and dairy farmers must keep a constant watch. Skilled management is necessary to prevent it, and quick antibiotic therapy to cure it. Given both, mastitis can be kept under close control; it does not always get them.

Robotic milking demands a much better understanding of these problems. As Bramley puts it: 'the piece of equipment is one thing. Its application in a dairying system is another area altogether.' The work required to explore this area will illuminate many dark corners. That information can then be programmed into the robot to make it much more sensitive than today's machinery. Other information can be added. Biosensors could keep constant checks on health, diet, reproduction or general well-being. Since a cow might choose to be milked five times a day, these checks could be carried out very frequently and allow rapid reaction to the first hint of difficulty. They could be linked to other sensors and video cameras monitoring many aspects of herd behaviour. Meanwhile the stockman or woman, freed from the chore of twice or thrice daily milking, would have much more time to devote to observation of the cows.

None of this will happen quickly. The prototype robot attached a teat cup to its first cow on a wet day in the summer of 1988, and the technology is very far from tried, tested and in full-scale production. Already it has provoked a complete rethink of commercial milking and, as Bramley says, the possibilities for improvement are very exciting.

Milk yields rise from more frequent milkings, so a rise in output of around 15 per cent will follow from free access to the robots; the robots could milk peak lactation cows several times and restrict nearly dry cows to one or two milkings. They could be placed singly in small grazing areas to serve around 30 cows, or centrally for serving a large herd. However they are used, they are likely to produce more milk from contented cows – and, perhaps especially in the case of over-worked one-man dairy farms, from contented farmers.

A third area in which politics and the dairy parlour meet is where biotechnology, together with genetic manipulation, promises – or threatens – much greater control over bovine reproduction. A number of possibilities are emerging from the laboratory to affect livestock breeding.

Geneticists have put together a breeding scheme dubbed MOET to speed up genetic improvement through multiple ovulation and embryo transfer. Recent schemes have used new techniques of predicting livestock performance and embryo transplant 'plumbing' linked with complex statistical analysis to double the rate of breeding progress achieved with AI. Cattle breeding companies, similar to those long familiar for pigs and chickens, are being formed to exploit these opportunities. As well as accelerating the improvement of dairy animals, embryo transplant technologies will see that every beef animal starts life as today's equivalent of Lindertis Evulse. Dozens of embryo Evulses – which are now likely to come from breeds like the Limousin, Charolais or even Belgian Blue as well as the traditional British breeds of Hereford and Aberdeen Angus – can now be recovered from their mother and reimplanted into foster surrogates, many of which will carry twins. It is suggested that this route will become as everyday as AI.

Other possibilities include deciding the sex of an animal before birth, altering the make-up of milk quality, spreading disease-resistance or other desirable genes, or cloning high-quality animals. As with pigs and chickens, the potential of the new high performance breeds will be best expressed through much more closely controlled management than has been traditional with beef cattle and sheep; and the cost of the bloodlines will increase the importance of achieving these levels of management control. The computer, and its expert systems, will be an important tool in achieving this.

Some of these developments will be very slow to come, particularly those which demand detailed knowledge of which genes do what. At present we have this knowledge for around 1 per cent of the genes in a cow. Even when the other 99 per cent of the genes have been identified, many limitations will remain.

A final area where politics and milk meet is the Milk Marketing Boards themselves. Every day since 1933 the Boards have collected the milk from tens of thousands of farms across the country and delivered it to millions of doorsteps – and in that time our daily pinta has become steadily purer until, with the Danes, it is now the purest you can drink in Europe. Churchill's remark that the best investment a community can make is putting milk into babies has been richly underwritten by the industry, even if the dividend to the individual dairy farmer has not always been as bonny as he might have hoped.

Now it is said that the Boards have served their purpose and must change to meet the needs of competition in the modern market place. Whether milk would be cheaper with that change is uncertain, whether it would be more reliably or purely produced unlikely. Whatever political decisions may be taken, the achievements of the last 60 years must be safeguarded.

# CHAPTER NINETEEN

# British Wheat in British Bread

Wheat and barley varieties bred in Europe filled our fields in 1970, and when we joined the Common Market the influence of Continental breeders might have risen. The man who reversed the flow was John Bingham. His first and in some ways still his most famous wheat variety was Maris Huntsman, which leapt to prominence in 1972 bringing with it an immediate 15 per cent jump in yield. It led the field for several years until other Bingham-bred varieties overtook it – and by 1973 we were exporting thousands of tonnes of Huntsman seed to French and other European wheat growers.

Bingham had joined the Plant Breeding Institute (PBI) in 1954. Given the number of years needed to produce a new variety he hadn't wasted much time. He stands beside George Stapledon in his contribution to our plant breeding, but where Stapes had a volatile Celtic temperament, Bingham is a reserved, even shy, East Anglian, happiest when surrounded by young plants at the PBI or on his farm in Norfolk. Since the introduction of Huntsman he has produced a series of winners. At times as many as 9 acres out of every 10 we plant to winter wheat have been drilled with seed bred by John Bingham, and our wheat yields have taken off. In the year that Huntsman was introduced we grew 5 million tonnes. By 1984 we were growing 15 million tonnes. Bingham and the PBI share the responsibility, but it is more than a domestic story. They did a lot of it from Chile by way of Mexico, North America and Japan.

At the end of the war the Americans took from Japan some short-strawed wheat varieties. They were interested in a group of genes, the dwarfing genes and in particular those from a variety known as Norin 10, which were to have the most powerful influence on world wheats.

Some years later, the Rockefeller Foundation provided the cash to begin the Mexican wheat breeding programme which Norman Borlaug was to turn into the Green Revolution. He saw immediately the importance of these short-strawed wheats, and used them as the basis for his breeding. Borlaug sent some of his breeding material to Chile, and there it was crossed with the wheat which had for so long dominated the English acreage, Cappelle Desprez. When the PBI entertained some Chilean visitors in the mid-1960s, they brought the cross with them.

Bingham had been using Norin 10 genes in his programme, but the cross with Cappelle Desprez immediately clicked. From it sprang a series of semi-dwarf wheats which have doubled the average yields of the early 1970s. Huntsman was not itself a semi-dwarf, whose first big success was Hobbit – a wheat which does not have furry feet although it does have a big head and short straw. It produced the same amount of plant material in total as the older, taller wheats, but divided its energies differently. While the old, tall wheats ended up at harvest with around 30 per cent of the whole plant as grain, Hobbit and its relations put 50 per cent of their biomass into grain, so their potential yield was higher. Also, their shortness allowed more nitrogen fertiliser to be used. Put more nitrogen on a tall plant and it falls over; in a wet summer the farmer is left with a tangled mess.

Shortness, high yields and nitrogen go together. Few have criticised shortness. High yields come in for no more than occasional objections. But nitrogen has been attacked in ways which have not greatly changed since William Gammie Ogg confronted the charge in 1947 that using bagged nitrogen was as bad as robbing graves – even though more than one person in three throughout the world is alive and fed by fertiliser from Haber's pressure cooker.

The keeper of the Rothamsted classical experiments today is Johnny Johnston, who has enough of the leprechaun about him to qualify for honorary membership of that tribe of gnomes and elves who traditionally stood as doorkeepers over the secrets of the earth. Leprechaun or not, he is a spritely and humorous guardian of the accumulated experience gained from soil science over nearly 150 years in Broadbalk, and if anyone knows the answer to such charges it must be he.

That experience showed that increasing the organic content of soil did little to improve the yield of crops. Farmers have traditionally kept on forking manure into the storehouse of their fields but according to the Rothamsted experiments it did not greatly increase the amount of food released by the storekeepers. As Johnston puts it: 'Organic matter has always been thought to enhance soil structure and improve the workability of the soil. Neither is easy to prove.'

Recently, however, that conclusion has begun to change. Soils in the experiments which have extra organic matter have given larger yields than others. They hold water better, have better structure and also provide plant foods in ways which fertiliser nitrogen cannot mimic. At the same time, adding fertiliser nitrogen still increases yields and gives its best responses on soils with more organic matter. The Rothamsted experience shows that plants do best with a mix of modern fast foods, traditional farmhouse cooking – and a large storehouse to back both of them up. So nitrogen cannot be accused of grave robbery.

We will continue to need bagged nitrogen in increasing quantities worldwide. But while Haber's enormous pressure cooker will always stand as the great industrial monument to chemical fertilisers, there are now glimpses of technologies which will produce bagged nitrogen with much less energy, and perhaps ultimately using biological processes.

One route has looked at an electrochemical process which would work at room temperature and pressure and be able to do the job in a way more like biological nitrogen fixation. Recently Dr Ray Richards, of the Nitrogen Fixation Laboratory at Sussex University, said of this that 'the development of a low-technology device for local production of ammonia seems to be feasible and it would serve agriculture in areas where high technology is inappropriate for various reasons. In turn, fossil fuel would be released to industry for alternative uses.' He added that this portable system could use 'wind, tide or sun as a source of electrical energy, air and water as a feedstock'.

Another approach has proposed straw as the source of hydrogen for small-scale ammonia production. John Thring and Associates have claimed that a plant large enough to be economic would need 77 000 tonnes of straw to produce 19 000 tonnes of fixed nitrogen, and that straw from a maximum radius of 9 miles would be sufficient to operate the plant.

A more modest aim is to help legumes fix more nitrogen than they do naturally. Workers at Rothamsted and the John Innes Institute have collected many different species of Rhizobium and hope to swap genetic material between them to produce super-efficient hybrids. In due course it may be possible to extend such genetic swapping so other plants, as well as legumes, can fix their own nitrogen. The nitrogen-fixing wheat plant is the Holy Grail of this particular quest and some of the finest knights pursuing it are to be found alongside Dr Richards at Falmer outside Brighton. Until recently they could see no end to their search; now they are more confident some scientific Sir Galahad will win through – in which case Sussex farmers will be the first to see the Falmer wheat.

Another criticism of bagged fertiliser concerns nitrates in our drinking water. Soil scientists agree that there has been 'a marked increase in the concentration of nitrate in drinking water which caused widespread public concern and controversy. This increase coincided with the period of increased nitrogen fertiliser use, so it is widely assumed that nitrogen fertiliser is to blame. Recent work at Rothamsted suggests that this assumption greatly over-simplifies a very complex problem and is not fully justified'.

Their work has established that little bagged nitrogen remains in the soil as nitrate at harvest. Nearly all the applied nitrogen is taken up in the crop or in the soil organic matter. After harvest, the soil becomes moist in the autumn rains, and this stimulates the soil micro-organisms to set about their labours. They break down soil organic matter, so producing nitrate. When there is no growing crop to absorb it, the nitrate is washed into ground water by the winter rains. This response also occurs on plots given farmyard manure, and Rothamsted experiments show that these hold more nitrate than those which are chemically fertilised. The organic plots therefore constitute a greater risk.

Furthermore, the largest amounts of nitrate are released when grassland is ploughed. This is especially true of old grassland which has been steadily accumulating organic matter, but occurs whenever grass is ploughed down – indeed, the traditional use of grass in rotations exploited just that reservoir of accumulated fertility. Together, these two findings make clear that substituting animal manures and rotations for bagged nitrogen would do little to reduce nitrate leaching. Instead, Rothamsted recommends that no fertiliser nitrogen should be applied in the autumn, and that winter crops should be sown early enough to use the nitrate released through the autumn. Both are now standard practice.

High-yielding crops need nitrogen and, whatever system is followed, even the best-farmed crops are at risk from leaching. The argument is about the consequences. One risk is to babies; high nitrate levels in water can lead to Blue Baby Syndrome, but fortunately the incidence is extremely low in this country, and no case has been reported since 1972. Another risk is that nitrates may cause stomach cancer. Evidence for this country from cancer research institutes shows that, where nitrate levels in water are highest, stomach cancers are low and falling. Even so, the scientists involved warn that certainty is impossible: 'the massive increases in fertiliser use may lead to an effect that will not become apparent for some years, so that trends of mortality must continue to be monitored.' This is a verdict of 'innocent but bound over to keep the peace'. It seems the sensible conclusion: what you are doing is harmless by all our measurements, but keep a very careful check on it indeed. It is reflected by legal requirements that drinking water may contain no more than a small amount of nitrate. Removing nitrates from water has been and still is inconvenient and costly, but modern methods are slowly making it easier and cheaper.

Nitrogen fertiliser is one of the most important ingredients in the modern agricultural kitchen. The full recipe demands all the other ingredients – the soil care, the seeds, the pesticides, the machinery and so forth – but nitrogen in one form or another will stay high on the farmer's shopping list. Like all ingredients it can be abused. It is powerful stuff, and the temptation to use it in unsuitable circumstances – say on thin, sloping downland chalk – has not always been resisted. Today, the pressures on farming mean that farmers are looking for every possible way of saving money. Wasting nitrogen is wasting money. Although we still do not fully know how to use nitrogen with minimum waste, we are learning fast.

Bingham's work with Norin 10 genes and the extra nitrogen they allowed was not his only breeding interest. Quantity was important, but he also wanted quality, and in many ways it is harder to breed for quality than yield. In those days, quality was put under the microscope at the PBI, as well as at Rothamsted and elsewhere; now, visitors can be shown it by the handful. It is a protein called gluten which looks like a cross between chewing gum and springy putty.

At Rothamsted they like to show you how a walnut-sized lump, thrown on to a hard surface, rebounds vigorously. But demonstrations can be unreliable. After one suitably showbiz build-up, the lump spreads over the floor like a dropped egg yolk. Nevertheless, springy it is (as long as too much water has not been left in the lump!). Indeed today each molecule is thought to be shaped as a tiny protein spring, and it is millions of these springs which put the bounce in British bread. These gluten springs are made up of more than 20 sub-units, some of which make better bread than others. Bingham and his team have made a lot of progress in breeding for better sub-units, and feel sure they can make more. Along with changes in the way we bake our bread, this means that home-grown wheat now supplies around 80 per cent of all the flour we use for bread-making. The 4 or 5 million tonnes of North American wheat we used to import are down to less than 1 million, and could fall to zero.

Another target is disease-resistance, from breeding in natural tolerance or immunity in other wheats and grasses, both cultivated and wild. This struggle is perhaps even harder than the search for quality, for just as insects find ways around the plant's defences so diseases can break down resistance. But as breeders begin to understand these defences, and as a wider range of plants and their genes is drawn on, so new resistant varieties emerge – though a fungicide is often used to give additional help from outside.

While all these changes were going on in the art and craft of wheat growing, so similar things were happening across the fence in the barley field. Joe Nickerson's biographer Ralph Whitlock put it like this: 'From time immemorial until 1976 wheat was generally sown in autumn in England, barley in spring. . . . J.N. was the first to appreciate the potential of autumn-sown barley. In the early

1950s he sowed 300 acres of spring barley varieties in the autumn. It soon became clear that, even allowing for the years when the crop was killed by frost and had to be ploughed up, the barley which had the longest growing period, on average, out-yielded all the rest.

'On a long visit to Bavaria in the late 1940s he was struck by the excellence of the crops of winter barley he saw. The climate of the upland farms of southern Germany was just as inhospitable as, and much colder than, that of the Lincolnshire Wolds, yet the Bavarian farmers were reaping splendid harvests.

'The variety which attracted him most was Malta . . . From a few grammes of seed he multiplied it until by the late 1960s he had enough to launch the new variety commercially.

'J.N. used typically forthright tactics. Armed with spades and samples, Nickerson representatives were sent out to farms in every part of the country. Their task was to demonstrate how these new winter-hardy barley varieties, committed to the soil in autumn, could revolutionise arable farming. Age-old farming pratice was about to be turned upside down . . . The revolution really got going in 1975.'

Today, a bigger acreage of barley is drilled to winter varieties than it is to spring, and Nickerson varieties have at times held as many as 9 acres in every 10 of that acreage. That change has meant that the vast bulk of the cultivation and drilling of cereals must be completed in the autumn. Much of it is done in September, which may be little more than days after the last of the previous year's crops have been harvested. That demands the reliability of speedy fieldwork, from larger and more powerful machines and implements. These machines have helped to turn some difficult, heavy soils into some of the most productive cereal land, especially for wheat.

Assembling the technology for these advances provoked much debate. Twenty years earlier, farmers had juggled seed, fertiliser and broad-leafed weedkiller. Now there were chemical growth regulators (which did for tall wheats what the Norin 10 gene did for the semi-dwarfs), grass weedkillers and fungicides as well. Different factions supported lower or higher seed rates, earlier or later dates for sowing, more or less fertiliser, growth regulator or fungicide, applied singly or together at earlier or later growth stages. At first these battles were fought in distant spots like Schleswig-Holstein and Belgium, but they soon spread to East Anglia, Perthshire or the Cotswolds. This was the period when a farmer observed that those who watched the Cup Final missed out on one piece of the puzzle. A burst of Wembley warmth accelerated the growth of crops held back for weeks by a cold, late spring, and by the time the television was turned off the narrow window for putting on a growth regulator had closed – well, almost.

A new occupation, crop consultancy, grew up to specialise in advice about these complications. If cereal growing had been a pleasant, easy way of making a living in the 20 years after the war, 'the late 1970s to early 1980s was a period of prosperity for cereal farmers unprecedented in UK agriculture in modern times', according to a team at Wye College. By 1984, high-input high-output techniques gave wheat yields at harvest which averaged well over three tonnes an acre, the highest in our history; by then many farmers regularly grew over 4 and some as many as 5 tonnes of wheat an acre. Dan Bullen would have been speechless to hear it was the first year this country had been a net exporter of cereals and a net importer of manufactured goods.

The consequences influenced the size of farms, the numbers who worked on them and the look of the countryside. We began regularly to export some millions of tonnes of grain a year. The quality could still be uncertain, but because of our very high yields we were growing it as cheaply as the Americans or the northern Europeans. Today, our growing costs can match or beat everyone except the Argentinians, Australians and Canadians. Since between them they grow 10 per cent of world supplies, there is plenty of room left for efficient domestic growers.

There was another consequence as well, and one which was to lead to something more serious than a misunderstanding between the Minister of Agriculture and the Russian Ambassador. A wheat mountain began to thrust upwards above the fertile northern European plains. Commentators echoed Dr Johnson's reaction to the Scottish Highlands without achieving his eloquence: 'An eye accustomed to flowery pastures and waving harvests is astonished and repelled by this wide extent of hopeless sterility.'

Doctor and commentators overdid it: an accurate fit between output and consumption was so unlikely as to be impossible. Sooner or later the resources poured into agriculture over 40 years must lead to surplus; then, they must be carefully withdrawn or other controls applied. Farmers understand that painful truth better than anyone since, as the group at Wye quoted above were later to remark: 'the decline in the profitability of cereals production can be directly attributed to productivity improvements achieved over the previous decade which generated massive surpluses and resulted in falling prices.' Farmers suffered from their own success, and little thanks they had from those who had provoked, cajoled and stimulated them into their earlier exertions. By 1985 the profits had disappeared; by 1987, a year of exceptionally wet and difficult harvest, the unprecedented prosperity had become a loss for all but the most skilful and determined.

The problems of surplus must be met, for the sake of the farmer, the taxpayer and the rest of the world. They are being so met. To the squeeze on price has now been added a mechanism similar to the standard quantity introduced by Soames 25 years earlier. When Europe's farmers produce more than a given amount of grain, next year's price is further cut in consequence. Set-aside has been introduced. So have payments for lower output in Environmentally Sensitive Areas (ESAs). It is sometimes suggested that the simplest answer would be to lower the levels of inputs everywhere, not just in ESAs. Though this approach will spread, it is unlikely to be a general solution. This is true for a number of reasons.

The first is that modern cereal varieties are more efficient than old varieties at all levels of inputs. Give them more nitrogen and they use it better; give them less nitrogen and the same remains true. Breeding has not been squeezing itself ever more tightly into a hi-tech dead end, it has been producing varieties which are more environmentally sympathetic. This will remain the case.

The second is that efficiency will remain a farming virtue. Again we can turn to Dr Johnson: 'that was the best garden which produced most roots and fruits; and that water was most to be prized which contained most fish'. Such robust common sense, long held as a principle by farmers, is needed for a world, and an island, where the more we can grow on fewer acres the cheaper the food and the more room for other activities, as well as other birds and beasts, plants and insects.

The third is that the chief cost of growing a crop is in land, labour and machinery, not seed, fertiliser and sprays. The best way to economise on growing cereals is to sell the farm; as long as you hesitate over quitting, high yields are the only way to meet these costs. As we move towards these higher yields on suitable soils, so we must plan, imaginatively and sympathetically, to use the land which cannot grow enough grain and is no longer suitable for modern farming. Some of it will still be farmed one way or another; much of it will find other uses.

The fourth reason is that other technologies as well as breeding are becoming more environmentally benign. Falmer wheats and lower use of bagged nitrogen may be years away yet; more effective phosphate fertilising is closer. Getting on for 17 million tonnes of phosphorus wash into the oceans each year. Of this 50 per cent comes from natural erosion, the other 50 per cent either from human sewage or detergents – which has led John Emsley to argue for 'making the phosphate which washed today's clothing grow tomorrow's food'. Phosphate fertilisers bond too tightly to the soil to be leached out, but since they use some 80 per cent of global production of rock phosphate, reductions would be welcome.

Once again, they are in sight. As so often in farming, an old partnership would take a new form. Rather like legumes and Rhizobium, plant roots link with fungi to form a mycorrhizal (which means simply fungal/root) association. The fungus becomes a courtesy root, which helps the plant to search more widely for available supplies of phosphorus. This mutual aid system works particularly well where phosphorus levels are low, and it is clear that mychorrhizae are important influences on yields worldwide. Rothamsted has identified the most effective among the 100 or so known species, and genetic engineers believe they will be able to make the process even more effective. If so, farming's phosphate applications may be reduced. More important even than environmentally sympathetic fertilising will be the slowly decreasing use of chemical sprays. To follow through these developments, we must go back to an earlier stage of the story.

Recently, a meeting took place in Bordeaux to celebrate the 'Hundred Years' War' against plant disease. Hostilities, as often, began by accident. The accident had two parts. The first was Medoc mixture, a brew of copper sulphate, lime and water sprayed on ripening grapes to make them taste like sink cleaner and so deter pilfering. The second was the cure for phylloxera, the disease which was destroying the French vineyards. Alexis Millardet, Professor of Botany in Bordeaux, brought in American rootstocks, grafted French vines on to them, and stopped phylloxera dead. It was an excellent early use of a natural source of resistance to protect against disease. It was also an excellent example of how solving one problem can cause another; for the foreign rootstocks brought mildew with them, known in America as wine-pest or sunscald and until then unknown in France.

During the 1880s mildew began to look as serious a threat as phylloxera itself. Re-enter Millardet, now a worried man; but one who, in the course of his travels, had noticed that Medoc mixture deterred more than petty thieves. It prevented mildew from developing. On April Fools' Day 1885 he announced that his modified Medoc mixture protected the vine leaves from attack by mildew and kept the plants healthy. He called the new formula Bordeaux mixture. Wine drinkers raised their glasses and have been drinking gratefully ever since.

This was the precursor of modern fungicides – although gardeners had always struggled to defeat disease. Sulphur's protective abilities had been known for centuries; lime had been in long use. In 1802 William Forsyth, George III's gardener, concocted lime, sulphur, tobacco and elder buds with boiling water, and applied it with a woollen cloth against mildew on fruit trees. Lime-sulphur and other sulphur mixes were in use in Europe and America throughout the first half of the nineteenth century, and sulphur dusting of vines became widespread in France in the 1850s.

If Bordeaux mixture had arrived a little earlier, European and American history would have been very different. It would have limited the damage of potato blight in Ireland in the late 1840s, for what was desperately needed in those circumstances was an effective fungicide. But it was not until a decade after the famine that fungus was first identified as the cause of blight, nor until some time later that cause and cure were linked. So the potatoes, along with large parts of Ireland, were left to rot. Other blights did damage only slightly less drastic. In Central Europe in the 1920s, repeated harvest failures led to famine. Potatoes, for example, are attacked by around 40 different fungus diseases, some two dozen viruses and six bacteria – and that is without counting the scores of insects and nematodes which enjoy potatoes as much as we do. Until the widespread use of modern foliar fungicides at the beginning of the 1970s, a range of rots continued to lower crop yields everywhere, and in many ways it is surprising that the toll was not even more devastating.

The new generation of sprays increased yields by 10 or 15 per cent. But for the fact that farmers had got rather used to miracles, this would have been just as startling as the arrival of herbicides. In some ways, it was more so. Whereas farmers felt guilty about weeds, for which bad farming was blamed, they more often felt victimised by disease; it came and went, was mild or severe, struck one field this year and another next and, apart from attempts to control some of the rots by seed treatment and crop rotations, nothing much could be done about it. Often enough, ignorance was bliss. When farmers were first invited to drive a tractor and sprayer through a ripening crop to keep it healthy, they wouldn't do it; it was absurd to knock standing corn flat to such a purpose. Ten or 15 per cent more yield changed their minds. Where 15 years ago almost no field of winter cereals was sprayed with a fungicide, today nine fields in 10 are treated.

A fungal rot attacks a plant rather as ivy attacks a tree. It wraps itself round the tissues, hooks and slips into the veins and sucks the sugars from the sap for its food. The plant turns yellow, shrivels and dies long before its healthy neighbours. But, since the disease spores blow on the wind or splash with the rain, those neighbours rapidly sicken too.

Through the 1970s, more and more plant medicines appeared on the market to help combat diseases. They produced the fine, bright, plump grains of a healthy crop instead of the shrivelled, discoloured pins and needles of a sick one – in the same way as fungicidal powder sprinkled on, say, athlete's foot, sees clean new skin replace the dead, decaying tissues. The best-known of these chemicals at the time, a spray called Bayleton from the German company Bayer, came to be thought of by many farmers as the penicillin of plant protection.

The treaments come in two groups. One, like Bordeaux mixture, protects the surface of the leaf; the other, like Bayleton, enters the plant's system to guard from within. Fungicides of this sort are safely used in human medicine as well as in agriculture. But one big difference between plant and human health is that we can breed for disease-resistance in plants.

Eyespot is a fungus which attacks the bottom of the wheat plant stem. It spreads from the exposed straw and stubble of a previous crop, looks like a clumsily applied beauty spot, but is much more than skin deep. It has the crippling effect of traditional Chinese foot binding, weakening the stem base so the plant falls over long before harvest. The wheats grown in the 1940s were likely to be crippled by eyespot. That meant ploughing, to bury stubble and fungus, and rotations, to stop disease carry over. Then the new wheat Cappelle Desprez arrived, which resisted eyespot. It was widely grown, and breeders spread its resistance to other varieties. This allowed cereal to follow cereal; and, since the disease no longer bridged from old stubble to new stem, early autumn sowing also grew in popularity.

Cappelle's resistance is no more than moderate, and these husbandry changes challenged it. But from the mid-1970s any weakness was made good by a group of fungicides known as the MBCs which successfully controlled the disease. By then, straw burning followed by minimal cultivations were starting to replace the time and energy consuming practice of ploughing. Successful eyespot control encouraged this trend. But any infected stubble or unburned straw challenged the next crop and the fungicide, and before long eyespot began to acquire MBC resistance.

Breeders looked for other plants carrying resistance, and found it in a wild Mediterranean goat grass. It is not the easiest thing to transfer genes successfully from a goat grass to a cultivated wheat, but they did it to grow the new variety Rendezvous – and now their task is to spread this resistance to other varieties. There is also a new fungicide – a product of the company we originally met as Pest Control Ltd – which controls eyespot successfully in wheats which lack resistance.

This constant infighting is typical of crop protection. Diseases probe the barriers, and scientists and farmers rush around mending their fences to keep them out. Since 1970, when the first mildew protection chemical was sold to farmers, the use of fungicides has risen fast. Today, it is a rare crop that gets no fungicide of any sort, and many get two or more doses. The chemicals are in general environmentally kind. Speaking at the centenary celebrations for Bordeaux mixture, Keith Brent of the Long Ashton Research Station said 'broader-spectrum fungicides do not seem to upset the balance of nature in any obvious way'. He added that mercury seed dressings were more toxic than most other fungicides, and some severe cases of poisoning to man and animals had arisen from eating treated grain. 'These materials have been withdrawn from use in many countries now, and despite their cheapness and effectiveness, it can only be a matter of time before thay are eliminated completely.' Some of the older surface fungicides have created residue problems, most notably with earthworms in orchards. Some modern systemic fungicides harm insects as well as killing fungi.

Chemical sprays can also leave residues on the food we eat and dark concern is sometimes expressed about their safety, lightened in this country neither by our habits of commercial and administrative secrecy nor by sensationalist claims of damage. Although maximum safe residue levels can be enforced, little is known about the possible long-term effects. A group from Imperial College reported recently that: 'to date there appears to be no evidence of harm arising from the consumption of foods which have been treated with pesticides according to manufacturers' recommendations, though epidemiological studies on residues in food are yet to be conducted'.

The British Medical Association is assembling evidence of these possible long-term effects; but it is difficult to pin down the influence of one chemical taken for a long time in tiny quantities, extremely difficult to do the same when many are involved, including not just pesticides but endless other factors such as smoking, drinking or tea and coffee consumption. Add the truism that one man's meat is another man's poison, and the labour of working out how over the years any one person may react to any one chemical becomes one for a toxicological Hercules.

As far as pesticide accidents go, there is one recorded non-fatal poisoning case on farms for every 100 domestic cases – most of which are caused by rodent poisons. Dr David Hessayon of the chemical company Pan Britannica Industries put the same point differently when he said that recorded pesticide accidents are 'a smaller number than accidents involving flowerpots, and half the number involving books and newspapers.'

He points out also that our standards of safety are illogical: 'In the EEC, a garden pesticide which causes slight reddening to the skin after four hours' exposure would be classed as an irritant. Of course there would be no irritancy in practice but the label would still have to bear a black cross and in the UK there would have to be the warning phrases "Keep off skin. Wash off splashes. Wash hands after use." Now look at another domestic product. It is a stronger irritant and in tests caused necrosis of the skin. Yet this non-pesticide bears no black cross nor do warnings appear to keep it off the skin. Such warnings would be impractical, because it is waterproof mascara for application around the eyes.

'As another example we can look at a moderately effective weedkiller which has not been launched as a commercial pesticide. The problem is that it contains 0.5 per cent of an ingredient which has been identified as a cause of skin cancer. It is also a co-carcinogen, increasing the tumour-promoting action of other carcinogens. Furthermore, it is also readily absorbed through the skin and cases of chronic poisoning as a result of skin absorption of this active ingredient have been recorded. Any government would have to look at these facts very carefully before granting clearance for sale under the present guidelines for safety. Such a product would have to bear many warnings if ever it was cleared for sale, but that neeed not stop you buying it. Any chemist shop will sell it to you as calamine lotion, with instructions for you to "apply liberally to the inflamed area of skin".'

Worries, whether about accidents or residues, are not confined to pesticides. We have seen how plants have produced their own poisons for self-defence. As techniques of residue analysis are refined, we find more and more natural poisons not only in our crops, but also in the moulds and rots which attack them. Hessayon had some fun with this too when he pointed out that the solanine in potatoes and the caffeine in coffee are much more toxic than most pesticides, that the average daily intake of common salt in this country is 10 per cent of the lethal dose, and that regulations compel the classification as poisons of many chemicals which are as safe as whisky.

It hardly seems a joking matter. Aflatoxins, fungi which attack nuts and soybeans, cause cancer. So does patulin, which comes from a brown rot in fruit and vegetables and a grey mould in starches. Psoralens, occurring in celery, parsnips, parsley, carrots and other members of that family, especially when they are diseased, stressed or going slightly mouldy, do the same again. Friendly old nursery food caramel has properties similar to known carcinogens. Even the changes brought about by cooking are now recognised to carry certain dangers. Ergot, a fungus of wheat, led to large numbers of stillbirths as well as causing constant outbreaks of a form of St Vitus Dance. An increasing number of fungal moulds are now suspected of causing cancer or other diseases, and many of these can be kept under control by keeping our food free of them.

Bruce Ames, a leading American expert on cancer, has said that cancer-causing chemicals are neither rare nor mostly man-made. In a letter to the Chairman of the Senate Committee on toxics and public safety he wrote: 'my own estimate is that over 99.99 per cent of the carcinogens Californians ingest are natural (e.g., natural toxic chemicals in plants, mold carcinogens) or traditional (e.g., cooking food, smoking cigarettes, alcohol)'. Other experts have given different assessments, which clearly indicate the uncertainties involved.

The task which now faces crop husbandry is to reduce these dangers, whether real or imaginary. Already some progress has been made. Japanese scientists have come up with an antibiotic fungicide, to protect rice from blast disease, which is highly specific and breaks down rapidly and safely in the environment. Antibiotic fungicides may be particularly helpful in the soil, where disease control has been working in the dark and where, short of total chemical or steam sterilisation, rots have been difficult or impossible to treat, so that worldwide this weakness in crop protection is thought to cost £20 billion a year. Now one natural fungicide isolated from oat roots may protect against the take-all fungus of wheat, while another produces an antibiotic which can spread quickly through the soil rather like a soil fumigant.

New approaches of this sort will make a better crop protection fence – whose importance is summed up in the old saying, good fences make good neighbours. Chemical fences could not be fixed like a line of hawthorn or barbed wire and when they blew about the countryside non-farming neighbours objected with all the vigour of the traditional moan: 'Your sheep are in my wheat – again!' Now crop protection is moving towards a new fence called integrated pest management. IPM is a mix of new and old technology, late twentieth-century monoculture tempered by understanding. The American biologist Paul Erlich has spelt out the difficulties in his book *The Machinery of Nature*: 'Plants evidently have been waging rather sophisticated chemical warfare against insects and plant diseases for hundreds of millions of years. Little wonder, then, that herbivorous insects usually adapt so easily to the crude attempts of *Homo sapiens* to poison them. Understanding the coevolutionary war between plants and insect herbivores puts the whole problem of predator-prey interactions and chemical pest control in a different light.'

Among other things, it is now recognised that carnivorous insects – those which eat pests – are harder hit by chemical controls than their prey. So the pests recover faster, then find their normal predators are absent. As Erlich puts it, 'pesticides can be extremely helpful tools when properly employed, but they must be used as scalpels, not bludgeons'. It would be impossible to train every farmer as a surgeon, especially when the experts still disagree. 'No topic in ecology is more controversial than the degree to which competition (and coevolution driven by competition) helps to shape ecological communities,' says Erlich. Nevertheless, the signs are encouraging. 'Ecologists are now able to design programmes of integrated pest management which avoid the pitfalls of the dominant spray-spray-spray programmes', and such designs will increasingly influence crop protection.

Put together, it works like this. Plant breeding plus genetic engineering help crops resist attack from insects and diseases; rotations and cultivations minimise the carry-over of pests; understanding threshold levels of damage and forecasting pest and disease build-up reduce the use of sprays; pesticides, biological or chemical, will become more specific to the pest and less persistent, so will not harm other organisms; they will be applied much more effectively so less chemical will be sprayed.

A utopian farming fantasy? It is happening already. Disease-resistance in tomatoes comes from genetic sources, not from fungicides; and insect pests are controlled entirely by biological means rather than chemical insecticides. While IPM is much easier to manage in an enclosed glasshouse or an orchard than in the field, its influence is slowly spreading.

One example in the field is control of the pea moth which has been worked out by entomologists at Rothamsted. When pea moth eggs hatch, the young larvae take only a few hours to bore into the pea pod; once there they are safe. To protect the crop, the larvae must be sprayed after they hatch and before they reach safety. Female pea moths are inconspicuous, so males are monitored in the knowledge that females will be there too. Traps are baited to attract males; when they catch 10 or more on two successive days the farmer knows females are emerging and about to start laying. The time taken to hatch varies with temperature, so careful measurements work out the most likely period. That is when the spray goes on. It's a lot more complicated than frequent insurance spraying, but it works much better and costs much less.

Another example started when Hugh Oliver-Bellasis came back from serving in a Guards' regiment to run the family estate in Hampshire. The background suggests a young fogey but he is a rarer beast, a traditional landlord with a radical streak. He had to farm the estate as well as he could, but he wanted to enjoy the old country pursuits and one of them was dwindling. Partridges were very thin on the ground. They had suffered like other wildlife in the 1950s when they were directly poisoned by some pesticides. By the 1970s the sprays were much safer but partridge numbers, unlike those of hawks, had not recovered. He wanted to find out why.

The Cereals and Gamebirds project was the result. Working with the Game Conservancy and scientists from Southampton University, Oliver-Bellasis looked at what happened when weeds were left unsprayed in the six-metre outer boundary round the edge of the crop. At first it rather appalled him: 'The thought of a dirty headland and weed ingress is totally against all that has been taught in the past. The results however show a significant benefit to farmland wildlife at no cost other than visual shame.' The research was to take at least five years, so his first task was to talk his fellow farmers into paying for it. They stumped up £575 000 to do so.

The scientist in charge, Nick Sotherton, adopts a briskly regimental sergeant major attitude to describe the work: 'We were trying to design a project which would give maximum benefit to game and wildlife but minimum aggravation, yield-loss and cost to the farmer.' The Game Conservancy already knew that poor chick survival was the problem, and that from birth chicks needed large amounts of certain sorts of insects if they were to flourish. These insects, abundant at the edges of cereal fields where grey partridge broods forage successfully, had suffered declining populations. They were killed by insecticides. But more importantly, herbicides had killed the weeds which the insects lived on. It was soon clear that this indirect effect was a far bigger influence on partridge chick survival than chemicals like aldrin and DDT had ever been.

Starting in 1983, unsprayed strips were left round the fields being studied. More broad-leaved weeds survived in these field margins, chick-food insects increased, chick survival rose and wild populations of grey partridges rose with them. The birds, bees, butterflies and small mammals had more to eat as well. Now, Nick Sotherton is trying to find out how this affects populations of insect predators and whether they can help control insect pests as a result.

Research institutions are getting in on the act – though there is a risk that declining science budgets will skimp on IPM. A major interest is pheromones, a message broadcasting system which is a sort of chemical BBC – though one in which regrettably many of the signals are about sex. Tiny quantities of chemicals are widely transmitted by many animals to help them organise their lives. Very often, they concern willingness to mate – it is the sex pheromone of the female pea moth which draws the males to the traps described above – but they also warn of attack or mark territory. Crop protection can use pheromones to disrupt behaviour directly, or to make chemicals less wasteful. Thus an alarm pheromone can keep aphids on the move and so increase the chances of their blundering into an insecticide. Or an attractant pheromone could lure predators into fields even when pest numbers are low, keep them there and stimulate them to search for their prey.

Genetic manipulation also plays a part. When a caterpillar munching through its lunch accidentally swallows a bacterium called *Bacillus thuringiensis*, it dies. The gene which makes the poison in the bacterium has been transferred to tobacco, and now tobacco plants give caterpillars indigestion and worse. This and other defences can be swapped around; insect growth regulators, antibiotics, viruses, fungi, predatory nematodes, bacterial diseases, anti-feedants – all offer natural materials which are highly specific in what they attack, then break down harmlessly in the environment. Compounds from such sources can be sprayed on crops, or genetic engineering could plug the relevant genes directly into the crop itself. Such measures will increasingly contribute to crop protection.

Computers will join in. Forecasting policies fall readily into computer programs, and enthusiasts are eagerly linking patterns of pest and disease development to weather forecasts to crop growth stages to pressing a button. The components are not yet firmly in place, but the early work is being done. The foundations for a much better understanding are being laid.

IPM is a response to Stapledon's red light. There were plenty of risks in the poor and unreliable diet we ate before the war, as there were when Stapes spoke. There are risks today in the assured supply of a wide range of plentiful, cheap foods – though they are a great deal less now than they have been historically. Recently, the focus has been on food poisoning rather than chemical residues, and some have laid the blame on the practices of intensive livestock production. There is no argument that contamination has occurred on some farms, nor that most of the problem arises from inadequate hygiene well beyond the farm gate, where it has been linked to a minority of catering institutes and to the use of cook-chill meals. New controls have been introduced to tighten hygiene regulations both on farms and through the rest of the food chain, and these will help minimise the risks involved.

Common sense has a part to play as well. As Elizabeth David once pointed out, some happily live on a diet of gin and chocolate which would devastate the rest of us. Others claim that they would willingly die for their favourite soft cheese, and if that is heaven for them, who are we to deny it? Statutory controls must ensure proper hygiene – and full information with clear labelling on the food we buy must be standard practice – but after that the individual must be allowed to choose. Those who wish to live and die on gin, chocolate and soft cheese must remain free to do so.

When people complain loudly about pesticide risks, they are saying among other things that our standards are now much higher – and there can be no question that public pressure has been important in raising those standards. As the Imperial College team put it: 'public pressure has permitted and encouraged responsible scientists, civil servants and industrialists to devise and implement effective controls, and this will remain true for the foreseeable future.' Since farmers will spend less, and the public will worry less, when fewer chemical sprays are used, both share an interest in moving towards the techniques of IPM and biological control. Much of the research will need to be publicly funded.

Technology will therefore stay at the heart of cereal growing. The troubles which the Russians have had with their wheat crop arise partly from inefficiency, and largely because their technology has been 40 years behind the times. Often enough they still grow wheat as we used to grow it just after the war, so it is hardly surprising their yields are not very high. Improvements in their technology will make a great difference to their output – and they are now taking place.

In this part of the world the Maris Huntsman of the early 1990s will be the first commercially successful hybrid wheat, which should give the same sort of yield increase of around 15 per cent that Huntsman provided. We have seen how a breeder produces a hybrid every time he uses the scissors to make a first cross as the possible starting point for a new variety. Clearly, to produce the thousands of tonnes of first cross seed for a commercial hybrid some form of mass production scissor is needed.

Chemicals have been discovered which operate as just such castrating scissors. Sprayed on the plants when they come into flower, the chemical snips out the male organ so that the female is fertilised by pollen blowing from a neighbouring plant. By choosing the parents with typical breeders' skill, useful agricultural hybrids can be produced. They may well come from the PBI, whose success brought it under the new ownership of Unilever.

Beyond hybrids lie the choices made possible by genetic manipulation. The range runs from much better resistance to pests and diseases to the production in cereal grains of types of food, drug or industrial chemical quite different from the content of the grain of Huntsman, Hobbit or other modern varieties. Other possibilities include improved cold-tolerance, better drought-resistance, or the ability to withstand higher levels of salinity. An obvious possible choice would be to take up the conventional breeding challenge to produce wheats which were better suited to making bread. It looks as though bringing all the ingredients together by genetic engineering may supply the answer. Not only will the engineers be able to insert into one plant the full menu of genes for making bread. They will also be able to design new genes which may be even better at the job than those now in existence.

# CHAPTER TWENTY

# Consumers, Pigs, Chickens and Welfare

Electronics liberate modern pigs. The transponder lets a pig eat in peace. Stephen Hornsey, in charge of 2000 sows at Lightwater Valley outside Ripon, says of 200 gilts rooting about in a large straw-filled covered yard: 'This system is the alternative they're talking about to sows kept in stalls or on tethers.'

The transponder is the key. Each gilt wears one on a stout plastic necklace; when she approaches a feeding pen the computer recognises her, lets her in and dishes out the right amount of food. When she has finished, she lets herself out. But Hornsey makes it clear that you can't just put on a piece of electronic plastic and leave it at that: 'It demands a much higher level of stockmanship. It's not just looking at a pig, you've really got to see her. When a pig is in a stall, all the information stares you in the face. It's very different when she's running about in a group of 200.' It was, in fact, just such difficulties which sow stalls and tethers had originally tried to meet.

The demands on a sow vary greatly through the year, and her food intake alters accordingly. Even so, it is physically impossible for a sow milking a dozen or more rapidly growing piglets to eat all the nutrients she needs. She is bound to lose condition as she milks off her back. Small groups of sows in farmyard or orchard which farrowed irregularly could adjust quite easily to these demands though they were always likely to do so on the principle, when the going gets tough the tough get eating. As herds grew larger, greedy pigs ate faster — and when the stockman put more food down to stop the shy animals from going short, the greedy ones ate faster still. When they had finished shoving and barging at the trough, they were quite likely to bully weaker animals in other ways.

As supermarkets demanded reliable supplies of high-quality meat at competitive prices, sows had to produce more piglets more regularly. That meant they must be in the right physical condition as well as being very carefully watched to know when they were ready to mate with the boar. Keeping each sow separate from her neighbour in a stall meant she could neither over-eat nor go short of food, she couldn't be bullied and it was much easier both to see any signs of illness and to keep track of where she was in her breeding cycle.

With economic influences also pushing producers towards closer control of livestock performance, stalls began to come in during the 1960s and within a few years nearly all indoor sows were managed that way. Within a few years also, welfare worries began to be expressed. To begin with, farmers who knew intimately the problems of managing large numbers of tough and determined pigs were likely to dismiss people who expressed these concerns as poorly informed cranks. This did little to satisfy critics, whose arguments grew louder as the economic influences changed.

Churchill's order, take it away and bring me beef, applied equally to pork. In 1947 we fattened less than a million pigs, or one in three of those we ate; it took a worker on the average wage half an hour to earn a pound of pork. Today we fatten 16 million pigs a year, still import over half our ham and bacon – and it takes less than quarter of an hour to earn a pound of pork. This fall in price has encouraged us to eat more pork. At the same time, however, for some people price alone has become less important. For them, eating no longer depended on efficient cheap food output but on new ideas about diet, new tastes, or simply on impressing their friends. Their attitudes often included concern for the environment and welfare.

Maurice Bichard, whose PIC supplies the pigs which Stephen Hornsey looks after at Lightwater, sees these changing attitudes towards cheap food as very important: 'When people are not worried whether eggs or bacon cost 50 pence more, then all sorts of things become possible.' For example, he points out that now the main pig plagues – swine fever, foot-and-mouth, swine dysentery and so on – have been defeated, what's left are lameness, infections of the guts and the lungs, and reproductive problems. Many of these are bacterial or viral in origin and are controlled by antibiotics and other drugs. All are at their lowest in the minimal disease herds which produce breeding animals for sale, where strenuous efforts are made to keep infectious agents like bacteria to very low levels. To apply similar hygiene to fattening pigs for commercial sale would be very costly, but there could be a halfway house which held fewer pigs than today's commercial fattening pens, and which would sometimes be left empty to be completely sterilised before new pigs came in. This would much reduce the use of drugs or other chemicals and could produce pork chops or bacon at a cost which affluent consumers might be willing to meet.

Some pig farmers have put their herds outside again. At first output fell, but they kept at it and today's outdoor sow produces nearly as many piglets as her indoor sister, and the extra costs of feed and labour are balanced by money saved on buildings. The land and climate of North Yorkshire are not suited to outdoor rearing so change there had to wait for transponders. Stephen Hornsey says they have now solved most of the early problems. Some were not new. 'We found there was aggression round the feeders. Shy animals sometimes left their food, and the greedy ones pushed in and ate it.' Changing the entrance and exit gates helped cope with that. There was also bullying in the group, especially when new animals were introduced, but careful observation and stockmanship helped control it.

There were benefits as well. The growing pigs had fewer feet and leg problems with straw instead of concrete underfoot. And boars could be kept alongside the strawyard, which encouraged maiden gilts to show their feelings; as a result, successful services increased.

The most thorough-going approach to the piggy good life has been pioneered in Edinburgh, where the School of Agriculture set up an experimental pig park where animals were allowed as much freedom as possible. They lived in an enclosure containing a pine copse, gorse bushes, a burn and a swampy wallow. They were fed a standard commercial diet, with extra on offer when the weather was fierce. Their behaviour was carefully observed.

The pigs built themselves communal sleeping nests which gave protection from the prevailing wind and good views of anything approaching. In the evening the younger pigs were likely to bring fresh materials for the walls while the older animals supervised any rebuilding needed and rearranged the nests. Daylight hours were divided between foraging and rooting, exploring, and occupations like carrying round bits of wood and stick. Farrowing nests were built by the sows away from the communal nesting site. After farrowing, the nest was protected from other pigs for the first five days, when the sow would occasionally leave her litter and the piglets began to explore their surroundings. Sometimes two sows would join up after farrowing and then forage and sleep together, though no cross suckling of litters was observed. Weaning took place naturally after three months.

The follow-up to this experience of semi-natural behaviour has been to build an indoor environment in which pigs could lead something more like an outdoor family life. Small groups of sows are housed together and their litters stay with them until they are sold for pork or bacon. This approach has remained largely experimental and for housed pigs the industry has so far proved keener to pursue the option of transponders than the ideas which the Edinburgh School of Agriculture has explored. This is partly because there has been no money to complete the research. With less government spending on research, welfare may be an area which all too often goes short.

As well as health and housing, breeding will change. It will not slow down. Indeed, Tony Brown, Technical Manager of PIC, recently forecast sows would before long produce 30 pigs a year, with significantly better food conversion rates than today – an overall improvement of around 50 per cent on present perform-ance. But breeding for lean pigs may take a step back, for very lean pigs can be so sensitive to stress that it kills them.

This development would not have surprised the novelist Aldous Huxley, himself a thin, highly sensitive, nervy man who was once told that 'most members of my type are in asylums'. Like the modern pig-keeper, Huxley was very aware that shape influenced behaviour. In a series of talks given in California he described the problem of what to do with 'powerful muscular men with a tremendous drive for domination. One of the answers in the Middle Ages was to put them into religious orders of knighthood and send them out to fight with the Mohammedans. This kept them out of the way as far as Europeans were concerned. At the same time means were found for protecting the people without much muscular energy by establishing convents into which they could retire.'

Huxley was rather close in type to the Landrace pig. It turns out that one likely reason why thin pigs and thin people – thin that is for genetic reasons, not because of starvation – are nervous is because both share nervous and hormonal mechanisms which burn off fat, increase lean and sensitivity to stress. According to Dr David Lister, of the Institute for Grassland and Animal Production, lean pigs have more receptors in their tissues which respond to hormones by provoking stress responses. Thin pigs and people may thus prefer living in with regular meals, a closed circle of acquaintances, a steady temperature and no loud noises. In this they differ greatly both from medieval crusaders and the Gloucester Old Spot, whose equivalent of fighting the Mohammedans is to live happily with donkeys, geese and children running round in an orchard, and to do it through the coldest winter and hottest summer.

The difficulty for the industry is clear. Consumers gave up eating fat pork and bacon years ago, but as pigs have been bred thinner and thinner so nervousness has increased. This can make them so stress susceptible they die, from the shock of a journey in a lorry, from too much exercise, or from handling and restraint in the course of everyday husbandry. It can also destroy the eating quality of the meat. Lister is looking for physiological mechanisms or drugs which can modify the receptors responsible for these reactions, to gain the benefits of lean meat without the unwelcome side effects.

Another approach to stress-susceptible pigs is that of Gary Duthie at the Rowett Research Institute. Duthie identified molecules known as free radicals, whose effect can be found in quantity in the blood of such pigs, as a possible cause of the problem. A free radical is a bloodstream burglar which breaks and enters healthy molecules to get at what it wants, and in doing so leaves chaos behind. This chaos is a cause of the pig's difficulties and can even lead to a fatal heart attack. Duthie thought he could do something about it.

The problem is one of law and order. To keep the bloodstream safe an effective police force is needed, and the bobby on this particular beat is Vitamin E. There are a lot of free radicals about – they are produced in every breath you take – and stress-sensitive pigs seem to be short of Vitamin E. Duthie found that feeding extra Vitamin E reduced stress attacks, and that things got even calmer when he added Vitamin C to the forces of law and order.

It occurred to him that what helped pigs could help us. We are usually well-protected against free radical attack, but smokers are at risk, partly because every lungful of smoke inhaled releases at least 1 trillion (1 million million) of these burglars into the blood, partly because the blood of smokers has a rather inefficient police force. Duthie found that extra Vitamin E gave smokers much more control of free radicals.

He then applied these ideas to heart attacks in humans. Fat cells leave real chaos behind them when burgled by free radicals. In particular, the breakdown products of cholesterol soon start to clog up the bloodstream, leading to coronary heart disease. High blood pressure and high levels of cholesterol are warning signs for doctors, and various groups of human beings are particularly at risk. Smoking, age, gender, personality, social class and where you live can all influence whether you die of a heart attack. You are most at risk if you smoke, are a middle-aged male, a go-getter, working class or live in Scotland.

Duthie thought these groups of people might have in common either too many free radicals or too little Vitamin E and C in the bloodstream. He knew smokers suffered from both. Age is important because it gives more time for burglary and so clogging has gone further. Gender could matter because there is more iron in men than women and iron leads to free radical formation. Go-getters suffer from a version of the Landrace problem. Working class and Scottish folk don't eat much fruit and vegetables and may not have enough Vitamin E and C.

So Duthie is now studying a large group of people in Aberdeen. He will find out what they eat, how they live and how the cops and robbers are battling it out in the bloodstream. Then he will ask a group of volunteers to eat large quantities of the two vitamins and will measure what difference this makes to the forces of law and order inside them. It may be that the work which started with stress-sensitive pigs will finish with a better understanding of coronary heart disease, and how to prevent it in those at risk.

Meanwhile, to the traditional techniques of pig breeding are now being added the resources of genetic engineering, which will initially have the effect of speeding up what breeders have always done. This will include better disease-resistance, faster growth rates and yet more productive sows. A version of BST is available for pigs. Porcine somatotrophin (PST) increases growth rate, lean meat and feed conversion efficiency in pigs as much as BST does in milking cows. But the changes could also operate in the opposite direction. Just as Bob Ørskov wants to see cows bred for better use of forage feeds, pigs could be bred to give improved digestion of fibrous feeds. They would not be given a rumen; rather, naturally occurring enzyme systems would allow them to digest grass and straw much more efficiently, which could considerably alter our pig-keeping habits.

None of the routes the industry may follow will lessen the steady fall in the number of farmers who keep pigs. Over the last two years almost all pigmen have made losses, and getting on for 2000 have left the industry, cutting herds to around 15 000. Pig keeping is notorious for its cycles, but this was a particularly fierce buckle in profitability.

Demands on management will grow because, says Maurice Bichard, future developments will be increasingly open to debate. The industry will have to find out what the consumer wants and be more aware of what suits the pig. Not everyone who looks after pigs holds the degree in agriculture plus the year's post-graduate work in farm management which give Stephen Hornsey his qualifications. But until more people of that calibre are spread through the industry, these new demands on management will be met more slowly – and will see more pig-keepers finally quit.

While pigs shift from stalls to transponders to PST to biotechnology, hens have also been on the move. The 1970s in particular were turmoil for eggs. The lion, symbol of the British Egg Marketing Board, was overthrown by the free market jungle. The Common Market brought new competitors, especially the French and Dutch, to shell the British consumer from purpose-built battery units just across the Channel. Within 10 years those units went bust, along with thousands of small domestic producers; but while they lasted the bombardment was intense. This fierce commercial competition was complicated by colour consciousness as consumers cracked into brown eggs.

In the late 1960s we ate white eggs from white hens – partly because they were more efficient at the job than their brown cousins. By the early 1980s we ate brown eggs, and by then brown-bred birds could do the job as well as the whites they replaced. Such strong, irrational preferences often confront the food industry. Americans, with their different perceptions of colour, never made the same switch and still demand white eggs. Many Europeans want their eggs white too, though the French, like us, prefer them brown.

Stonegate Farmers Limited met the turmoil by bringing in hygiene and quality control, computers and solid-state electronics, high-speed conveyors and automatic handling; as egg packing, much of it still a cottage industry, was rapidly upgraded to meet the demands of modern food processing premises. Freshness was fundamental: the aim was to get eggs laid that morning to the supermarkets' central stores by evening. To achieve it, packing stations had to be on the farm. This drove Stonegate to add egg production to its established packing business. Bill Martin took charge of introducing the laying hen to Stonegate, at a time when the welfare organisations were putting a magnifying glass over eggs. 'The word went out that we must go back to free-range. Housewives and supermarkets were both demanding it. I remembered my formative years, all those chickens dying in the orchard, and thought, here we go again.'

In 1981, one free-range flock supplied Stonegate with eggs; today there are 80. They depend on the willingness of egg eaters to pay more for their pleasure. They produce slightly fewer eggs than battery birds, eat a bit more, bully each other a bit more, and a little more labour is needed to look after them. Drug bills are up, though not much, for no Stonegate hen gets medication while in lay. Apart from the wormer drugs given when needed to free-range hens, all other disease prevention comes from inbred resistance and a vaccination programme identical for every growing pullet, free-range or battery. The development of poultry vaccines has been one of the great success stories of modern animal medicine. Even so, the greater difficulties of management with free-range hens mean slightly more of them die – from disease rather than from predation, for electric fencing and other modern aids can keep foxes away.

As a result, a free-range hen needs nearly 6 pence to cover the cost of laying an egg, compared to around 3.5 pence for her battery sister. When her daily round is done, Stonegate lorries must visit 80 free-range farms to collect 5 per cent of the company's output, while the other 95 per cent come from just 18 farms; so the transport costs are higher. All in all, housewives may have to pay 50 pence a dozen more for free-range eggs.

Demand for the moment has reached a plateau, with very small increases in consumption each year. Bill Martin says 'we are in the business of marketing the eggs people want to buy. If free-range demand rises, we shall supply it.' The demand is greater in the South than in the North, and he reckons that Stonegate's 5 per cent is roughly typical for the egg industry as a whole – though some would say total free-range demand is as much as 10 per cent.

Another initiative pioneered by Stonegate was the barn or perchery system. Aware of the management difficulties at free-range, Bill Martin set out to find a system that was a new approach to deep litter. 'I went to Switzerland, where batteries are to be phased out by the mid 1990s, and found the Swiss had not thought about what to do next. But they told me to go and see Doctor Rosemary Wegner outside Hanover, who runs a small animal welfare unit for the West German government. She and a young research scientist had developed a system which excited me. With them, I drew up the basic plans for a perchery.'

The birds laid their first eggs for Stonegate in 1983. They are kept in large pens with perches at different levels and separate nest boxes and are trained to lay in the nest boxes but not to sleep in them so as to avoid fouling. As with free-range, there are slightly fewer eggs, more food gets eaten, there is more bullying, and more birds die – in Stonegate's experience mortality in batteries is 3 per cent, in percheries 5 per cent, and at free-range 10 per cent. Demand for perchery eggs has so far stayed low, but Stonegate and others are ready to supply it if it rises.

Today's industry is dominated by just four companies: Dalgety, Hillsdown, Thames Valley and Stonegate. Between them they supply 50 per cent of the eggs we eat, either from their own farms or from large producers contracted to them. The other 50 per cent is supplied by 12 000 small packing stations drawing from a host of producers who face two difficulties. A sound business needs to keep at least 30 000 hens – compared to the 800 which would feather a flock-owner's nest just before the war – and many small producers have fewer hens than that. In 1988 the producer was paid around 32 pence per dozen, or 11 pence less than the NFU's calculation of the cost of battery production. It seems inevitable therefore that the ferocious free market in eggs will continue to demand size and efficiency in laying units, even more so in the Europe-wide market after 1992.

This fierce competition, and the reluctance of the great majority of consumers to pay more for free-range eggs, locks industry and hens for the moment into batteries. Meanwhile flock-owners believe their birds are healthier, safer, less subject to bullying and cannibalism, altogether easier to manage, in short better-off in batteries in all ways but one – welfare. They also know that welfare is an increasingly important issue, and that the industry must recognise this.

Bill Martin accepts cheerfully that legislation will change the way eggs are produced. 'I am delighted that the universities are doing research on animal behaviour to find the ideal environment. We may well find that cages with exercise areas, perches and nest boxes are needed, and the industry will respond. What it will ask for is a lead time which is commercially sensible.

'Also, the whole of Europe has to agree. The debate is going to be lengthy indeed with some of the southern Europeans. In fact, it is just possible that Europe may have to divide itself on animal welfare, with cross border movements prohibited.'

One British scientist looking at welfare is Ian Duncan, a quietly merry Scot with a grizzled beard and a twinkling eye. He and others have summarised the limits which cages place on a hen's behaviour. Birds in cages flap less, scratch the ground less and of course dust-bathe less. They preen more, stretch more, and shake their heads more – no one is quite sure why but it is thought to be because of frustration and conflict. Caged birds can be flighty. Put a simple but unfamiliar object in the cage and they will shrink away when birds in pens will ignore it.

Nesting behaviour is clearly quite different. In a battery, birds must lay where they are. Outside, hens hesitate between various nests, quite often abandon them, and choose different nests both between clutches and from year to year. In deep litter, hens behave more as though out of doors, change their minds, and in some strains prefer the floor to the nest boxes supplied, which leads to fouling, breakages and egg eating by the birds.

Feather-pecking and cannibalism can afflict birds in all systems; in cages, they are believed to be substitutes for ground pecking rather than aggression. Indeed, there is less aggression inside cages than out, perhaps because there is too little space, or because the bird at the top of the pecking order is too close to allow others to express aggression.

Clearly, birds have needs which they cannot express in commercial cages and are driven to act in ways which do not meet their real needs. What is much less clear is how far this unusual behaviour means real stress and loss of welfare. Feather-pecking and cannibalism, which as we have seen are not confined to cages, must mean pain. So must injuries to feet and legs.

Finding out what the animal is feeling is a more difficult, but developing, skill. One way of doing it is to give a bird a choice and see what it does – which, in some examples, has been to choose outside runs before a battery cage, familiar neighbours rather than an empty cage but an empty cage rather than strange birds, and litter rather than wire mesh underfoot. But, say the boffins, beware. None of this tells you how strongly the birds feel, not all of them feel the same way, and we don't know how much this minority is upset if it has to fall in with what most birds choose. Furthermore, hens are impatient; offer them a small reward now and they will choose it ahead of a bigger reward later.

Ian Duncan has used choice and motivation to ask hens about sex. Hens live in single sex groups: are they frustrated? Duncan put cocks and hens into a divided cage with a weighted door between them, and found that while cocks would push through the obstacle vigorously, the hens weren't bothered; they seemed just as happy to stay where they were. He also found that cocks pushed through just as enthusiastically to fight strange cocks next door, but not to get at male birds which they already knew. When he covered the door so the birds could not see each other the cocks made no effort to push through. Clearly they were not influenced by smell, and equally clearly they had not learned to associate the door with the bedroom. To Duncan, it suggested that the sex-life of chickens might be arranged round the old belief, out of sight, out of mind. He is now working with a much richer and more complicated environment to see whether he can confirm this hunch.

Hens in batteries cannot dust-bathe. Again, Duncan's work suggests that the urge to bathe is stimulated by dust and if it's not there a hen thinks of other things. They cannot nest. Their urge to do so is not in doubt. For between one and two hours a day they display nesting behaviour, and when they can't consummate it, it shows – in stereotyped pacing, hormonal imbalance and a raised heart rate.

Outdoor hens nest in loose material. First they lower the keel into the chosen pile, next they work it around a bit, then they turn their whole body this way and that to mould a comfortable shape. These preliminaries satisfied, they settle to the job while pecking up more loose stuff to tuck in around the nest.

All or any of this could be important to a hen. Duncan found out that moulding the shape is much more important than pecking up the loose stuff, and that hens were as happy moulding in a bean bag as in straw. When he offered them a choice between DIY nests and pre-moulded polystyrene the hens chose the made-up nest but – rather like a housewife adding an egg to a pre-mix pud – then went through normal nesting behaviour before settling into it. Duncan believes that offering hens such a nest site in a cage would sharply reduce the frustration they now experience. And, if they laid eggs in the nest reliably, a different egg collection method could put an end to sloping cage floors and might cut down on cage-dusting.

Newly-laid eggs are wet and as they roll down to the collecting point they can pick up a ring of dust; producers are legally forbidden to wash eggs, so instead the floor is dusted twice a week. The best-designed and managed modern houses are so dust-free that this problem does not occur; but many still use a big soft bristle brush, or a feather duster to keep things clean. Measurements show that the most frightening thing in the everyday life of a battery hen is the twice-weekly dusting. Duncan believes the bristles may look like a fox or stoat, the feathers like a hawk, and suggests that dusting in the dark might help. It may seem a small change but he believes it would be important, because other work has shown that chickens will work harder to avoid a fright than they will to get to a nest or to food. As well as 'out of sight out of mind', it seems hens respond to another platitude, 'anything for a quiet life'.

The most painful experience in chicken husbandry is debeaking, which is done to stop feather-pecking. Mike Gentle, who works with Ian Duncan, has found that the nerves grow back after debeaking to form a tangled mass called a neuroma. The same thing happens to our nerves when a limb is amputated, and then we commonly feel phantom limb pain – a feeling of pain in the limb no longer there. Gentle has found electrical patterns from neuromas similar to those from phantom limbs, and thinks chickens may get phantom beak pains after debeaking. In any case very little debeaking is done these days – no Stonegate hen is ever debeaked – and what still occurs may happen in free-range flocks to stop cannibalism as well as in other systems. But as a result of Gentle's work debeaking is likely to be made illegal very shortly.

Chickens spend much time pecking and Ian Duncan thinks it should be possible to give them something like the cuttlebone provided for pet budgerigars. Birds peck for curiosity and calcium, and a mix of plaster of Paris and oyster shell grit could give chickens a more satisfying target than their neighbours' feathers. It might make them eat less too: Duncan thinks calcium-pecking is greatest when hens make eggshells; if there is no calcium to peck, they peck at their food instead.

Altogether, the modified future cage could contain four birds, a couple of nest sites, a perch, an exercise area, a flat floor and an oyster-shell-grit-and-plaster-of-Paris pecking point. Mayfair it's not, but even on the ideal chicken farm cages have something to be said for birds who like the quiet life. Hens don't like a mob, and a lot of hens together can fall into football hooliganism, so keeping them in small groups has much to be said for it.

We are also likely to see more free-range birds and more deep litter egg production. Free-range as we know has difficulties with disease, predators, unless the management is good, and bullying. Deep litter has the problem in our climate, that if the bacteria in the litter stop working, then the house rapidly gets very cold and damp and then diseases strike. It is, says Ian Duncan, quite simply a disaster when the bactria stop working. Bill Martin guesses that by the year 2000 the national flock will be down to 32 million birds, of which on present trends four million will be free-range and one million in percheries. The rest will be in cages which will be greatly different from the battery cages of today.

So much for the egg. Meanwhile, the broiler battleground has continued its cut-throat competition as poultry meat grows into bigger and bigger business. Stimulated by supermarkets, agribusiness, advertising, nutritional hype and convenience and price, our appetite for broiler chickens swells. There is no sign that this hunger is sated. The industry believes that 'in terms of value for money, health and versatility, chicken has the attributes which most closely match the modern consumer's requirements'. Chicken rivals beef as the meat with the most, and we already eat more bird than beef. If the graph shows no sign of faltering, within not very many years we will eat more chicken than all other meats put together.

Price counts. It takes someone on the average wage three-quarters of an hour to earn a pound chunk of beef sirloin, half an hour for the same amount of lamb, quarter of an hour for pork – and under 10 minutes to earn a pound chunk of chicken. In 1986, when Ross Breeders celebrated its thirtieth anniversary in the industry, the souvenir newsletter said: 'That genetic science and selective breeding has been at the heart of it all can be judged from these figures. In 1956 a 3-pound bird in 56 days on 9 pounds of feed was considered a fair achievement. Today's aim for 1986 is a 5-pound bird in 49 days on 10 pounds of feed – a physical improvement unmatched in any other sphere of animal genetics.' It means that as the years pass the chicken gets cheaper, and the less we pay the more we eat.

Half the chicken we eat disappears down the national throat in catering establishments; much of it goes down fast, for example as

Kentucky Fried Chicken, some more slowly as pre-cooked recipe chicken dinners. Once these recipes were established through the catering trade, they spread into the home following increased ownership of domestic freezers, and yet more chicken-eating was then stimulated by microwave oven ownership.

This versatility, which underpins constantly rising consumption, has a long history. Napoleon, who knew that an army marched on its stomach, was an early fan of chicken as a fighting man's fast food. A modern version of the dish served at the battleground of Marengo reads: 'Get the butcher to joint a tender young chicken, and then, after flouring, fry the pieces in butter and olive oil, adding a good flavouring of shallots and parsley. When the chicken is nicely coloured, and almost done add one tablespoon of tomato purée, half a gill each of dry white wine and gravy or stock, a pinch of crushed garlic, some mushrooms and a few diced prawns. Cook for a few minutes and serve with a fried egg on a piece of fried bread for each person.'

The ingredients, it is said, were those which the chef had to hand and simply threw into a frying pan when Napoleon demanded his dinner, and the dish named in honour of the victory can now be bought ready-cooked from the supermarket by any fast-food addict with a microwave. Alongside it in the display cabinet may be found recipes from Italy to India, each complete with what the trade calls a 'delicious sounding' description on the pack. We eat more and more products of this sort which, along with the whole range of convenience foods, have liberated many women from the chores of the kitchen. Arguments for more fresh free-range chickens will thus continue to encounter the buying preferences of working women who buy through caterers and supermarkets.

Sun Valley celebrated 25 successful years of growth in 1986, when it produced its own souvenir newsletter. By then it could claim to be the country's largest producer of fresh products, selling 30 million broilers out of a national total getting on for half a billion – a figure which meant that production of table chickens had increased just on a hundredfold since the early 1950s. It backed the selling operation with a team of demonstrators whose attack might have overwhelmed the victor of Marengo himself. 'Working from home, the demonstration force is run as efficiently as an army battalion from the company's Hereford headquarters. In charge is Liz Adams, who plots the positions of everyone in the team in much the same way as an army commander would position his troops.

'It is a system which works for Sun Valley and suits the major supermarket companies right down to the ground. They can offer their customers an added attraction and with the help of demonstrations will certainly sell more of the company product. An ever increasing demand for new product creations ensures the continuing growth which will help the company survive in its second quarter century.'

If we can judge by the Americans, who in a year each eat twice as many broilers as we do, our gluttony for cheap, convenient chicken has still some way to go. The increase ahead will not be as dramatic as the hundredfold rise of the last 35 years, but before too long we could be eating a billion birds a year.

# CHAPTER TWENTY-ONE

# *Cultivated Soils*

$B$obby Boutflour told his students that no soils were too high, too thin, too wet, too dry, to stop modern farming from growing splendid crops. He taught at a time when the soil was seen simply as a resource whose output must be maximised, with every acre fully exploited by the farmer. In the course of fulfilling these demands, we took our soils for granted – for while farmers depend on soils as citizens on cities, both are so familiar we often accept them without further thought.

Sit in a helicopter looking down on the City of London. The skyscrapers, churches, blocks of flats and offices, pubs and clubs are the clods and crumbs of soil. The squares, churchyards, roads, streets, and lanes where cars and people pass are the major channels in the soil through which air and water move and the larger plant roots penetrate. The halls, corridors and stairs, the rooms and cupboards are the narrow gaps between the grains of soil where smaller roots move around as readily as people move around flats or offices. Desks, filing cabinets, drawers and shelves, the insides of boxes and jars are the minute spaces between individual particles of sand or silt, right down to the tiny platelets which slide over each other to give the slippery feel of clay. Plant rootlets and root hairs work into such tiny gaps to pick up the food essential for survival and growth as hands reach into drawers, shelves and boxes to take out papers, clothes, bread or bottles of beer.

This country contains more soil types than cities and they are at least as different from each other as Glasgow from Bournemouth. A single farm may have as many as 20, a single field as many as five different soils. Black peats run into brown loams spread into silvery greensands. Clays alone come in greys, blues, yellows and reds, the loams can be anything from thin, cold, grey and wet to deep, warm, red and freely draining.

Like cities, soils are animal, vegetable and mineral. Soil minerals run from coarse sands to fine clays with rich varieties in between which depend on the rock from which the particles were originally worn, and which differ as a city of marble differs from one of steel, concrete and glass.

The vegetables are plants, which include everything from freshly buried straw, bits of tree or newly decaying roots to unbelievably ancient humus; the results of these mixtures can vary from the plum pudding of peats to the dry toast of sand dunes. Humus, the cement which holds the soil together, is made by the decay of plants and animals. It is fundamentally important in maintaining soil structure but it does not do the job alone. Minerals help – as they help support cities – and other vegetable matter also joins in to give soil its structure. So do the microbes, which exude gums that stick soil particles to each other. Between them, these hold together the clods and crumbs and keep open the pathways between them. Larger channels, the earthy equivalent of roads and streets, are kept open by cultivating the soil or by the action of worms and growing roots. The building blocks which keep open smaller channels are glued together by humus. Some weakly-glued soils, where the return of organic matter is inadequate, can collapse and then these channels may begin to break down.

The decay of vegetables to form humus takes place very slowly. Under normal farming, a 1 per cent change in total organic matter in the soil may take 40 years. No system of crop farming makes much difference to this. Ley-arable systems and rotations like the traditional Norfolk four course have much the same effect as growing continuous corn. Only long periods under grass, of 25 years or more, lead to significant increases in soil organic matter.

Because of its extreme age, the amount of humus varies very little whatever the annual additions of dead plants. It is difficult to say just how old it is, but figures between 300 and 2000 years are given. It is quite likely that much of it is more, even a lot more, than 2000 years old. An awful lot of farming would be needed to damage durability of this sort.

Some of the decayed material is younger, some of it only recently added and very young indeed. In its first 100 years of decay it is much less durable than humus – which means a single-minded Dan Bullen could make a dent in it during a farming lifetime. No one has proved that a minimum amount of plant matter must go back to the soil over such a period to maintain structure. Some soils seem all but indestructible. Others certainly need more plant remains than they get at the moment in the form of the roots and debris of each succeeding crop.

The array of living plants and animals which fills the ancient city of the soil is vast. Leave out large, familiar ones like badgers or foxes, and the task of the rest is to break down the vegetables. This is what happens to a piece of leaf. 'The more resistant material is softened by fungi, then it is eaten by mites which continue the decomposition possibly with the aid of a microbial population in their gut; and finally the undigested material is excreted and forms the food supply for a whole chain of other animals until it is converted into resistant humus-like material.' The foxes and voles have the sharp-eyed appearance of property developers, but it is the microbes which get on with the real work.

They are most vigorous under grassland. There, the total soil biomass in an acre can weigh 30 tonnes, and fungi can make up 65 per cent of this; 20 tonnes of fungi is the equivalent in weight of around 400 human property developers, or about one for every 12 square yards – which even for the City of London would be on the high side. Large numbers of bacteria, perhaps as many as three billion in a single gram of soil, do not amount in weight to more than around one human property developer for each 300 square yards, which would still be excessive except perhaps in the most fashionable urban areas. As well as microbes, there may be three million worms an acre, though under typical British pastures the figures are likely to be much lower, at perhaps a million, equivalent to about one human developer every 700 square yards.

Tot all this up and under an acre of grass there may be the equivalent in weight of nearly 500 human property developers an acre, or one every 10 square yards. The figures are much lower in typical arable soils, which are likely to hold the equivalent of perhaps 75 workers out of sight beneath the farmer's feet. Unlike their human counterparts, they knock down the new and turn it into the old. In doing so they consume and release the energy and food held in these newly dead plants, before getting eaten in their turn. Sir John Russell, the most distinguished soil scientists of his day, put it like this: 'Nutrients can be used over and over again by an unending succession of organisms. An atom of nitrogen never loses its value; it might in the course of a single day form part of a fungus, a bacillus which decomposed it, an amoeba which ate the bacillus, and a bacterium which decomposed the dead amoeba.' Thus the microbes, especially the bacteria and fungi, are together responsible for this feast of recycling or decay, which maintains the soil fertility.

Cities can become slums, as soils can lose their fertility – though in this country the experience of urban decay has been much commoner than the loss of soil structure and erosion. Neither issue was an immediate concern in 1947, when the country was as determined to exploit its soils as to rebuild its battered cities. The few who worried that wartime cropping risked battering our soils were soon faced with the evidence of rising yields. The earth was there to produce, the work of the farmer was to make it produce more, and year after year it did so. It was not until the late 1960s that two very wet harvests in succession caused difficulties which threatened ever-rising output, and added to a feeling in some quarters that our arable acres were being put under severe pressure by the techniques of modern farming. As a result, Sir Nigel Strutt headed a team to investigate our soils.

Read today, the most notable thing about the Strutt Report is the absence of concern about erosion. The team worried about whether modern farming was damaging structure and so the soil's ability to grow crops. It decided there was no general problem because there was no general soil. Many soils got an A1 rating. They were entirely tolerant of modern methods and it was quite wrong to suppose that all-arable rotations were causing harm everywhere. On other soils structure was threatened, though not irreparably, either as a result of faulty and over-intensive cropping which led to lower organic matter, or through using heavy machinery.

There was no profound attempt to look at modern practices of fertilising or spraying because practical evidence of harm was inconclusive and the science of soil ecology was inadequate to the task. What was clear was that wet was the threat. When wet, some soils run to a slurry with little structure or strength. Circle round the risks of modern farming as it might, the Strutt team kept coming back to this: our weather was far more of a threat to our soils than our methods and the best way to meet it was by good drainage. 'It is impossible to have good soil structure without good drainage, either natural or artificial.' Where drainage was inadequate and could not be improved, then cropping should be abandoned and the land put back to grass. Otherwise, what was needed was more drainage, followed by higher output.

The Strutt Report was cautiously confident about what was going on under the farmer's foot; but it did refer to 'the economic difficulties of combining modern methods (which are, of course, inevitable) with perfect soil health', and warned that 'modern methods of farming obviously necessitate much greater attention to what is happening below the topsoil, which in turn means knowledge of the subsoil itself'. Many farmers responded to those warnings by digging down to look, but that still left too many who had mislaid the spade.

The Report was the first wide-ranging look at the effects of post-war farming on the soil. If it did not convince doubters, in the next few years their views were buried under bumper harvests. Draining was essential to the new – as to the old – agriculture, soils went back to being reliable producers, and it was not until the early 1980s that doubts surfaced again, this time about erosion.

Erosion is often thought of like tooth decay, the steady rotting of a resource. It is more like a blow in the mouth. Heavy rain falling on unprotected and sloping soil will often threaten to punch out a few teeth. Crop cover may be too thin to hold soil particles, and the ground may have been compacted by machines so that the rain finds penetration hard and runs across the soil surface to form gullies. When the machines have travelled up and down the slope they leave ruts to channel the water and increase its erosive power. Larger fields mean fewer hedges and ditches to intercept these channels. The fine seedbeds prepared by modern machinery are vulnerable to rainfall, and loss of organic matter in some soils also reduces resistance to storms of rain. Today, more than 30 per cent of our arable soils are at risk from these processes – though no more than 20 per cent of these, or a little over 1 million acres, are thought likely to be losing significant amounts of topsoil.

Wet autumn weather causes most loss, though erosion can occur at any time with prolonged or heavy rain. Roy Morgan of Silsoe College, who has been studying erosion in our cropland, said of the extremely wet autumn in 1987: 'Any field that could erode probably did.' He is echoed by John Boardman at Brighton Polytechnic, who through that autumn saw the Rottingdean Council pay £1 million to clear away eroded topsoil from roads and housing estates. Such serious assaults occur once in five years, with losses of between 5 and 10, or in extreme cases as much as 20 tonnes of soil an acre. They are most likely on thin, light sandy soils which, if constantly cropped, can be forced out of arable farming within 50 years. Heavier clay soils are most unlikely to suffer in the same way.

Erosion is therefore a problem which is severe locally rather than nationally. The experts say that on the South Downs, in North Norfolk, in parts of Shropshire, Nottinghamshire and Somerset, and on the red sandstone of the West Midlands, horrible things have happened. Other soils, especially the durable and resistant clays, are unscathed. Any cropping can lead to erosion, and historically every time such soils have been cropped they have been at risk. Huge amounts of erosion occurred worldwide for centuries before modern farming was thought of – most of our fertile valley-bottom soils are the result of erosion many millennia ago. However, today's big fields, heavy tractors and widespread planting of winter corn increase the risk on susceptible soils. To minimise the risk means keeping crop cover wherever possible (which requires carefully worked-out rotations), using crop residues on or in the soil when the crop itself cannot be growing, and working the slope round the contour instead of up and down. In some cases it will mean giving up cropping and going back to grass.

These safety measures can be expensive, and in the short term there is no economic incentive to adopt them. In the longer term though, as the pressures on all farming build up, these marginal arable fields are the most likely to be pulled out of cropping and returned to the soil-conserving protection of permanent pasture. Although that would be the most secure answer, other changes in farming practices could also help.

One of these changes concerns improved understanding of what is going on underfoot. Professor Jim Lynch, of the Institute of Horticultural Research at Littlehampton, recently said that 'the once neglected rhizosphere is set to become the centre of attention in agricultural research'. The rhizosphere is the rooting zone of the plant, and Lynch went on to say, 'the ultimate goal is to improve modern agriculture by replacing chemicals wherever possible with biological methods of pest control and "natural" fertilisers'.

Roots 'leak' various chemicals, particularly carbon, into the soil, where they become a source of food for microbes. The carbon may be eaten by bacteria, which are in turn eaten by other small soil animals, thus releasing nitrogen which can then be taken up by the roots. Other bacteria and fungi can also help plant growth, and could be added to soil to increase fertility. Others help defend roots from attack by diseases. Lynch describes one defender which 'can behave as a parasite, coiling its own threads around the threads of the pathogen. It then produces enzymes that break down the wall of the pathogen, allowing it to penetrate and so kill the harmful fungus'.

Some microbes are very good at exuding gums which help to stick soil particles together and can thus increase stability – something which Lynch has done successfully in the laboratory. As well as adding microbes in this way, plants could be bred to leak particular substances which would favourably affect the microbial community. Altogether, Lynch anticipates 'a deluge of information on the rhizosphere' to tell farmers much more about the roots, microbes and soils underneath their feet.

A completely different influence will come from changes in farm mechanisation. The engineers who have given us heavyweight modern machinery are now thinking again. One possible development is fast tractors, machines which will be both speedy on the move and quick on the uptake. It used to be said of horse cultivations that they either started something which the weather would finish or finished something which the weather had started. It is often now said of tractors that they cultivate to undo damage that previous operations have inflicted. Avoid the damage, and much of today's need for cultivations would vanish. So engineers now ask why light, speedy tractors could not crumble the soil into a seedbed by the impact of fast-moving tines rather than by power and weight. As always, there are pluses and minuses. The power needed to pull a plough rises rapidly as the speed increases. Very well, say the engineers: redesign the plough. Grip, however, goes up with speed; this will help to balance the need for more power.

Tests show that when a tractor comes equipped with the suspension of a car, drivers willingly go as much as half as fast again as in a bumpy unsuspended tractor. Tractor drivers who get bored grinding along in low would welcome whizzing along at speed – and when they take these new machines on the road, motorists would less often overheat in long queues behind 150 horses harnessed under a single bonnet.

Once they start thinking like this, engineers quickly throw off their inhibitions. Air and earth may be vitally different to farmers but aerodynamics and terradynamics are engineering cousins. So why not try variable geometry, the ability of some modern aircraft to change shape so they can fly either very fast or very slowly, in ploughs as well as planes? It would be streamlining in reverse. Planes are designed in wind tunnels to reduce the drag, which shows up as swirls and vortices and air patterns as the wind tears past. Ploughs and cultivators would be designed to increase the swirls, helping to whisk and crumble soil particles as they hurtle past. To an engineer, that would be a far more elegant answer than a monster tractor rumbling along on double or triple wheels hauling half a tonne of metal through the earth behind it. The new machines would need reasonably level, flat fields and one of the side effects could be less erosion.

As for quickness on the uptake, the modern Massey-Ferguson claims its intelligent tractor has brought a revolution as big as Harry Ferguson's hydraulics. The chip in the tractor tells the driver about forward speed, wheel slip, optimum fuel use, area of ground covered – and before long could hook up to that variable geometry cultivator to make sure that soil whisking was always happening with the lightest and most effective touch. It could also hook up to a map of the farm to log in just where the wet patch starts or the weedy patch ends, where the crop is growing dense and lush and where it is meagre. As a result, different husbandry treatments could switch in and out while the machine kept on the move. In effect, an intelligent machine of that sort would move agriculture much closer to the sort of detailed knowledge and individual treatment which horticulture lavishes on its crops – and as with horticulture, such activities would concentrate on the best soils, rather than on thin, light, erosion-prone slopes.

A completely different approach to rethinking our present farm machinery is the gantry. John Matthews, the jovial Director of the AFRC Institute of Engineering Research at Silsoe says of the gantry, 'it will probably span 15–20 metres of crop, its wheels perhaps travelling on the surface of the porous backfill of stones or synthetic material installed as part of the drainage system of the field.' This moving bridge will carry all the implements now hitched to tractor or combine – cultivators, drills, sprayers, fertiliser spreaders, or harvesting machinery. Because the gantry works over a wide level surface, it will be extremely precise in operation. 'Power for cultivation with the gantry may be only about 12 per cent of today's power level, and the vehicle may be made to operate with an efficiency very much higher than today's tractors, where up to 40 or 50 per cent of the power is often lost in wheel slip and rolling resistance. Thus for the cultivating process the power may be only 5–10 per cent of today's levels.'

Fertilisers and pesticides will go on much more accurately with the gantry, whose sensors will show where the crop needs more or less help, while the onboard computer will vary the amount of chemical accordingly. Sprays will be targeted by air jets or electrical attraction so that less of the active ingredient is needed. As with other intelligent machines, all the operations carried out by the gantry will be electronically recorded and fed into the farm management computer daily. Such a machine, working over highly fertile, level soils, would see erosion kept to an absolute minimum.

Matthews's vision of the future goes well beyond the gantry. It links machinery with the brains of the computer, the eyes of the camera and the feelings of bio-sensors to produce the robotic farm worker of tomorrow. 'Look', he says, 'it won't be *One Man and his Dog* in 10 years' time, it will be *Robot and Flock* – automated dogs competing to lose fewest points when rounding up the ewes.' He grins to show he's not entirely serious, but adds, 'A robot sheepdog is a very tough challenge for a computer scientist. We're a long way from doing anything like it. By contrast, we already have computer programs which can farm better than all but the very best farmers.'

This does not mean that the robots are about to take over our farmland. It does mean that routine can and will be handed over to video cameras, infra-red sensors, temperature gauges and other artificial eyes, ears, noses, tongues and fingers all linked to mobile computers which will feed their information directly back into the farm office. There is an old saying that the best fertiliser is the farmer's boot. In future, says the Professor, the best fertiliser will come from booting up the farm computer.

According to Professor Matthews, we shall end up with the Information Technology (IT) farm. He described it when he spoke to the Oxford Farming Conference two years ago. The benefits include better quality in growing and storing food, more reliable supply from season to season and cheaper supply from savings on all the farm inputs consumed by animals and plants. They include less waste, and so less pollution; by fertilisers or chemicals, by noise and smell, or by eroding the basic resource of the soil. They include less boring and repetitive work, less use of machines and fewer accidents.

Perhaps above all these benefits mean that farmers will have much more detailed knowledge of what is going on across the acres of their farm and what, if anything, to do about them. The options will be presented in clear detail with all the relevant background information – from what's happening to the weather to what's happening to the markets – built in. Professor Matthews expects to have a full computer simulation of such a farm by 1990. Within two years, he expects this model to be in place on working farms. Within 10 years it should be part of the mainstream. 'Perhaps,' he says, 'for a major farm one is looking at a system costing as much as a combine harvester and increasing margins of output over input by half of this each year.'

Quite apart from the geewhiz-kiddery of all this, it means a change in farmers' attitudes which will be highly beneficial to their work. No more than five years ago, they felt safer doing too much too soon rather than too little too late. This often meant more of everything than was necessary. On the IT farm, all farmers should be able to devote themselves to doing as little as possible as late as they can, although as Matthews says: 'There will still be the challenge of beating the neighbours, or beating the farm's own record. There will still be national record yields of crops or milk, and there will still be competitions. Whether the winning entry will include not only farmer and farm name, but also the computer hardware and software name, I leave you to judge.'

# CHAPTER TWENTY-TWO

# Diversity, Extensify

Modern farming has given us the luxury of choice. Five million acres could go out of intensive farming in the next 10 years. Some suggest 10 million may go out in 15 years. Whatever the figure, it's a lot of acres, perhaps as much as 25 per cent of all we farm at the moment. The catchphrase to cover this hole in the agricultural landscape is diversification.

This means whatever you wish it to. At one end it links intensive farming to the food chain by encouraging farmhouse cheese-making, or ice-cream and yoghurt production, or making hams and traditional sausages, or herb preparations, mustards or pickles. It means new crops like cuphea and meadow foam, new livestock like deer, goats, wild boar or snails. It grades down through less intensive farming, perhaps in an Environmentally Sensitive Area (ESA), perhaps by planting broadleaf woodlands, perhaps by set-aside, or by non-chemical or organic farming. Then it stretches into non-farming, ranging from farmhouse or farmyard tourism to beating ploughshares into golf clubs to horsiculture to water sports to nature reserves. At the bottom end it falls off into land turning back to scrub, but that is abandonment rather than diversification and much resisted because of the desolation of the 1930s.

Of these possibilities, the most agriculturally important are organic farming and the more extensive farming encouraged in ESAs. For years, organic farming laboured under the derisive label muck and mystery. It was unfair, but it was not hard to understand. The muck was clear enough — but all farmers with any livestock used that. The difference was that organic farmers were much more likely to talk compost than dung. In this they were supported by two champions, Sir Albert Howard and Lady Eve Balfour.

Howard's *An Agricultural Testament* was published in 1940. Its argument would today be called holistic: 'Soil fertility is the condition which results from the operation of Nature's round, from the orderly revolution of the wheel of life, from the adoption and faithful execution of the first principle of agriculture – there must always be a perfect balance between the processes of growth and the processes of decay. The consequences of this condition are a living soil, abundant crops of good quality, and livestock which possess the bloom of health. The key to a fertile soil and a prosperous agriculture is humus.'

Lady Balfour's *The Living Soil*, published in 1943, followed up on the work of Howard and others: 'Fertility, as will presently be shown, depends on humus. The accelerated growth induced by chemical fertilisers has the effect, among others, of speeding up the rate at which humus is exhausted. As this depletion of humus proceeded, troubles began.'

The answer for both Howard and Balfour was compost. This faced them with an immediate difficulty, for their advocacy occurred at a time when all the pressures on food supply demanded more, fast. They were not unaware of it. Howard wrote: 'the correct relation between the processes of growth and the processes of decay is the first principle of successful farming. If we speed up growth we must accelerate decay.' But throughout the 1940s the demands for speeding up were so great that compost making got left far behind. Nevertheless, the faithful held on to the message and in recent years as the demand for speed first receded, then in some instances began to reverse itself, it has again been heard more loudly. Richard Mayall, who has been farming organically and making compost since 1949 says frankly: 'Forty years ago, I was called a crank. For the next 35 years I was called a crank. In the last five years, everyone has started to come and ask how we do it. It's the most exciting thing which has happened in my farming life.'

The mystery came from those organic farmers who were also soil mystics, for example the bio-dynamic supporters of Rudolph Steiner, whose recipe for burying herbs or weeds in the bladder of a stag, or a bovine mesentery, before digging them up and adding them to the compost heap, raised eyebrows among more conventional farmers whether organic or hi-tech. Howard himself commented: 'I remain unconvinced that the disciples of Rudolph Steiner can offer any real explanation of natural laws or have yet provided any practical examples which demonstrate the value of their theories.'

Both Howard and Balfour attempted to place organic farming on an experimental basis, though both were wary of science whose concern with the parts, they felt, stopped it from seeing the whole. Now, nearly 50 years later, attempts are being made to put organic farming on to a more scientific basis. Elm Farm Research Station near Newbury is devoted to this end, and other Institutes and Universities are showing interest, but the efforts are tiny compared to research devoted to hi-tech farming. They will, however, both grow and begin to dovetail with existing research – for like conventional agriculture, their main concern is to provide crops and animals with the nutrients for growth, and to protect them from attack by various pests.

The two knightly champions were certain that modern farming was bad for soil, crops, animals and people. They believed it was unsustainable. In that, they unquestionably over-simplified. The Frenchman Chateaubriand said: 'Forests precede and deserts follow civilisations', and since he died in 1848 he was not blaming modern farming. The slow loss of nutrients had been gradually undermining the most 'balanced' rotation of all, the Norfolk four-course rotation – though the numbers involved in these sums are open to challenge. Recent experiments have measured nitrogen from legumes as giving from 20 per cent to nearly all the nitrogen needed in a rotation, so uncertainty about legume nitrogen's precise contribution is likely to continue.

Aberystwyth University is studying nutrient flows on the Mayalls' farm, but the computer has not yet sorted out the answers. Mayall is particularly interested in not losing the nitrogen so carefully accumulated by clover and dung, so he looks forward to getting the information, but whatever the mathematical truth the sale of farm produce always means a loss of nutrients. There are then further natural losses through leaching, denitrification, or the volatilisation of ammonia from organic manures. The only way to avoid a slow run-down of fertility is therefore to import nutrients. The survey of organic farming carried out by Anne Vine and David

Bateman of Aberystwyth University recognised the difficulty of getting enough nitrogen to the right place at the right times, and concluded that 'the more successful organic farmers were bringing substantial quantities of nutrients on to their farms'. A number of the farmers they talked to said that this practice was essential to their farming.

The difficulty is lessened on mixed farms. Howard and Balfour were quite clear about the importance of livestock husbandry, both for successful composting and for ensuring a proper rotation of crops and grass. Richard Mayall's system depends on 180 dairy cows. Another organic farmer, who does not rely on composting, is Barry Wookey. In his book *Rushall, the Story of an Organic Farm*, he wrote that 'since all organic farms should have stock, animal husbandry is very important'. The animals both eat the legumes grown to fix nitrogen and return dung to sustain soil fertility and nitrogen levels.

One way or another, by keeping livestock, by growing legumes and grass/clover leys, by buying in manure or organic fertilisers, or by composting, the nutrients can be supplied. But as Wookey comments: 'May . . . is a month for organic farmers to go away fishing! The growth of all crops tends to be slow, and seeing one's neighbours' fields, with many units of bag nitrogen to help them, growing away so much faster than one's own is enough to try the patience of Job. The stock seem to chase every blade of grass as soon as it appears, the hay fields can scarcely conceal a hare, and the corn seems to grow downward rather than up.' One result is that yields and output of both crops and stock are smaller – and estimates of how much smaller vary widely.

Vine and Bateman concluded that organic cereal yields were around 90 per cent of those on conventional farms, and livestock output around 70 per cent. They also said that low-input organic farms – those which did not buy in large amounts of nutrients from outside – had yields closer to 60 per cent, and point out that 'any significant extension of organic production would seem to imply an increasing proportion of lower-yielding farms because of limited availability of off-farm sources of organic nutrients'.

The Mayalls, who farm the beautiful red sandstone soils of Shropshire, grow around 36 hundredweight an acre from first wheats and 32 hundredweight from second wheats, while their neighbours would hope for getting on for twice that. Barry Wookey wrote that 'my own view, having been trying to farm organically for the last 15 years, is that we can only hope to produce about half the output of a "chemical" farm'. Whatever the true figure, which will vary from year to year, for different soils and for different farming systems, organic productivity will be lower. Also, the ups and downs in output from one year to another are likely to be more vulnerable to the weather, and perhaps to attack by pests.

Organic farmers in this country can cope with insect pests. Richard Mayall recalls bad aphid attacks but says they never seem to do much damage; he believes that his organically grown wheat has thicker cell walls which are tougher for aphids to penetrate. Barry Wookey comments that 'most modern farmers spend hours tramping their fields looking for the first sign of disease or the first aphid. It is not enough to walk them once a year – they have to be walked regularly every week during spring and early summer, and each disease found has to be assessed to determine whether it will be economically sensible to combat it by spraying. Some farmers become nervous wrecks at this time of year as they are persuaded to spend more and more on sprays of one sort or another. The organic farmer, who relies on a healthy soil to produce a healthy plant which can stand attack by most of the common diseases, can go fishing quite happily because, even if a disease does appear, he may not spray against it. Ignorance is bliss!'

There is often less disease on an organic farm. Studies by the Dutch at their experimental farm at Nagele put this down either to the decreased availability of mineral nitrogen, or to more parasites and predators. Nevertheless, one reason for lower yields on organic farms may be that low levels of disease – sometimes unrecognised, sometimes ignored – are somewhat lowering output.

Weeds are a different matter. Richard Mayall says, 'on the organic system of farming the biggest single problem is weed control'. Although in his cereals he manages by cultivations, in vegetable crops much weeding is done with the hoe: 'We always go through the potatoes once by hand to remove any rogue weeds we have missed with the mechanical cultivator. As far as the smaller vegetables are concerned, it involves inter-row cultivations and walking through to clean the weeds between the plants by hand. It is a bit of a laborious job and its a very specialist job but it is essential as part of the rotation to keep the ground clean.'

Barry Wookey described how he manages: 'Quite obviously, not allowing annuals to seed means that in a cereal crop there must be no weeds to go to seed, as any that are present will have flowered and seeded by harvest time, and hoeing cereals on a large acreage is just not practical. The method we use to prevent seeding is the "weed strike" or "false seedbed" technique, which involves preparing the ground for planting some 10 to 14 days before drilling actually takes place. With normal weather conditions and a little bit of luck, all the weeds in the top 2 inches or so will start into growth, ideally to the white string stage, where they are very vulnerable, and the subsequent mechanical actions of drilling and harrowing will eliminate the majority of the weeds and volunteer cereals . . .

'With leys, of course, preventing annuals from seeding means topping with a mower just before the seeds are set – too soon and the plant will put up another flower, too late and the seeds are viable whether cut or not.

'Perennials too can be a real problem. The worst is, I suppose, couch . . . followed by docks, nettles and thistles. With no sprays to help us we rely on the bastard fallow to control any build-up of these problems. In a field's last year as a ley we cut hay and then immediately break the ground up. Thus we have what are normally the three driest months – July, August and September – to work the ground to kill off the ley and any perennial weeds that might be there. This is really the only opportunity we have of doing this and it is vital to the maintenance of clean fields.'

Organic farming is said to demand more labour than conventional farming to produce its output – and once again, there is considerable debate about how much. Richard Mayall says that the only crops which require extra labour are the vegetables; other cropping is similar to conventional farming. The biodynamic farm at Nagele uses nearly four times as much labour as the conventional farm, an increase only partly explained by the fact that the former runs 20 dairy cows, the latter none.

Sir Kenneth Blaxter, previously Director of the Rowett Research Institute, has said that 'if we wish to maintain production using half our present inputs of support energy, manpower would have to be increased 15-fold'. But Anne Vine and David Bateman feel labour requirements are little different between the two systems: 'Differences are so small that there is no evidence to support the view that organic farms offer more jobs in practice than conventional ones. Both types of farm are perhaps restrained by economic considerations rather than shortage of work to be done.'

It is at least certain that organic farms need no less labour. At the moment, organic farmers are highly motivated enthusiasts, but as the movement spreads, the motivation may thin out. It is easier to use a herbicide than a hoe, to stack a heap of fertiliser bags than make a heap of compost. Enthusiasm for the return of wooden handles and hard work will not be helped by falling returns, as more organic food is grown and the price drops – a difficulty already confronting free-range egg farmers. But as far as cash returns go, whether organically grown food is better for you is less important than whether people believe it is. If they do, they should still be willing to pay more for it when supplies are much more freely available. Research has failed to find significant benefits from, or even differences between, food grown in different ways, though people are still looking – but given the fact that many lucrative dietary fads have no basis in reality, that too is perhaps unimportant.

Another difficulty concerns appearance. The mucky egg, scabby potato, weevilly apple and sluggy lettuce of the late 1940s may be welcomed by organic enthusiasts should they reappear today. Most people have preferred their food to look like Hollywood, which means much cosmetic use of sprays. The supermarkets' demand for quality imposed this pattern; now their concern about residues is changing it. This has put the consumers' choice of unblemished fruit and vegetables in conflict with the consumers' demand for reduced use of chemicals. The answer will be to offer more expensive and possibly blemished organic food alongside cheaper conventionally grown pin-up produce, and let consumers choose.

There is another conflict between much modern eating and most traditional food production. Hamburg is the home of the steak which bears its name, but an early American version was described by its backer Dr James H. Salisbury as 'the muscle pulp of lean beef made into cakes and broiled'. Salisbury believed that fruit and vegetables fermented in the human stomach to cause various diseases, and even mental derangement. To avoid these dangers, he proposed that we should eat quantities of lean meat with no more than small amounts of fruit and vegetables.

The Salisbury steak, the central item in this early faddist health diet, could have come from any cow in an organic system, but today's hamburger is governed by the rules applying to fast-food restaurants. Tight specifications for delivery times and quality standards govern vast daily supplies of food and the way they are grown. The resources of beef feedlots, helped out by the trade in cull dairy cows, are needed to supply steaks and hamburgers. All this makes it tough for Old Macdonald's farm to supply new McDonald's franchise. So long as the markets for both Old Macdonald and new McDonalds keep growing, we can expect to see more farming of both types.

The difference between beef feedlot and open cattle range – indeed, between many intensive and extensive forms of farming – seems a bit like tap water compared with bottled mineral water. The label on the bottle tells you it is pure, good for you, and delicious; it is also more expensive, and nobody offers to pump it into your house through a network of pipes. In a better world, perhaps, we should all be able to get spa waters from our taps, and for little more than tap water costs – but it isn't going to happen. Even if it did, we wouldn't want to use it for making the tea or cooking our food in. In the same better world, there should be far more organic farms than there are now, and far more organically grown food should be available. This development will indeed take place. But we are never going to feed the world on the produce of organic farming, and mass production of tightly specified basic foods for the supermarkets and the catering trade is generally unsuited to organic methods. It is now quite clear, however, that the mission to revive the fortunes of organic farming will succeed.

Another important move towards less intensive farming is happening in ESAs. Although they cover less than 1 per cent of the farmed landscape, they already spread from the Channel coast to Scotland, from the Suffolk river valleys to Wales. They have two aims: to manage and maintain some of our most beautiful countryside, and to do it by encouraging less intensive farming. Both cost money.

One ESA now covers a large part of the much-loved, much-farmed South Downs. In his book *Nature in Downland*, the naturalist W.H. Hudson quotes 'the very words of one now dead, who had himself carried the shepherd's crook and worn the shepherd's greatcoat for many years on these hills: "If a ewe happened to get overturned on a lonesome part of the hill the ravens and carrion crows would come and pick out her eyes before she was dead. This happened to two or three of my ewes, and at last I got an old gun and shot all the crows and ravens I could get nigh. Once I shot an eagle, but that was the only eagle I ever saw. Since the hills have been broken by the plough, such birds are seldom seen. There haven't been any wild turkeys either for many a year".'

Hudson takes these words from a piece written in 1854 by M.A. Lower, so the breaking by the plough must have happened 50 years earlier during the Napoleonic Wars. The resulting loss of eagles and wild turkeys did not stop the price of wheat from rising to £36 a ton – a price which was not exceeded in money terms until 1971 and has never been exceeded in real terms (£36 in 1815 is just about £1000 in today's money).

Hudson himself, writing in 1923, listed the following birds which had disappeared from the Downs: raven, kite, common buzzard and honey buzzard, hen harrier and Montagu's harrier, bittern and reed pheasant, bustard, stone curlew, blackcock, chough, guillemot, razor-bill, kittiwake, and shag. He wrote also of the turf: 'The Downs are nowhere tame, but I seldom care to loiter long in their cultivated parts. It seems better to get away, even from the sight of labouring men and oxen, and of golden corn and laughing bindweed, to walk on the turf. This turf is composed of small grasses and clovers mixed with a great variety of creeping herbs, some exceedingly small. In a space of 1 square foot of ground, a dozen or 20 or more species of plants may be counted, and on turning up a piece of turf the innumerable fibrous interwoven roots have the appearance of cocoa-nut matting. It is indeed this thick layer of interlaced fibres that gives the turf its springiness, and makes it so delightful to walk upon.

'But all the tilled downland is not turf: there are large patches of ground, often of 20 or 30 to 100 acres in extent, where there is no proper turf, and the vegetation is of a different character. Some of these patches have a very barren appearance, and others are covered with grass and flowers in the spring, but in summer are dry and yellow or brown, when the turf all around keeps its verdure. This difference in the vegetation is not caused by a difference of soil, as one is first apt to imagine, but to the fact that the ground of some former period has been tilled.'

Somewhere around 35 years ago, there occurred 'a spectacular effect on the show on the Downs this year both of common plants like the cowslip, ragwort and rock rose, and of rarer plants such as the Pasque flower and some of the orchids.' The author of those words, Dr A.S. Thomas, warned that this would be temporary. It was caused by the disappearance of rabbits as myxomatosis killed them, and Thomas knew that the removal of their grazing would lead to an increase in coarse grasses and woody plants which would crowd out the small, interesting herbs.

Some 10 years ago another author wrote of the early spring which saw 'the appearance of cowslips and the early purple orchid. These were followed, as spring passed into summer, by such flowers as the common spotted orchid, the bee orchid, self-heal, pink centaury, ragwort, marsh agrimony, viper's bugloss, and the rock rose; and then in July and August by harebells, lady's bedstraw, knapweed, autumn gentian, St John's wort and various kinds of thistle and tall, yellow daisy-like flowers. It used to be possible to walk along the gallops and pick 50 different kinds of wild flower.' That is Marion Shoard, describing the unsuccessful attempts to save Graffham Down from the plough.

Despite this history it remains true that anyone who walks the South Downs Way today still gets great joy from the experience. No doubt the pleasure was more intense when wild turkeys and bustards ranged across the Pasque flowers and orchids thick along the hillsides. Perhaps the beer tasted better in the Richard Cobden in Cocking, its flavour helped by Cobden's support for the Repeal of the Corn Laws which removed the ploughs from the Downs for the next 70 years. Even when those ploughs came back in 1914 and again in 1939 they left pockets of wildflowers and wildlife still clinging to steep slopes hidden among the immense whale-backed hills, and could do nothing to stop the wind singing through the grass, corn and trees, nor lessen the long views of waymarks like Chanctonbury Ring or the Devil's Dyke. All these retained their power to delight.

Now, something of the pre-war feel may return. The plough will not vanish as in Cobden's day; indeed there are places where it is in harmony with the riches of the landscape. Elsewhere, though, it should never have broken the downland grass; when it did so it scarred through the thin soil into the chalk, often so deeply that the hillside was swept away to the valley bottom by the storms of autumn and winter. On such sloping, shifting ground, corn-growing is at best a struggle, at worst a sin. Now, it is to be encouraged to stop. Throughout the South Downs, farmers have signed up to restrict the intensity of some operations over nearly 35 per cent of the whole ESA. The voluntary nature of the scheme gives no guarantee of protection either to the most vulnerable or necessarily the most beautiful areas; but a start has been made which will almost certainly spread.

It is not just in blocks of countryside called ESAs that intensive farming can and will restrict itself. The Silsoe Conference in 1969 was an early attempt to reach a compromise between farming and conservation, and the resulting Farming and Wildlife Advisory Group (FWAG), with its local county organisations, has done much to help those who want to balance modern farming and conservation. The multi-authored volume *Countryside Conflicts* (itself a reverberating thump on the conservation drum) said of FWAG – and its intention to show that wildlife conservation and profitable farming need not be incompatible – that it 'appeared remarkably influential'.

All conservation costs money. The Countryside Commission's Demonstration Farms project, which ran from 1975 to 1982, met the economic implications of conservation head on. It wanted to know both whether existing views and features pleasing to the eye could be conserved and if new and appealing landscapes could be created, and it studied 10 farms to find the answers. ' "Beauty" and the "beast" were not the only marriage candidates. Multiple union was sought on each of the farms, for all of the interests involved, namely: farming, forestry, sporting, recreation and the three aspects of landscape conservation: visual, biological and historical. The challenge was to discover whether a multi-purpose plan could be worked out and implemented for each of the farming and landscape situations, based on the broad interpretation of the landscape.' The aim to plan for wildlife in the context of farming profitability accepted that 'from the outset, it was clear that the adoption of the complete farm approach would entail additional expenditure'.

When this turned out to be small, the final report on the project could argue convincingly that 'financial resources were not a constraining influence on how many conservation works could be undertaken on the ten farms.' Unfortunately that was not the whole story. The report went on to say: 'The project highlighted the relevance of opportunity costs in situations where the conservation of large and important features was directly in conflict with the commercial interests of the occupiers. This mirrored the position of other commercial farmers, who have been faced with similar conflicts in such areas as the Somerset Levels, Exmoor, and the Halvergate Marshes.'

These costs arose as cash was lost from not farming areas set aside for conservation. They ranged from £720 to £9950 per farm. But the Commission was not downcast by this, saying: 'too much should not be read into these figures. Only in the case of two farms was any mention made concerning compensation or some form of financial help or official recognition to reduce the financial burden. Otherwise the goodwill and personal wishes of the farmers concerned were such that opportunity costs were overlooked.'

The project assumed that conservation as a public good should receive public funds. Farmers should be paid income supplements for specific conservation tasks. At the same time, offenders damaging scheduled or protected features should be made to pay a yearly sum equal to the full amount of the annual gain derived from the act of destruction. Totting up the figures in an attempt to get at nationwide costs, the final report concluded that somewhere between £32 million and £96 million would be needed, depending on how much the nation wanted to conserve, and suggested that with adequate support up to 75 per cent of the nation's farmers would be ready to draw up 'complete farm' plans.

whole farm plans.

In 1981 the Wildlife and Countryside Act took a large step in that direction, though its support of management agreements was controversial. In 1985 the Food and Environment Protection Act changed the rules some more. Today, especially in the ESAs which have grown out of the 1981 Act and from changes brought about in Brussels, those rules have moved closer to the proposals outlined by the Demonstration Farms project. They include both payments to manage parts of the countryside in sympathy with tradition and wildlife, and tighter rules about some modern farming practices. The changes have been criticised by some conservationists, but have quite clearly pointed out a new way.

This accepts that the wildlife which once came free with food production – or which at least appeared to, though the shepherd who got himself an old gun knew better – no longer does so. The problem was summarised by Gerald Wibberley: 'Conservationists want essentially the products that low fertility brings. Modern British agriculture stresses all that goes with high fertility.' Since efficient modern farming no longer has wildlife as an automatic and welcome bonus, costs are involved in managing the countryside for low fertility. ESAs are a good start. They will lead to lower fertility. But they are still a compromise between farming and conservation. Where high-output food production is needed, wildlife will remain under pressure. Where the two can cohabit, well and good. Where the need is for habitat to preserve wildlife, farming must fit in. That will mean more cash.

The Royal Society for the Protection of Birds, for one, has recognised this. For example, it spent £750 000 to buy the Old Hall Marshes in Essex, and then obtained a grant from the EEC to cover half the cost of the necessary and expensive improvements. Ian Prestt, Director of the RSPB, commented to the *Shooting Times* that the site had 'slowly been degraded and there's no doubt at all that with proper management we should be able to bring back avocets, godwits, bitterns, herons and all sorts of things. It's now just largely dried fields that have gradually been transformed to improve the sheep grazing on them. It's almost negative management. They've kept it as rough land'.

In other words, putting farming first, even extensive and non-chemical farming, had not helped the birds. The improvements they need demand carefully controlled grazing, much new fencing, regulating the surface water – and all the live and deadstock to achieve this. By 1986 the RSPB owned over 100 000 head of cattle to help in maintaining the habitats which it owned. Some of its member criticised it both for contributing to the beef mountain and for taking money from Brussels to do so. But the Society was right: it was spendiong a lot of money on the wildlife, as part of that activity it had to fit farming into conservation, and to reduce spending it took what cash it could from the taxpayer. It is an example which needs to be far more widely followed, and one Prestt has spelled out frequently. In an interview with the *Observer* in 1982 he had stressed; 'it is the government's failure to produce the cash that is the real cause of the destruction of our wildlife heritage'.

Richard Mabey, for one, agrees with him. In *The Common Ground* he wrote: 'Men who work the land have, I think, a relationship with their basic resource that is qualitatively different from that of other kinds of producer. It is an intimate, risky affiliation, at the mercy of factors which no agricultural technology can control, and often earning small and precarious financial rewards. At present, most small farmers may only be able to scrape a living by continuing to improve the productive capacity of their land, and, if we are to ask them to hold back for the good of the community, we must at the very least be prepared to make sure that they do not suffer financially.'

It is not a new conclusion. Over 40 years earlier, one man had already reached it. In 1941 the Scott Committee on Land Utilisation in Rural Areas had been formed; it was to conclude that modern farming and the rural landscape were in harmony, that there was 'no antagonism between use and beauty'. S.R. Dennison disagreed. In a minority report, he argued that traditional farming would always see impoverishment and must go; modern farming would rely on increasing efficiency and specialisation and must be encouraged. If beauty was wanted, then farmers must be paid as 'landscape gardeners and not as agriculturalists'. Thus he echoed the views of Repton and Gilpin expressed nearly 200 years earlier – views which only now are beginning to edge their way into public policy.

# CHAPTER TWENTY-THREE

# *The Biotechnology Future*

A Dan Bullen born in 1989 would recognise the farming climate. It is as it was just before the Repeal of the Corn Laws, though now with the important difference that it is international. The Americans, who have called for an end to all farming subsidies and all farming protection, are in effect calling for a global Repeal of the Corn Laws. Mrs Thatcher, still uncomfortably close to thinking that the main business of farmers is to bank government subsidy cheques, wants to get the state further out of farming. She wants less support for scientific research, and little or none for the extension service ADAS. She wants to diminish the role of agricultural marketing boards like the Milk Marketing Boards which have done so much to slow the disappearance of small, distant, nationally unimportant dairy farmers.

Against these powerful influences, Brussels believes that some protection must continue. But even in Brussels protectionist fervour burns less strongly than it once did, and from time to time the flame gutters in the brisk winds blowing from the free market. The guttering shows up in steadily lower prices for everything European farmers grow.

State intervention and state support were of central importance in changing agriculture from a craft to an industry, and few would now argue they should continue at the levels of the last 40 years. The change which they inspired would have come in any case but more slowly, just because the farming scientific hare has constantly outrun the farming policy tortoise. But government support gave farmers such confidence to invest in new technology that in some ways the policy tortoise has led the science hare by the nose. Together, they accelerated the change from craft to industry, from an agriculture based on mixed farming and rotations to one based on specialisation backed by engineering and chemistry.

As Howard Newby has put it, 'the technological transformation of British agriculture is not the product of the "hidden hand" of the market, but of quite deliberate policy decisions, consciously pursued and publicly encouraged . . .' This policy drove farming through the revolution we have followed. Now another revolution is on us and the scientific hare this time is led by the R & D divisions of multinationals and not by the state. This can lead it on an erratic course, as the BST story shows.

The central problem recently has been surplus production. Surpluses have led to expensive storage, expensive disposal costs, trade wars, falling world prices and falling domestic prices – but biotechnology, by its ability to raise yields even more sharply, now promises to make many of farming's previous problems insignificant. The technology will operate strongly on production, as with BST, but even more strongly on breeding – and as we have seen, breeding has been at the heart of increased productivity. Whatever the sector, whether pigs or peas, cows or corn, poultry or potatoes, 50 per cent of the rise in yields is reckoned to be due to breeding.

If traditional breeding was bingo, breeding with biotechnology is Lego. The pieces are the genes which control such basic processes as reproduction, growth, lactation and health. We now know just how to click them neatly together once we've found them, but at present the box of pieces is frustratingly empty. That means there is a limit, rapidly reached, to how many new models can be made, and the major task is to find a lot more pieces.

Grahame Bulfield, Director of the AFRC Physiology and Genetics Research Station at Roslin outside Edinburgh, puts it like this: 'Gene identification is a serious problem. Most traits of commercial importance in farm animals are controlled by many genes whose number, nature and chromosomal postion are almost totally unkown to us. The major challenge facing animal scientists in the next few years is to devise strategies to identify these genes; this will be essential before the widespread use of transgenic techniques becomes possible.'

Genetic Lego comes in a number of sets, and you can use and re-use the pieces to make completely different models. Among the sets are those for bacteria, plants and mammals. According to Bulfield, the mammals' set when full would hold 100 000 pieces, and at the moment has around 1500 pieces in it. He reckons it could be 20 years before the box has enough in it to be useful, and perhaps 100 years to be full – and that long before then we will have become Lego experts without enough pieces to make many of the models which interest us.

The pieces in the mammals' set can be clicked into cows or chickens or mice, while the plant pieces can move just as readily from trees to grasses to brassicas. Quite a lot of the pieces can be used in both sets at the same time. Human genes fit easily into the mammals' set. It seems that once nature hits on a method – say, for making milk in mammals – it sticks to it. The machinery which leads from genes to milk is very similar indeed in us, in cows and sheep, and in duck-billed platypuses. This sort of similarity keeps popping up. For example the gene which controls cell division in yeast has been found in humans where it is also involved in controlling cell division.

The Lego set for mammals first began to interest farming in 1982. An American called Palmiter clicked the rat growth hormone gene into a mouse. The result would have caused the farmer's wife to drop her knife in amazement, for the mouse grew twice as fast as its normal brothers and sisters. The possibilities for domestic livestock were obvious and scientists everywhere got stuck into the necessary research.

So far, no farmyard animal has yet emerged to amaze the farmer's wife a second time. Many of the attributes of farm animals are controlled by a large number of genes working together and it is difficult or impossible to assemble these from the 1500 so far in the box. Even when the necessary pieces are there, it is very expensive to click them into place. But where the end product is produced by just one gene, and is difficult or expensive to make in other ways, Lego already has a practical place. Thus there are some very ordinary-looking sheep at Roslin with a very extraordinary characteristic.

These sheep have had a human gene clicked into them. It is the gene which makes factor IX, a blood-clotting protein which seals cuts and stops blood gushing like Bank Holiday beer. Sufferers from haemophilia B cannot make their own factor IX and have to top up with it regularly. It comes from the blood transfusion service which extracts it from the blood bank, and recently haemophiliacs have died of AIDS contracted from the blood which supplied their factor IX.

John Clark in Edinburgh successfully clicked the necessary gene into sheep so that factor IX is made in milk. It is planned to extract the factor IX from the milk and give it to haemophiliacs. This will remove the danger of AIDS and should be a cheaper way of making an essential drug than the present method. Factor IX made like this may, thanks to sheep, be available to help haemophiliacs within 10 years. But it may not be much help to sheep farmers. One small flock of lactating ewes could be sufficient to fill the world's needs of blood-clotting factor IX to treat sufferers.

Grahame Bulfield believes that chickens will take over the lead soon because the six multinationals which breed commercial chickens have the scientists, the money and the markets to exploit the opportunity. At first it was difficult to put new genes into chickens. The embryo of a new-laid egg already holds 60 000 cells and no Lego user could guarantee to click the chosen gene into every single one of them. The single cell formed when the egg is first fertilised can be removed from the bird and the new gene clicked into that, but it is then very difficult to put the embryo safely back in the chicken.

Bulfield and his team got round that by using foster eggshells. The single cell was removed and put into a broth in a jar. A day later it was moved into another broth in a borrowed shell and five days later moved again. In all, after incubation for 22 days, a chick emerged none the worse for its unprecedented early life in borrowed jar and shells – the first time a warm-blooded animal had been reared outside its mother from the moment of fertilisation. That achievement makes it much easier to click genes into chickens. Two new models which even the existing rather empty Lego box might supply before too long are resistance to Marek's disease and the ability to pre-determine sex – obviously useful when only one sex lays eggs.

The new technology allows the breeder/scientist to alter one thing at a time. Conventional breeding usually alters many genes at once, some of them disadvantageous. For example, breeding for high milk yield from concentrates in dairy cows also selected against insulin production, and that lessened the cow's ability to digest coarse forages like straw; high-quality bread wheats come with lower yields; and very thin pigs are more likely to be stress-prone. Life for farmers and their livestock would be much easier if the good could be separated more readily from the indifferent or bad.

Dramatic changes will take place as the plant box of Lego pieces fills up. Chemical and organic farming are certain to grow closer as biotechnology moves in on the plant. The immense resources of Shell, BP, Unilever and ICI – all of whom have been buying up traditional crop breeding companies – are now in part targeted on the designer seed.

Michael Bevan, a molecular geneticist at the Institute of Plant Science Research, has described how progress has already been made with clicking resistance to pests into plants. For viruses, 'two strategies have been developed to make plants permanently resistant to a wide variety of viruses which are serious plant pests.' For insects, as we know, 'the toxin gene products from *Bacillus thuringensis* have been used for several years to control a wide variety of insect pests in agriculture. The isolation of these bacterial genes has led to the creation of plants that are spectacularly resistant to browsing insect pests'. Herbicide tolerance can be bred into plants so that only the safest and most effective herbicides need to be sprayed. But, like Bulfield, Bevan warns that 'we have to understand in much greater detail how plant growth and the plant's response to the environment are regulated. Only with this knowledge can the fledgling industry of agricultural biotechnology take flight'.

When it does, crops will be very different. Oilseed rape might produce many different types and grades of oil for both food and industrial uses. The John Innes Institute of the AFRC, which is working on rape, is even more excited about peas. When the House of Lords Select Committee considered biotechnology recently the then Secretary of the AFRC Professor John Jinks told their lordships that John Innes was 'trying to make the pea an all-purpose source of protein, starch and oil . . . By genetic manipulation we are raising the starch content of some of the varieties. We are raising the oil content of others, and in yet others we are manipulating the protein content, not just the amount of protein but the kind of protein. What we hope is that in the not-too-distant future you can grow the pea for any of the purposes for which you currently grow oil crops, protein crops or starch crops.'

Ultimately, when the seeds of all crops contain their own fertiliser factories and their own chemical defence works, the farm fertiliser spreader and sprayer could join the horse hoe and the scythe in the farm museum. The cereal grower would then be back at the point he left 50 years ago, of drilling the seed, shutting the gate and leaving the field until harvest time came round – with the difference not that there was nothing more he could do but that nothing more was needed. It is hard to see how this could be described as anything other than organic farming, though one of a biologically very hi-tech sort.

There are, of course, two views about these possibilities. One believes they represent the triumphant culmination of nearly a century of trial and error in breeding and growing safe and reliable supplies of food for a rapidly increasing population. The other thinks they will pose risks of undesirable and potentially pollutant side effects – summarised by one American as 'the rutabaga which ate Chicago' theory.

Andrew Johnston, of the John Innes Institute, recently put it like this: 'In the UK the antagonism to genetic engineering is not as fierce or as widespread as in the US or in parts of continental Europe, but the question of the "planned release" of genetically manipulated organisms is certainly one that the scientific community must address now and for the foreseeable future. It is clear that there are real problems associated with the evaluation of any environmental threats perceived to be due to the deliberate release of genetically manipulated organisms; there is little or nothing that can be done to control the spread of pollen or microbes whose genomes have been manipulated by the introduction of novel genes and it will be difficult to estimate the influence of such genetically altered varieties on the environment. There are no easy answers to this problem; the scientific community is clearly aware of it and all that one can hope is that individual cases will be treated with rational thought and not hysteria.'

Some of this novel breeding will be for specialised chemical purposes, as new industrial inputs will be needed from farming. Dr Ken Sargeant spends his time in Brussels considering how farming and industry will fit together. He points out that 'it was the breaking of the link between agriculture and industry, by using first coal and later petroleum fluids to replace many agricultural raw materials, that swept away the constraints placed by agriculture on industrial development'. Plastics and man-made fibres are just two of the consequences. Now, says Sargeant, as the oil threatens to run low, we are moving back towards new links between agriculture and industry: 'The enhanced control now being achieved over the performance of plants and animals has brought farming to the threshold of massive change which will probably witness the decline of commodity products and the emergence of specialised planned cultivation of both plants and animals as a part of integrated operations aimed at specific markets. Some of these markets could be outside the area of food, but to capture them, farming will need to be modelled more closely on pharmaceutical fermentation than in the past.

'If doors are to be opened for the production of non-food products from agricultural raw materials then science and techno- logy must provide the key. The production process must be viewed in chemical terms. Plants must be regarded as chemical factories that use the energy of the sun to convert carbon dioxide, water, fixed nitrogen and a few other chemicals into saleable chemical products. Animals must be seen as chemical factories that process plant chemicals into higher value mixtures. Micro-organisms must be encouraged as living helpers of plants and animals . . . they must be discouraged where they compete and cause disease. Above all, the various activities in the chain, including the industrial process- ing, must be viewed as a whole so that every one contributes optimally to the success of the overall process.

'Fortunately our understanding of the chemical processes involved is growing rapidly. In particular we are gaining in our control of the genetic apparatus that guides the chemical processes of all living things.'

Two Danish scientists, Finn Rexen and Lars Munck, have been exploring the practicalities of this through work on a crop refinery. They say that 'from an industrial point of view a cereal plant is a fascinating raw material containing the building blocks for a wide variety of commodities of major importance to our daily lives'. The two main chemical components are starch and cellulose. Both vary considerably between varieties of the same species, which suggests that a specialised industrial cereal could be bred which would be as valuable for its straw as its grain. On harvesting, it would be carted whole to the crop refinery and broken down into components which could supply these industries: food, feed, textiles, paper, board, cellulose, synthetic polymer, fermentation, fuel and specialised chemicals. These local bio-refineries would 'harvest, separate and pre-treat the different botanical constituents of a range of crops and guarantee the industries a stable supply of homogenous raw materials all year round'.

Whole crop harvesting would demand new crops. The refinery, working all year round, would swallow crops like shrubs or coppice trees, elephant grass or cuphea, with the new patterns and colours they would bring to the landscape – and genetic engineering would join mechanical engineering to insert novel high-value ingredients into crops both old and new. A prototype bio-refinery is already working in Denmark, where its technical and economic performance will be closely watched.

Straw would become a valuable product. Throughout the European Community, paper and hardboard manufacture could swallow up 20 million tonnes of stems and save on imports of wood. Or the stems could be compressed and used as fuel. Recent chemical developments have taught us how plant cells are built up and so how to strip them down to their base chemicals. This can be done using solid state bio-processing. Tubes can be made with enzymes bound to the walls, which strip away chemicals from straw stems passed through them. Bio-degradable plastics can be made from straw. In America, laundry bags are already made of such materials. Where hygiene is especially important, as in hospitals, the laundry bag is thrown into the wash still surrounding the clothes, disintegrates and is washed away with the dirt.

None of this is going to happen while cereals and oil are at their present prices, but over time the balance is likely to shift in favour of renewable cereals. Even before that happens, we may have found that the limits to using fossil fuels are atmospheric, not economic. As we burn the oil and coal, so the greenhouse gas of carbon dioxide builds up; it could so upset global climates that we have to change our habits. Using crop wastes for energy would mean that each spring the newly growing crop sponged up afresh into its tissues the carbon dioxide given off when it was burnt the previous winter. Fired by sunlight, the energy could go round and round instead of accumulating.

In their recent submission to the House of Lords Committee investigating biotechnology, the Agricultural Genetics Company – a commercial organisation established to exploit discoveries made in plant sciences by AFRC Institutes – unequivocally confirmed what the civil servants and academics have argued: 'The next decade will see the establishment of a new relationship between agriculture and industry as a result of the increased control that can be exerted over the processes in both sectors. Agriculture will move away from being biased in favour of the producer and will move towards the end user.' The AGC submission went on to say that 'agricultural research discoveries must be linked to the needs of the processor'. What this might mean is suggested by what happened to the market for fats.

Margarine began life in 1869, when a French chemist called Megé-Mouries churned the oil from kidney fat with milk and sliced cows' udders. This unpromising approach led through other animal and vegetable fats and through various new processes to a manufactured product a bit like butter. The makers could mix in different oils and still come up with a similar product, and this flexibility allowed them to switch to cheaper oils and sources of supply as these became available. They called their product butterine, a name to which the dairy trade objected, as it did to the use of yellow colourings to mimic the appearance of butter. Butterine lost the first battle but not the second, and margarine has been winning the war more or less ever since.

Dairy farmers have suffered the consequences, but at least the oils for margarine come from farmed land somewhere in the world. A similar confrontation now looming for the protein market could have a very different outcome. We have already seen single cell protein produced in industrial fermenters and continuously harvested to supply animal feed. This technique provides large amounts of microbial protein, often from bacteria. For various reasons it has made little headway as animal feed in Europe or

America but it is more widely used in Russia and some Third World countries. In principle, the approach could supply humans with protein, as could the somewhat similar use of the blue-green algae Spirulina. In practice, Europe and America have looked to textured vegetable proteins and myco-proteins for possible alternatives to protein from meat.

An OECD report on textured vegetable proteins derived from soya said that 'a full meal, from a first course of "vegetable meat" with gravy to a "cream" cake, could be, theoretically, prepared almost entirely from soya products'. These proteins not only emulsify, thicken, extend, and stabilise; in doing so they 'make it possible to render a product crunchy, pasty, dense or frothy'. Myco-protein, a fungus which can be harvested from industrial fermenters, may be better still. It was described by the government chemist Dr Coleman in his evidence to the House of Lords Committee referred to above: 'Myco-protein is made from a filamentous organism, so if one aligns the fibres, when one eats it, it has the texture of flesh.

'It tastes very good. It comes out of the process rather like bland blotting paper, but with the food technologist and with all the flavourings and colourings that can be obtained these days, one can make it into chicken, beef, game pies, hamburgers or upmarket things like canapes – it has great potential.'

The product itself comes from RHM and ICI. Sainsbury's have been using it to make pies and say of it: 'It's a natural product derived from cereals so it contains no animal fats and no cholesterol. It even contains things that beef doesn't – healthy things like dietary fibre. And weight for weight the myco-protein product contains fewer calories than meat. It looks like beef. It tastes like beef. It has the goodness of meat. We've used myco-protein to make an exciting new pie. And we've followed the principles of healthy eating through.'

Another possibility again is to use the fermenter to produce not protein as such but the different amino acids which together make up protein. These could then be combined in differing amounts to supply precisely tailored nutrients. Yet another is to culture animal cells directly. Dr John Randall of the Institute of Agricultural Engineering at Silsoe has said: 'it may be that the ultimate in animal welfare is achieved by engineers developing machines and systems to produce meat and animal products without recourse to the animals themselves. Such biotechnologies are already emerging on a laboratory scale and it will be the responsibility of the biochemical engineer to design full-scale environmentally controlled bio-reactors for food production'.

Maurice Bichard of PIC has echoed this. 'It's quite possible to think of cells from a pig being grown in a dish in a laboratory and producing pigmeat outside the animal's body. It would require rather sophisticated control and maybe high cost, but I don't think those are the issues. We've got to decide whether that form of meat production would be more acceptable to people than the present systems of animal production.'

Finally, it will become possible to insert the genes for protein manufacture – say of the milk protein casein – into a crop plant and to harvest and recover it directly from the field without going to the trouble and expense of getting a milking cow to harvest it for you. If it was put into sugar beet, it could then be extracted in a modified beet factory.

These approaches resemble the search for animal and then vegetable fats which preceded the successful marketing of margarine. Such battles are far from new. William Cobbett, writing some 20 years before Dan Bullen's birth, objected vehemently to the disappearance of home-made bread and home-brewed beer. Commercial bakeries were attacked on nutritional and economic as well as moral grounds; and if commercial beer was bad, tea was worse: 'The drink which has come to supply the place of beer has, in general, been tea. It is notorious that tea has no useful strength in it; that it contains nothing nutritious; that it, besides being good for nothing, has badness in it, because it is well-known to produce want of sleep in many cases and in all cases to shake and weaken the nerves.'

The protein debate will doubtless echo such conflicts. There is no telling how the different technologies involved will emerge from the continuing processes of research and development – though the fact that Sainsbury's already market a myco-protein pie is one clear pointer. While some of the technologies involve growing crops – textured vegetable proteins (TVP) start with soya, and casein production could start with sugar beet – others need not go on to the farm at all. The choice between a beef steak or a myco-protein, Spirulina or TVP pie, may become as familiar as that between butter or margarine – or between clothes made of natural or artificial fibres, and tables made of plastic or native hardwoods. These choices, governed by cost, comfort or style are already common, and we can expect to see more bio-industrial foods like TVP or myco-protein in mass markets and catering, as well as more natural foods like beef and lamb to fill the growing demands for mother's cooking.

The multi-authored volume *From Farming to Biotechnology* has spoken of 'the increasing transformation of "food" into "nutrition"', and emphasised that 'the greater awareness of nutritional criteria is not reducible to a return to natural wholefoods. These criteria can equally be met by a balanced diet of bio-industrial food or the products of organic agriculture suitably improved through genetic engineering'. The same authors have pointed out that 'once the basic biological requirements of subsistence are met, the "natural" content of food paradoxically becomes an obstacle to consumption. If increased intake is to be promoted while also observing current dietary recommendations, then food must be more highly processed to reduce the content of calories, unsaturated fats and sugars.

'Conversely, industrial techniques of "animal" protein production can be easily adapted to meet these dietary requirements . . . given their capacity to convert low-value carbohydrates into high-value proteins, these direct industrial methods will accelerate the transition from crop to biomass production in agriculture.'

The implications for farmers over the next 50 years will be at least as profound as those which have occupied them since 1947.

# CHAPTER TWENTY-FOUR

# Why are They Down on the Family Farm?

The problems which seemed so intractable 15 years ago as we joined the Common Market have got harder, not easier. The 1970s were a mini-golden age which saw output, investment, incomes and land prices high. Now, surpluses have led to a rapid switchback. Farmers are under growing pressure, and argue that supply management of some sort, such as quota or set-aside, is needed to save their bacon – while others insist that lower prices will sort the sheep from the goats as readily in agriculture as in other industries. A world in which genetic engineering can cross pigs, sheep and goats can surely find a link between supply management and price to balance the interests of consumers and producers.

Meanwhile, farmers will continue to form a smaller and smaller part of the food chain they underpin. Over 60 per cent of the value added through the chain goes to food processing and retailing and around 25 per cent to businesses which supply farmers with their needs. That leaves farming with about 15 per cent of the total mark-up. The return on capital in food retailing is up to 30 per cent, on food distribution 25 per cent – and on growing the food is today just about 0 per cent. Farming income is now at its lowest level since the war – and half that income must be spent on servicing accumulated debt.

To the economist, this points to the fact that farming is over capitalised. So it is. But it is far from in control of all its costs, particularly its greatest cost – land. It used to be said that rising farm incomes led to rising land prices, which led to higher rents and so to higher costs for food growing. That happened in the 1970s, and when incomes fell in the 1980s so did land values. Now, with farming returns and incomes still falling, land prices have been rising again. The booming house market has pushed up the price of farmhouses and land has piggybacked up with them.

The price of other inputs needed to grow food also keeps rising, but the squeeze on farmers by forces they do not control is no longer simply a domestic matter. The team at the top of Agriculture House is a strong one – among other things, it has been the first to take farming's case to the public rather than simply to Whitehall and Westminster – and farmers have a good Minister of Agriculture. But the decisions which affect farmers are seldom taken in Knightsbridge, Whitehall and Westminster. Often enough, they are taken by Heads of State, influenced by national and international concerns a long way from the farm gate, or in the boardrooms of multinationals which take a global view of available resources. The results would be easier for farmers to live with if surpluses in one part of the world were not accompanied by starvation in another.

That the family farm has more or less survived the revolution so far has been due in part to state support. It was also due to its ability to grapple with the changes demanded by mechanical and chemical farming. The experts argue about farm size and efficiency, but once a farm is above the middle range – around 200 acres for dairying, say 400 acres for arable, though of course differing greatly for other enterprises and soil types – efficiency is likely to drop away or at best to be maintained. So middle-sized family farms, efficiently worked, have not been at a severe disadvantage simply because of their size, and have probably been among the most productive in the land.

Now, vanishing state support and dwindling CAP support for farming will increase the pressure on smaller farms. This will either drive their owners out of farming altogether or further into part-time farming. There is already a great deal of the latter, though nobody knows quite how much. It looks as though the 100 000 smallest farmers in this country – those with an average size of 30 acres – usually gain no more than 10 per cent of their income from their farms. They have been part-time farmers for decades already. More and more, this will be true of small to middling and then of middling to larger farms. Farmers must become rural entrepreneurs as well as food producers – otherwise, as food producers, they may vanish altogether.

They certainly threaten to do so in America, where it is suggested that by the year 2000 at least 80 per cent of the country's food will be grown on 50 000 very large farms. This compares with today's total of over 11 million farms in the European Community. Brussels has fought to slow the economic realities behind this trend, but the split into fewer very large full-time farms and a lot of smaller part-time ones cannot be resisted for ever in Europe. It could well be hastened by biotechnology. If so, it would be prudent to hasten slowly, partly for the farmers, much more for the rest of us.

It is easy enough to take farmed land out of production, but some of the consequences can be unwelcome. Farmers are being encouraged to plant woods on part of their cropland, which sounds a sympathetic land use. But soils under woodland, including broadleaved woods, are much more acid than under grass, and if a lot of farmland was wooded it could seriously affect water quality. Further, suppose that only the less dramatic fears about the 'greenhouse effect' actually start to happen; then we might be glad of a reserve of soils which could quickly be brought back into food production.

Over the last 50 years farming, like many other industries, has been accused of going too far too fast. Farmers have argued that they had little enough choice in the matter if they were to grow the food which was needed, but they also accept that there is truth in the charge, and many would like to go more slowly if they could. Yet the fact that we all live in a greenhouse now seems positively to encourage us to throw stones, and some go on coming farming's way even though it has reacted more quickly than many industries to the concerns of its critics. While we debate what to do about acid rain or the greenhouse effect, our farming is already changing – which is one reason why we are world leaders in many areas of farming biotechnology as the chemical slowly gives way to the biological revolution in agriculture. It could be a very important leadership to hang on to.

In all this change, some things will stay the same. Farming will as always be about converting sunlight into food, and this process will more and more be concerned with the husbandry of renewable resources. Sir Kenneth Blaxter, former Director of the Rowett, said in his retirement address as President of the Institute of Biology that 'the primary challenge is to devise an ecosystem for man which has a long-term stability and which does not erode the basic biological and physical resources on which we all depend'. He went on to describe that as 'perhaps the greatest biological challenge that man has ever encountered'. It is a challenge we have been meeting for some 10 000 years, since the first agricultural revolution of the neolithic.

One other thing at least will be unchanged. The day jockeys keep quiet on the going, undertakers on the gone and auctioneers on both is the day farmers will shut up about the weather.

# Index